Aggies by the Sea

AGGIES

BY THE SEA

TEXAS A&M UNIVERSITY AT GALVESTON

Stephen Curley

Texas A&M University Press ■ *College Station*

The paper used in this book meets the minimum requirements
of the American National Standard for Permanence
of Paper for Printed Library Materials, Z39.48–1984.
Binding materials have been chosen for durability.
∞

Library of Congress Cataloging-in-Publication Data

Curley, Stephen J.
   Aggies by the sea : Texas A&M University at Galveston / Stephen
Curley. — 1st ed.
     p. cm.
   Includes bibliographical references and index.

   1. Texas A&M University at Galveston—History.   2. Oceanography—Study
and teaching (Higher)—Texas—Galveston—History.   I. Title.
GC31.6C87   2005
551.46′071′1764139—dc22

                                       2005005322

   ISBN 978-1-60344-810-9 (paper)

Unless otherwise noted, all illustrations—including those from the *Voyager*
yearbook and the TAMUG Archives—are from the Archives of the Jack K.
Williams Library, Texas A&M University at Galveston. All illustrations from
the *Galveston Daily News* are reprinted with permission of the *Galveston
County Daily News*.

Frontispiece: Collage of TAMUG images. Created by Joseph Leibrecht.

To Joseph F. Curley, my father and my hero;

and

to Betty Curley, my wife and my muse, whose

love and support inspire me even when the

going gets tough.

Contents

Preface

The student yearbook of Texas A&M University at Galveston is aptly titled *Voyager.* It is an evocative name for the publication of an institution intimately connected with the sea. The forty-year history of Texas A&M University at Galveston has been a rough but rewarding voyage.

In 1958, the community of Galveston launched a concerted effort to convince Texas A&M to run a state maritime academy and to convince the State of Texas to fund it. The job was not easy. The eyes of Texas have traditionally (even legendarily) been cast toward its enormous dry land, not its sea coast. After four hard scrambling years, a subcommittee of the Galveston Chamber of Commerce finally persuaded the Texas legislature to pass the enabling bill. Governor Price Daniel signed it into law. And on February 24, 1962, the Texas Maritime Academy was established.

The response was underwhelming. In that first fall semester of 1962, only twenty-three cadets showed up for maritime classes in the YMCA building on the campus of Texas A&M. And recruiting new cadets proved at least as difficult as coaxing operating funds from the State. It seemed that the small academy was destined to struggle every year for what it needed to survive. The first summer cruise of its first training ship *Texas Clipper,* in 1965, might be seen as a metaphor for those early years. The ship broke down four times. Still, despite the lowered expectations of her critics, she managed to get where she was headed—finally—and arrived back home with her mission accomplished.

In 1970, the outlook for the Texas Maritime Academy was bleak. It had never reached its projected goal of enrolling two hundred students. Its biggest class, in 1967, was only 141 students—and enrollment was shrinking. In 1971, the academy would move into its new Pelican Island campus: a ship's dock, a classroom and office building, and an engineering laboratory building. All four years of undergraduates moved to Galveston (freshmen and sometimes sophomores had previously been taught at College Station), but students were rattling around in spaces that were unmistakably designed for a larger school. In 1972 only eighty-nine cadets signed up for fall courses. Luckily, help was on the way: some prescient administrators at College Station were planning to add undergraduate science education at the Galveston campus. That would change everything.

The Texas Maritime Academy became part of the College of Marine Sciences and Maritime Resources in 1971. The next year, before a single science undergraduate was admitted, the name was lengthened to Moody College of Marine Sciences and Maritime Resources. And then in 1973 (the year I joined the faculty), the actual transition began: the first twenty-three marine sciences students showed up on campus. New students included the first women (seven of them) and the first African American (one). The next year enrollment shot up, and it continued to climb throughout the rest of the decade. From 1972 through 1979, the undergraduate population of Moody College (the shortened name was adopted in 1977) increased by more than 600 percent to 640 students. The 1970s ended with faculty, staff, and students feeling on top of the world. The campus was indeed beginning to look like a real college campus: it had a dormitory, a student union, a swimming pool, tennis courts, and a big new classroom laboratory building. And, of great symbolic importance, it changed its name to one that was immediately and happily identifiable—Texas A&M University at Galveston.

Things began to turn sour at the start of the 1980s. Undergraduate enrollment hit the doldrums: it began an 18 percent decline over the next seven years to 524 students. Worse, the dwindling population of the campus caught the unwelcome attention of a fiscally tightfisted Texas legislature. TAMUG became one target of an ill-defined legislative attempt to save money by closing or combining campuses around the state. It was a scary time. However, after the smoke cleared in Austin, TAMUG was still standing. Not only that—the main campus at College Station offered renewed support to the Galveston campus. With the completion of a library building in 1986, TAMUG literally turned a new page.

Its second big growth spurt, from 1986 to 1993, increased enrollment by more than 150 percent to 1,337 students. Along the way, word got out that TAMUG did an exceptionally fine job of educating students. The influential national rankings of US News & World Report placed TAMUG in the top ten of its category. Only four other Texas universities—and they were all private institutions—made top-ten rankings in their categories. This widely publicized report enhanced TAMUGs academic reputation and made it easier to attract new students from all over the nation to the specialized programs in Galveston.

In 1992, TAMUG and the Texas A&M College of Geosciences merged to form the Texas A&M College of Geosciences and Maritime Studies. During this unwieldy administrative marriage, which gradually fell apart until it was entirely dissolved in 2001, TAMUG lost its way and its autonomy. From 1993 to 1997, TAMUG enrollment declined by almost 17 percent to 1,111 students. But there were counterindications. For one, the physical education facility opened. Even more significant, the

State ranked TAMUG faculty members as the third most productive in
Texas in terms of research dollars, ranking below only the two flagship
institutions, Texas A&M University at College Station and the University of Texas at Austin. In 1999, the inaugural issue of *Time* magazine's
Princeton Review named TAMUG among the top five hundred colleges in
the country.

The third big growth spurt began in 1998. As this book was going
to press in 2004, enrollment surpassed the sixteen hundred mark and
showed signs of further increases. TAMUG has recovered much of its administrative autonomy. Research dollars keep pouring in. Construction
of an engineering building—the largest structure on campus—and planning for a new science building promise continued growth. The campus
employs about 250 staff and 140 faculty members. Today's TAMUG students can choose among nine undergraduate majors, a double major,
several license-option programs, and two graduate programs, all focused
on the ocean.

I have been asked whether the forty-year history of the school teaches
us any lessons. I believe it does; I've identified three of them.

First, when the main campus sneezes, the Galveston campus catches
pneumonia. Periods of growth and prosperity in Galveston are ushered in by eras of good relations between the campuses, separated by
150 miles. Whether you call it a college (or part of a college) of Texas
A&M University, part of the TAMU System, or a branch campus of Texas
A&M University, TAMUG rises or falls depending upon the close or
not so close relationship of the people in charge of both campuses. The
current relationship between administrative heads could not be better.
Would that it had always been so.

Second, despite the proverbial claim that money does not solve problems, money has solved many problems during the history of TAMUG.
And conversely, lack of money has created problems. Fighting for legislative funding has been a chronic struggle. TAMUG is a relatively small
campus that is both part of Texas A&M University (issuing A&M degrees) and a free-standing campus responsible for its own utilities, police department, dormitories, and the like; TAMUG is a separate line item,
independent from main campus, in the state budget. In other words, it is
neither fish nor fowl. Or it is both. The Texas legislature often seems genuinely, and understandably, puzzled about how to deal with TAMUG.
The past four decades illustrate that when the money comes in, the institution grows.

Third and perhaps most obvious, undergraduate enrollment is crucial to the continued well-being of TAMUG. Periods of decline—the late
1960s, the early 1980s, the mid-1990s—have coincided with loss of support and funding. Periods of growth in the the mid-1970s, late 1980s,
and from the late 1990s to the present have coincided with administrative creativity, eras of good feeling between TAMUG and the legislature
and between TAMUG and the main campus. And, of course, increased

enrollment brings with it increased revenue: money to fuel construction, to fund salaries sufficient to attract and keep quality people, and to finance bold academic initiatives.

Visitors from College Station have sometimes remarked that today's TAMUG reminds them of the way the main campus used to be. Their response is probably triggered by Galveston's more intimate scale, but I like to think they also sense the "Spirit of Aggieland" in TAMUG. In 1876, the Agricultural and Mechanical College of Texas enrolled its first six cadets; in 1962, the Texas Maritime Academy enrolled its first twenty-three cadets. From such humble starting points, legendary voyages are launched.

Acknowledgments

I took on the project of writing a book about the history of TAMUG as a labor of love. In August, 1973, when I began my teaching career as an instructor in the Moody College of Marine Sciences and Maritime Resources, the school was so small that every student enrolled in an English course was in one of my classes. The institution was obviously still in its infancy, changing its name twice more in the next six years, until finally settling on Texas A&M University at Galveston. The school and I grew up together. Now I find I have been teaching for almost three-quarters of its existence. That suits me just fine.

I recall sitting in my office on the first floor of the administration building and watching roseate spoonbills wade in the marshy area that years later was to become the foundation of the classroom laboratory building. Beautiful wildlife but no human life: not a single person was outside. Of course since we had only about a hundred students, this was not too surprising. I wished to myself then that someday I could look out of my window and see students walking from here to there on the campus—that it would look like a *real* college campus, full of life. I got my wish. Now there is hardly a time of day or night when one can look in any direction without seeing students going to and fro. TAMUG teems with life, both extracurricular and academic.

I would like to thank the following individuals who answered questions or were interviewed for this book: Milton Abelow, Jane Bedessem Carpenter, John Calhoun, Ted Chang, William Clayton, Tom Cromer, Karl Fanning, Vi Florez, Bill Glenn, Carl Haglund, Karl Haupt, Bill Hearn, Kyrm Hickman, Patrick Lynam, Donald Harper, Shelly Henry, Paul Hille, Gerald Hite, Shane Hunt, Jason James, W. Mike Kemp, Jenny Kettler, Ernest Kistler, John Kovacevich, Jack Lane, Donna Callenius Lang, James McCloy, William McMullen, Bill Merrell, John Merritt, George Mitchell, Bill Orange, James Ortiz, Valerie Ortiz, James Perrigo, Al Philbrick, William Pickavance, Sammy Ray, Bill Russell, Steve Scanio, David Schmidly, A. R. "Babe" Schwartz, Jack H. Smith, Sam Stephenson, Erwin Thompson, Judy Wern, and Sarah Wilson.

xiv

Acknowledgments

Special thanks go to Bob Byrne, Cherie Coffman, Nicole Joiner, Jenny Kettler, Diane Verrett, and Natalie Wiest. In using the archives and circulating collection of Jack K. Williams Library, I profited from the helpfulness of the friendly staff. The campus administration also let me use material from the institution's files. I thank student government for making their archives available to me. And I am grateful to all the student editors and writers who published the *Voyager, Channel Chatter,* and *Nautilus* over the years. I would like to thank Mary Lenn Dixon, editor-in-chief of Texas A&M University Press, whose kind and perceptive comments helped bolster my sometimes flagging spirits during the long process of publication. Bill Hearn, James McCloy, John Merritt, Donna Callenius Lang, Sammy Ray, and Bob Stickney aided me by reading earlier versions of this manuscript. Joseph Leibrecht helped me with illustrations and contributed the photographic collage. I have been helped by many, but any errors introduced into this history are entirely my own.

My wife Betty, whose influence is greater than I can say, has understood from the start, supporting my efforts during this long project and tolerating my need to research the detail in the evenings and on weekends.

And finally, my hat is off to the many men and women—students, faculty, and staff—whose investments of industry, imagination, and intellect during the school's first forty years have helped realize the dream that is today's Texas A&M University at Galveston.

Aggies by the Sea

Loomings
May 1958–August 1962

THE fabulous fifties redefined postwar America. On the one hand there was the Cold War with its attendant anxieties: the specter of nuclear weapons, the frenzied building of private bomb shelters, the Red Menace, and McCarthyism. On the other hand there was the Baby Boom with its attendant hopes: a burgeoning economy, plenty of jobs, a home-building explosion, and expanding educational opportunities—especially in the sciences and technology.

Most schools can tell you what day they were born; almost none can tell you what day they were conceived. The A&M undergraduate campus in Galveston can—it all began on May 21, 1958. In other respects, that Wednesday in Galveston was not extraordinary, just a typical late spring day with temperatures in the comfortable seventies and a few scattered showers. For entertainment, you could plunk down ninety cents (forty-five cents for children) at the State Theater downtown to see Bob Hope and Anita Ekberg cavort in *Paris Holiday*, plus a cartoon and news features. But increasingly, people were staying home to watch television. That night they could choose among *I Love Lucy, Leave It to Beaver, The Millionaire,* and *Wagon Train*; those with a taste for reality programming might opt for *This Is Your Life* or the celebrity game show *I've Got a Secret*. Kids got plenty of exercise playing with two new toys, the Frisbee and the Hula Hoop.

In the news was the ticker tape parade of the day before in New York City for the young piano sensation Van Cliburn of Kilgore, Texas. It looked as though guerrilla fighter Fidel Castro would soon have to concede victory to Cuban dictator Batista. In baseball, as usual, the Yankees were running away with the pennant in the American League: Mickey Mantle had won the previous night's game with an inside-the-park home run. In the National League Duke Snider looked like the Brooklyn hero of old, winning for the Los Angeles Dodgers on an eleventh-inning

1958

In 1958, a committee of Galveston businessmen is established to help create a state maritime academy. They ask the A&M College of Texas to run it.

3

homer; and thirty-six-year-old Stan "the Man" Musial had just earned hit number three thousand, putting him seventh on the all-time record list.

The Agricultural and Mechanical College of Texas, reported the *Galveston Daily News*, would grant undergraduate degrees to 937 students on the upcoming Saturday. The local Ford dealership ran an overly hopeful (or understandably desperate) advertisement for what would become the most celebrated automobile flop in history: "All Detroit knows it! The EDSEL look is here to stay—watch the others copy it next year." You could tune up the family car for $4.50 ($3 off the regular price), rent four rooms and a bath for $40 a month, buy a two-story home for $7,500, and you could buy women's summer shoes for $4.50 or carrots for a nickel a bunch. For only $1.25 a month, said a Southwestern Bell ad, "Many housewives are adding kitchen telephones in their homes. They're mighty convenient."

The newspaper also had a special section for National Maritime Day, first proclaimed in 1935 by President Franklin D. Roosevelt to commemorate the launching on May 22, 1819, of the *Savannah,* the first ocean steamship to make the Atlantic crossing. Calling the vessel a steamship was a stretch: it was a steam-assisted ship that ran out of coal after eighty hours of engine use; it chiefly used sails on its three masts to catch the wind from Savannah, Georgia, to Liverpool, England. In 1958, President Dwight Eisenhower reiterated Roosevelt's proclamation with a new reason to celebrate: the keel for the world's first nuclear merchant ship, named *Savannah* after the earlier historic vessel, would be laid that year, thereby ushering in the new era of nuclear power for the merchant marine. Like the prediction in the Edsel ad, this one too was shaky.

Galveston was celebrating Maritime Day on May 21, a day early. The special section touted the city's maritime prowess: it was "One of America's Leading Grain Ports" and the "World's Greatest Sulphur Port"; a lemon-yellow molded sulphur mound remains a landmark for those crossing the bascule drawbridge to the Pelican Island campus. Galveston was the "No. 1 Cotton Port," and, in the era before containerization, "America's Port of Quickest Dispatch." That night many civic leaders and their spouses spiffed up for the annual banquet in the Grecian Ballroom on the southwest end of the Galvez Hotel. Rear Admiral Walter Ford, deputy administrator of the federal Maritime Administration, was the featured speaker at this "combined social and serious affair." Members of the Galveston Propeller Club, the Galveston Chamber of Commerce, and the Galveston–Texas City Traffic Club jointly sponsored the banquet. In his prepared remarks, Ford made brief mention of the existence of state maritime academies.

In 1874, he explained, the federal government had passed legislation authorizing the creation of these academies. The nation needed well-educated and trained officers to run its merchant ships. The 1862 Morrill Act, which had granted public land for state colleges that would foster "agriculture and the mechanic arts," had been part of this same national

push for vocational education. In 1876, it resulted in the creation of such
schools as the Agricultural and Mechanical College of Texas. Four state
maritime colleges existed in 1958: State University of New York Maritime
College (established in 1874), Massachusetts Maritime Academy (1891),
California Maritime Academy (1929), and Maine Maritime Academy
(1941). There was also a national academy, the United States Merchant
Marine Academy (1943). Graduates were merchant marine officers, li-
censed by the United States Coast Guard. These academies, said Ford,
bolstered domestic and foreign commerce in times of peace and ensured
that we could depend on our own merchant fleet in times of war.

In thanking Ford for his address, local banker Robert K. Hutchings—
"perhaps casually," according to a later account of the conversation—
asked a question that would lead to the creation of a great educational institution: "Why can't Galveston have a maritime academy?" After all, the
West Coast had one, in California, and the East Coast had three, in
Maine, Massachusetts, and New York, not to mention the national academy at Kings Point, also in New York. It seemed only fair and reasonable
to put one on the Third Coast. It would be a boon for the Texas economy.

On such chance remarks is history based. Ford responded to the notion with encouraging warmth. Yes, the Maritime Administration would
"like to have one state academy on the Gulf Coast," he said. But—and
here he was insistent—the federal government would be receptive only
if the proposal came through official channels directly from the State of
Texas. In other words, the people of Galveston, not Washington bureau-
crats, had to come up with the idea. That was all it took to galvanize the
citizens of Galveston.

The very next day, they went to work. Chamber of Commerce President Edward Schreiber wrote to Ford expressing "appreciation for your
generous offer to furnish us with detailed information that might assist us in locating a merchant marine academy at the Port of Galveston."
Ford wrote back immediately. His letter begins with typical bureaucratic jargon: "Pursuant to our conversation and your letter of recent
date, I am pleased . . ." and so forth. A handwritten postscript softened

Galveston and Aggie Football

People debate whether the first A&M foray into Galveston was with
oceanography, or the marine lab, or the maritime academy. In truth it
started on the gridiron. The relationship between College Station and Galveston goes back to the nineteenth century. On November 30, 1894, the
newly organized football team of the Agricultural and Mechanical College
of Texas played and won their first on-campus game 14–6. Their opponent? Galveston's Ball High School, founded in 1884. The game was played
on what is now Simpson Drill Field, next to the Memorial Student Center.

the tone: "We certainly enjoyed our visit to Galveston." And his advice was right to the point. He enclosed detailed instructions about creating and operating a state maritime academy. Perhaps even more helpful was his putting Galveston in contact with Ralph Leavitt, president of the Maine Maritime Academy Board of Trustees. As a Maine state senator, Leavitt had led the successful effort to pass the legislation required to establish his state's academy in 1941.

Schreiber quickly appointed a Galveston merchant marine academy committee chaired by the personnel director at Todd Shipyards, Emmett O. Kirkham. The charter members of that committee were the general manager of Todd Shipyards, Lester Briese; W. H. "Swede" Sandberg, the general manager of Galveston Wharves; the assistant superintendent of public schools, Bedford McKenzie; furniture store owner and Chamber of Commerce President Edward Schreiber; and the vice president of Lykes Brothers Steamship Company at Galveston, J. J. Thompkins. Kirkham wrote directly to Leavitt.

Leavitt replied warmly, "I have been anticipating that I might receive a letter from somebody in Texas." Leavitt made his unqualified support clear at the outset: "I have long thought that Texas should have such an

Emmett O. Kirkham: The First Committee Chair

It was fitting that the person chosen to head up the effort was an educator turned maritime businessman. Emmett Oran Kirkham, born in 1914 in Elwood, Texas, had taught school and served as principal at Elwood School; later he was the superintendent of Freestone Consolidated School. He had a B.S. degree in chemistry, physics, and biology from Sam Houston State Teachers College. From 1940 to 1942 he taught in Galveston schools. During the Second World War he left teaching for a second career in the shipping industry. He worked at Todd Shipyards in Galveston, where he advanced from payroll clerk to director of personnel and labor relations for the Galveston-Houston divisions.

In 1958 the Galveston Chamber of Commerce appointed him the first chairman of a committee to investigate the possibilities of establishing a merchant marine training academy. The next year he stepped down as chair, but he continued to serve as an active member until the creation of the academy in 1962. He was appointed to the Texas Maritime Academy's first advisory Board of Visitors. For eighteen years he continued to serve as a member, and he was appointed chairman from 1970 to 1977.

Kirkham was present at the dedication of the Pelican Island campus and chaired the effort to plan for its future construction. At the time of his death in 1982, he was the labor management consultant for Todd Shipyards Corporation and Tampa Shipyards, Incorporated. On November 1, 1986, in recognition of his years of selfless service, the campus dedicated its original classroom-laboratory-administration building as Emmett O. Kirkham Hall.

Academy and am more than pleased to be of service." His three-page letter was full of practical starting advice for committee members: first they had to decide whether the academy would be independent or part of an existing state-run college. Over the next few years, Leavitt would write more than thirty friendly letters of advice to the committee. He was a staunch ally, known for his political savvy. (In 1955, he had led the successful fight to continue federal support for state academies. When a new political appointee accused Leavitt of misinterpreting what the writers of the Maritime Act of 1958 had had in mind, Leavitt gave him a withering glance: "Young man, don't tell me what was in their minds. I wrote the Act.") The committee favored having an academy run by one of the state's two flagship institutions of higher education. But which one?

On August 15, the "Proposed Merchant Marine Training Academy Committee" met at 10:00 A.M. at 315 Tremont Street. Only three of the six members attended. Chairman Kirkham explained the purpose of the committee: "to explore the possibilities of establishing a merchant marine training academy in Galveston." Notice that at this point they were talking only about "possibilities"; there were no guarantees that their efforts would prove fruitful. The first order of business was to enlist the aid of State Senator Jimmy Phillips of Angleton to introduce legislation that would create a maritime academy in Texas. Phillips eagerly took on the job: he believed that if local support were strong enough, either the University of Texas or the A&M College of Texas would be happy to sponsor and later administer the academy.

The second order of business was to contact A&M, which had a large underutilized building at Fort Crockett that might house an academy. It would not take much space, they thought; the Maine Academy had started with only twenty-eight students and three teachers. Sid Holiday, general manager of the Chamber of Commerce, contacted Albert Collier,

In 1958, the Texas A&M Marine Lab came to occupy part of the former army barracks at Fort Crockett; the rest of the building was being considered as the home of the prospective maritime academy. During the First World War, Fort Crockett was used to assemble troops; during the Second World War it guarded the coast against German U-boats and housed German prisoners of war.

director of the A&M-run marine lab at the former military installation. Collier, who had been appointed chief scientist of the laboratory in February of 1958, was interested. He bounced the idea off A&M administrators at College Station. They too welcomed the notion. Thus Collier became the committee's liaison with A&M's College Station campus. Things were beginning to look good on paper, but by the year's end the committee had nothing tangible to show for many hours of hard work except for the prospect of a great deal more work.

1959

In 1959 members of the Galveston committee would continue plodding along until they suddenly were confronted with their first major challenge: a twenty-eight-year-old legislative obstacle to creating a maritime school in Texas. What they did would show what determined teamwork could accomplish.

In February of 1959, the new chamber president J. W. "Bill" Lain appointed Galveston–Texas City bar pilot Captain Sherman B. Wetmore as the new chair of the committee. Wetmore accepted on condition that Kirkham, who cited increasing job demands as his reason for needing to step down as chair, remain a permanent committee member. The committee reassured State Senator Phillips that Galveston was big enough for both an A&M-run maritime academy and a UT-run medical center. All agreed that an academy would bring great prestige to the city and the state.

Seven months later Wetmore and Kirkham, meeting at a private office in Todd Shipyards on Pelican Island, were struck by the untapped potential of neighboring undeveloped land to the west, on the harbor line. Wouldn't it be a great spot for the maritime academy's campus? Their pipe dream would prove remarkably prescient. For the moment, however, most of the practical discussion centered on how to use the upper half of A&M's Fort Crockett building to teach, berth, and feed about fifty cadets. Collier said his colleagues Kenneth McFarlane Rae, professor of oceanography, and Dale Leipper, professor and department head of oceanography, were intrigued by the possibility of offering courses in oceanography and meteorology to the new cadets. Leipper had a dream that Galveston could become the Woods Hole or Scripps Institute of Texas. Even more important, Leipper said, upper-level A&M administrative officials were interested. The committee eagerly accepted an invitation to speak directly with the A&M chancellor and president.

The committee carpooled up to College Station. On March 3 they met with Dr. Marion Thomas Harrington, president of A&M College of Texas and chancellor of the A&M College System, to ask that their proposed academy be made a part of A&M College. Harrington received them warmly. He seemed in favor of their proposal but then asked a suspiciously loaded question: Did they know about any existing legislation authorizing a nautical school? The committee members looked at one another like deer caught in the headlights of an oncoming tractor-trailer. No, they answered. Harrington sprang his surprise: from a neatly stacked pile on his desk, he distributed copies of a statute passed by the 42nd Legislature of the State of Texas on May 28, 1931: "Article 291 b., Nautical School Authorized; Management by Board of Directors of Agricul-

These three Galveston leaders—as the captions in the *Galveston Daily News* (November 18, 1963) make clear—played key roles in creating a maritime academy in Galveston. Left to right: Banker Robert K. Hutchings got things rolling when he asked whether the U.S. Maritime Administration would support such an academy. Shipyard executive Emmett O. Kirkham headed up the first year's effort. Harbor pilot Sherman B. Wetmore succeeded him and saw the project through to fruition.

tural & Mechanical College." There was silence as committee members read what they had been handed. This twenty-eight-year-old piece of legislation allowed "interested citizens" to establish "in one of the harbors of the State of Texas a Nautical School for the purpose of instructing boys in the practice of seamanship, ship construction, naval architecture, wireless telegraph, engineering and the science of navigation." A&M College would appoint a superintendent to administer "said school," the only specified activity of which was to arrange "from time to time" for "cruises from and to the harbors of Houston, Galveston, Beaumont, Port Arthur and Corpus Christi."

So far, so good. But as Wetmore said, "The last section of the act was a dilly." Section 4A pulled the rug out from under their feet: "It is hereby declared to be the intention of the legislature only to allow interested citizens to support such school, and . . . it is understood that the State shall never be called upon to appropriate any money for the support of this school at this or any future time."

In other words, the 1931 Texas Legislature had told A&M officials to go ahead and start the enormously expensive program if they liked but without the state funds it needed. Not only that—they were forbidden from *ever* asking for money to run this program. It may sound as if maritime education had been singled out for harsh treatment, but such was not the case. In its historical context, this was a typical piece of Depression legislation, passed when the state had plenty of interesting notions but little with which to fund them. At the time, A&M had been looking to expand in a number of new directions: the 1931 Texas Legisla-

Sherman B. Wetmore: The Founding Father

Sherman Baldwin Wetmore, born in New York City in 1903, moved to Galveston in 1913. He graduated from Galveston's Ball High School in 1920 then the New York State Nautical School (now the State University of New York Maritime College) in 1922. He was a mariner to the bone: both his father and his son graduated from that academy.

Early in his career he worked for American Export Lines, operators of the vessel *Excambion*, which would become the first *Texas Clipper*. Captain Wetmore saw distinguished service in the U.S. Navy during the Second World War, receiving twelve American Medals including the Legion of Merit with combat V and gold star, the Bronze Star with combat V, and the Navy Commendation Medal. He also received the Croix de Guerre with Silver Star for rescuing one hundred men from a torpedoed and burning French tanker. His last active duty was command of more than a hundred minesweepers in the Formosan Straits. In 1959, after thirty-four years of service, he was promoted to rear admiral and placed on the retired list of the U.S. Naval Reserve.

From 1959 to 1962, he chaired the effort of a Chamber of Commerce committee to establish a maritime academy in Galveston. The task was daunting, the obstacles many. Had it not been for Wetmore's untiring and creative leadership, the Texas Maritime Academy might never have been established. In 1962 he was appointed chairman of the first Board of Visitors and named the Galveston Maritime Man of the Year.

He worked to find a training vessel for the new school and even helped sail her from the Hudson River, where she had been mothballed for seven years, to Todd Shipyards in Galveston. As a Galveston–Texas City pilot, he often took *Texas Clipper* in and out of her dock at Pier 19 and later at Pelican Island. He was also instrumental in working with Texas A&M to acquire the hundred-acre Pelican Island campus donated by George Mitchell.

In November of 1990, TAMUG accepted the donation of an oil portrait of Admiral Wetmore and recognized him as one the founding fathers of the campus. Wetmore died in Galveston on April 21, 1995; fittingly, it was San Jacinto Day, the day on which Aggies worldwide muster to recognize those who have passed on.

ture was willing to fund a firemen's school (which continues to this day) but balked at a nautical school. Because of the Depression, the notion of a nautical school had gradually rusted away for more than a quarter of a century, like a ship in the reserve fleet at Beaumont.

The meeting and the dream of a Texas academy could both have ended there. But that was not Harrington's purpose. Apparently, after Collier had told him of the local push for a maritime academy, Harrington had uncovered the only impediment in their way. Rather than wanting to dampen their enthusiasm, he "challenged the committee" to get the legislature to delete that funding restriction and then return for another meeting at College Station. It was a big challenge. Obtaining

legislative consent to fund a new educational institution is always a
daunting prospect. But the committee accepted the task, they said, "with
enthusiasm and hope."

Amazingly, they were able to do the job in two weeks! Once back in
Galveston they assembled a crack political team, including Texas State
Senator Jimmy Phillips of Angleton and State Representatives Jerome
Jones of Galveston and Peter LaValle of Texas City. In less than a week,
Jones and Phillips introduced an amendment to repeal the restriction
against funding a "Nautical School." It passed the House and Senate
quickly and Governor Price Daniel signed the bill into law on March 27.
At last the Galveston committee members could point to some tangible
progress.

Now loaded for bear, they wanted to push on immediately. But cooler
heads prevailed: the experienced legislative team advised them to wait
until the next session before requesting funding. It was one thing to get
theoretical approval but quite another to get real money. As the politicos
put it, it would be better to "let a sleeping dog lie" than to startle the legislature into opposition by hasty action. The Galveston maritime academy committee was expanded to include John A. Parker (co-chair), Duke
Files, John Higgins, David C. Leavell, J. W. Lain, Van D. Mercer, John Me-
hos, Charles Ott, Edward Schreiber, Jack Smith, Jake Webster, and Bryan
Williams Jr.

In July the Galveston contingent returned en masse to College Station with the amended restriction. Harrington, who had just stepped
down from the presidency but was still chancellor, was favorably impressed and ready to help them. He appointed faculty members Leipper
and Collier to advise them and to investigate what College Station ought
to do to plan for funding, offering courses, and running a maritime academy 150 miles to the south. Everyone was so optimistic that a startup
date as early as fall of 1961 sounded reasonable.

The Galveston committee gathered information and support from
key sources including the U.S. Maritime Administration; the four existing state maritime academies; U.S. Representative Clark W. Thompson;
the Masters, Mates & Pilots union; and Gulf Oil Corporation. Wetmore's
personal contacts proved particularly valuable: in 1922 he had sailed on
New York's *Newport* with classmates Jack Everett, now the national Maritime Administration training officer, and Vice Admiral Harold Moore,
now the president of New York Maritime College.

In September of 1959, Wetmore encountered some opposition at the
Propeller Club National Convention in Detroit. The Houston delegation, perhaps a little jealous of Galveston's prospects, split five to five
over a routine resolution commending the Texas effort to establish the
fifth state academy. Wetmore had decided to withdraw the resolution to
avoid the political embarrassment of a debate. However, he never got the
chance. The parliamentary chairman in charge of the more than ninety
resolutions—the last order of business before tired delegates drove to

the airport to go home—was known for his efficient ability to refuse to see or hear anyone rising to take the floor. Thus without a discouraging word, the resolution passed unanimously. Two months later Wetmore received pleasant news: the secretary of the Navy commissioned him as a rear admiral on the same day he was placed on the retired list of the Naval Reserve. A humble man, Wetmore continued to prefer the title of captain in personal correspondence, but he willingly used the title rear admiral to lend prestige to the Galveston effort to create an academy.

1960

In 1960 the country was riveted to television sets, watching Senator John F. Kennedy and Vice President Richard Nixon engaged in a series of the first-ever televised presidential debates. In Galveston, the likelihood of a Texas maritime academy seemed remote.

Opposition to the formation of a Texas maritime academy came from two camps that usually had little else to agree upon. Some shipping executives—especially graduates of the National Maritime Academy at Kings Point—saw no need for a Gulf Coast academy. Texas boys, they said, ought to apply to *their* alma mater, Kings Point. And some spokesmen for maritime unions could not think of a reason to have any maritime academies in the first place. At a legislative hearing one union official said: "The guy you have to depend on is the guy who started out, as did I, and thousands more who went to sea as ordinary seamen, able bodied seamen, who studied on their own. There is no provision for this guy today. We keep getting these young, fancy boys out of the academies that can't hold water." So there you had it: management said a local maritime academy would be too low class, while labor said it would be too high class. (Ultimately, the president of Masters, Mates & Pilots said he was willing to endorse the Texas Maritime Academy, but given the conservative bent of the Austin legislature, it was deemed politically unwise to announce what might be seen as left-wing support from a union.)

And then to top it off, on February 23 Dr. Leipper delivered a shocking message from College Station. The Galveston committee had been expecting happy news, but what they got was doom and gloom: A&M said it was backing off from its earlier support of the academy. Some deans and other officials, according to the memo, "had found reasons why it was impracticable for A&M to administer a maritime academy." But the hidden reason for the cold shoulder was, of course, money. The University of Houston had made a bid to enter the state college system, and along with its bid came an enormous demand for additional funding. Texas public colleges had been told that state appropriations in the next legislative session would be inadequate to fund current projects, let alone new ones. All their presidents therefore signed "a mutual agreement not to ask the State Legislature to fund new projects." It was a defensive move, designed for self-protection. The memo concluded by leaving it "up to the Galveston committee to decide upon any further action." In other words, A&M would sit on its hands. The effect was chilling: without A&M endorsement, the Galveston committee could not address the Commission on Higher Education; and that was the only way to get funding. With that avenue cut off, the academy was dead in the water.

On February 26 Wetmore, Parker, the new chamber president Ted
Waterman, and State Senator-Elect A. R. "Babe" Schwartz (replacing
Jimmy Phillips, who had resigned from the State Senate) decided to go
straight to the source. They traveled to Arlington to address the Board of
Directors of the A&M System, meeting at Arlington State College. They
asked the question point blank: If Galveston got the money from the legislature, would A&M operate the school? The Board responded yes to
this carefully worded conditional question. They said they had never yet
failed to follow legislative directives. And to show their goodwill in a formal way, the board passed a resolution recognizing the "desirability for a
Maritime Academy in Texas." Chancellor Harrington, reported Wetmore,
"advised the committee to go direct to the Commission on Higher Education albeit without the blessings of A&M."

But that door, too, would shut in Wetmore's face: the commission's
executive director, Ralph T. Green, told Wetmore that no such proposal
could even be considered without first obtaining the "formal, official approval" of A&M. There was seemingly nowhere else to turn. The last
week of February and the first week of March were to go down as the
most debilitating in the four-year effort to create an academy. Wetmore
recalled that "almost all concerned were ready to abandon future efforts." Privately, he and co-chair Parker "admitted to each other that the
chance of eventual success seemed unreal."

Fortunately, they discovered more than one way to skin a cat. In mid-
March the new A&M president James Earl Rudder brought with him a
much more encouraging message. Rudder, a retired major general and
hero of the D-Day invasion, was not about to let a little thing like academic politics thwart the dream of hardworking Galvestonians whom he
had come to admire and genuinely like. While he was in town to visit the
A&M Marine Laboratory, Rudder told the Galveston committee informally that there was historical precedent for a school to become authorized without prior approval from the Commission on Higher Education.
A local community, he said, since it was not under the authority of the
Commission on Higher Education, could go directly to the Legislative
Budget Board. Furthermore, he assured them that if they got the okay,
he "would do everything possible to administer a first rate maritime
academy." He smiled at the Galvestonians; they smiled back at him and
looked at each other. Taking the broad hint—given his military background, it seemed more of a marching order than a hint—the committee began to lay out a detour around the roadblock.

They used inside pull. State Representative Peter LaValle, who had
served on the House Appropriations Committee, had a close working
relationship with key members of the Legislative Budget Board (LBB),
including its director. Meanwhile the speaker of the Texas House, Wag-
goner Carr, was running for state attorney general. He promised LaValle,
coincidentally his local campaign manager, that the Galveston legislative

delegation and the chamber committee would definitely get a chance to make their case in person before the LBB in Austin. Representative LaValle and State Senator Schwartz, citing the 1959 legislative authorization for the academy, convinced the Legislative Budget Board to look at a forthcoming two-year budget for the academy. It did not hurt that Schwartz was able to wave in front of their noses a written document from Rear Admiral Walter J. Ford—the federal official who had answered Hutchings's question at the 1958 Maritime Day banquet about a Galveston academy and who was now the acting U.S. maritime administrator—promising to pay $75,000 in federal funds to Texas when it started to operate a maritime academy.

That budget came from an intriguing cooperative effort between an Aggie and a Longhorn, rivals on the football gridiron but collaborators in the interests of Galveston. With assistance from Don Walker, who was the business manager of the University of Texas Medical Branch and a friend of the committee, Wetmore worked up a tentative budget based on the costs of remodeling Fort Crockett and operating an academy. Wetmore had obtained sample budgets from other state academies. Walker used his considerable fiscal experience to recast the figures into a format designed to please Texas government officials. The budget asked for $120,000 from general state funds, supplemented by $75,000 from federal funds. To make it legal, the committee publicized their budget at any venue where influential people would listen—meetings of civic clubs, public hearings, and political rallies. In June, LBB examiners came to Galveston to tour Fort Crockett and review the budget. Not only did they deem the budget "realistic," but according to Wetmore they also "evinced much more than routine interest in the possibility of establishing a maritime academy." Texas boosters themselves, the LBB staff loved the idea of an academy. In the short run, it would allow young Texans to make their mark on the maritime industry, and in the long run it "would create vistas of opportunities to provide facilities for the study of all marine sciences and technology." The examiners and their staff even gave the committee insiders' help: they "rearranged and adjusted" the budget "to conform to state Standards." Things were looking up.

Sure enough, on July 21, the Legislative Budget Board scheduled a hearing for this academy budget, extraordinary in having been prepared by a local chamber of commerce with help from the University of Texas during the official silence from the A&M campus that would eventually operate it. Score one for an unprecedented collaboration between selfless Longhorns and conniving Aggies. The LBB was "cordial and noncommittal" about the budget. The Galveston team could not predict what the final decision would be, but at least their budget had received a hearing.

The year ended with a flurry of activity for the Galveston committee, but after the dust cleared, there was still no academy in Texas. All the Galveston team could point to—and it was a gargantuan accomplishment—was that they had managed to keep the project alive despite long odds. They still had to convince a fiscally conservative state to commit money to run an expensive educational program. It seemed daunting. In Texas, one of the few states without a sales tax, most politicians ran for office on the no-new-taxes platform. As 1960 drew to a close, wrote Wetmore, "the majority of Galvestonians were understandably pessimistic."

Meanwhile there was some concern that if Texas did not get its act together quickly, another state along the Gulf Coast might snap up the opportunity to host a maritime academy. In truth, the Southern Regional Education Board (the accrediting agency) in October had asked officials whether they had any interest in a regional maritime school in Mississippi, Louisiana, or Florida. But nothing ever came of this disturbing news. Apparently no other state was interested or organized enough to beat out Texas.

The regular session of the legislature opened in January with a happy political surprise: the Legislative Budget Board had included in its recommended budget an item funding the Texas Maritime Academy. The item appeared in both the House and Senate appropriations bills, which had to be reconciled with each other before any appropriations were authorized. What is written into a bill, of course, can also be scored out. It was slippery footing for the academy subcommittee of Wetmore, Parker, and Jack Spring, who met weekly with the Galveston legislative team of Senator Schwartz, Representative LaValle, and Representative Maco Stewart (who had replaced Jerome Jones).

Galveston, smelling victory, redoubled its efforts to win over the state legislature to approve the academy budget item. Demonstrating political astuteness, the committee persuaded the Massachusetts Maritime Academy to change its schedule so that its training ship *Bay State* would dock in Galveston for four days, beginning March 13. Every member of the Texas Senate and key members of the House were invited; thirty accepted the invitations. They were treated like royalty, welcomed at the Galveston airport by the Kirwin High School band and the Ball High School Tornettes drill team, driven to the harbor, and piped aboard the ship by uniformed cadets. Galveston pulled out all the stops: the visitors attended a reception at the Jack Tar Hotel and then had dinner at Gaido's restaurant.

The event had been scheduled to conclude at 9:00 P.M. so that legislators could be flown back to Austin, but nature interfered. High winds and a tornado alert grounded all planes. The chamber happily spent more of its budget to put the VIPs up at motels for the night. The partying and lobbying continued. According to historian Henry C. Dethloff in his *Centennial History of Texas A&M University, 1876–1976*, "That one event probably did more to sell the Legislature on the need for a maritime school than all of the other letters, appearances, and publicity combined."

1961

The year 1961 was golden for the proposed academy. Everything went its way.

But the event ended with a mishap. Wetmore, in his official capacity as harbor pilot, guided the *Bay State* to the sea buoy in heavy seas with gale force winds and then disembarked to the pilot boat alongside. Just as he let go of the ship's ladder, the pilot boat dropped into a wave trough and he fell, slamming his knee on the boat's deck. Wetmore suffered a serious knee injury that required surgery, four months' hospitalization, and extensive therapy. Fortunately, his co-chair John Parker was able to take charge of the committee during Wetmore's lengthy recovery period.

During the regular legislative session, supporters of the academy must have felt as if they lived in Austin. They testified at numerous meetings of both House and Senate subcommittees of the Appropriations Committee; A&M President Rudder was often at their side to lend his support. Constant vigilance was needed to prevent the maritime item from being removed from the budget. It was almost axed when the three Galveston legislators—Schwartz, LaValle, and Stewart—had to leave Austin to attend the funeral of Galveston County Judge Theodore Robinson. They asked the House Appropriations Committee to take no action affecting the Texas Maritime Academy until they returned. Appropriations Committee members said they understood and assured the Galveston delegation that the Texas Maritime Academy would not be discussed in their absence.

However, there is an old saying in Texas that no one is safe when the legislature is in session. Although Representative Stewart had planned to spend the night in Galveston, at the last minute he decided to return by private plane to Austin. Why? Call it a lucky hunch. Back in Austin, he walked into the ongoing night meeting of members of the Appropriations Committee just as they were getting ready to slash funding for the proposed Texas Maritime Academy. He had caught them red-handed. History does not record what was said, but the upshot was that Stewart managed to squelch the adverse action.

All the hard work paid off. By the end of the special legislative session (called after the end of the regular session to deal with unfinished business) in July, 1961, the budget item finally passed—one minute before the midnight deadline. Actually the time was gerrymandered. Wetmore recalled that "clocks in the legislative halls were turned back" to avoid having to call another special session. Governor Price Daniel signed the bill in August. State funds for the Texas Maritime Academy had been appropriated at last. By the summer of 1961, State Representatives LaValle and Stewart and State Senator Schwartz had managed to appropriate state funds of $261,000 for the first year and $174,000 for the second year of the Texas Maritime Academy.

The extra startup funds were earmarked to rehabilitate Fort Crockett, housing the A&M Oceanography Department laboratory. Plans were modest. Students would be accepted in 1962. After their first year at the College Station campus, they would inaugurate the Galveston campus in September, 1963. Attorney General Will Wilson (a major force behind

shutting down illegal gambling in Galveston) handed down a favorable
opinion in September of 1961 to allow plans to go forward. "I trust that
this will clear the way for the start of construction on the new Merchant
Marine Academy, which I know will mean a great deal to Galveston and
Texas," said Wilson.

All was not entirely well, however. An overly cautious Joint Conference Committee had attached to the appropriation a rider that made
actual state funding contingent upon the academy getting a ship and
enough federal money to maintain it annually. The rider was unneces-
sary; in the setting up of previous maritime academies, the federal government had always honored its end of the bargain in this respect. But
never had it made such a promise part of its contract with a state. The
rider was yet another monkey wrench thrown into the works. President
Rudder told the Galveston committee that A&M would not activate the
school until this matter of the ship was decided.

The Galveston committee now set about convincing the Maritime
Administration to add a ship-plus-maintenance paragraph to its standard contract form. The first proposed addition, written by LaValle
and Stewart, was turned down by Washington. Then a Washington
counterproposal was turned down by the Texas attorney general. This
long-distance ping-pong game was getting nowhere slowly. The two
sides needed to sit down together at the same table. Congressman Clark
Thompson arranged a conference in Washington, D.C., on November 27.
The decision makers were all there: representing Texas were Wetmore,
Parker, Assistant Texas Attorney General Pat Bailey, and A&M assistant business manager Walter Berndt; representing the federal Maritime

Hurricane Carla: Killer Storm Hits Galveston

In retrospect, the agonizingly slow legislative process turned out to have
been fortunate. Had the Texas Maritime Academy been founded by September 10, 1961, as originally hoped, it would have been in the path of a
devastating storm. Hurricane Carla, a force 4 or 5 hurricane (authorities
disagree), packed top winds estimated at up to 150 miles per hour when
it made landfall between Port O'Connor and Port Lavaca. Before it was
downgraded from a hurricane on September 12, Carla was responsible
for at least forty-two deaths and billions of dollars in property damage.
It dumped almost seventeen inches of rain on Galveston and caused high
tides of over nine feet. Waves broke over the seawall and wrecked Galveston landmarks like the Balinese Room at 20th Street and the well-known
Murdoch's Pier (the naked pilings of the latter can still be seen off the
seawall). Windows in the Fort Crockett building were blown in, allowing
wind-driven rain to soak its interior. Galveston, its low-lying areas under
four feet of water, suffered tremendous damage from tornadoes spawned
by the killer storm. It was the worst hurricane to hit Texas since the Great
Storm of 1900.

Administration were Deputy Maritime Administrator Julius Singman, General Counselor Larry Jones, and Captain Jack Everett (Wetmore's former classmate). With no rancor on either side and a friendly eagerness to get things over with, they quickly hammered out this acceptable compromise in stultifying bureaucratic prose: "Under the contemplated operations and maintenance of such training vessel provided for in this Article 5, the assistance payments provided for in Article 1 are more than the budgeted and contemplated annual maintenance and operation expenses of said vessel."

In other words, it was a done deal: the federal government had explicitly agreed to pick up the yearly tab for running the training ship. There were no longer any disagreements. In early December the maritime administrator and the attorney general of Texas informally notified A&M President Rudder that the amended contract was satisfactory to both parties. Wetmore received the news from Washington by Western Union telegram: "Agreement as discussed during Washington conference approved by Maritime Administration on December 5, 1961 and mailed to General Rudder for appropriate action."

Rudder immediately began the administrative action to create the Texas Maritime Academy. As required by Maritime Administration regulations, he appointed an advisory Board of Visitors. Its charter members included ex-officio members Dr. W. J. Graff, dean of instruction at Texas A&M; Captain Thurman Gumpton (USNR), commandant of Eighth Naval District; and Captain John T. Everett (USMS), U.S. maritime administrator. Regular members were Rear Admiral Sherman Wetmore (chair); Captains Charles Glenwright, Robert L. Jones, Neal Storter, and Wesley Walls; Judges Peter LaValle and John Parker; and Russell Brierly, Emmett O. Kirkham, Dam Low, J. C. Rudd, and Dallas Gordon Rupe.

1962

In 1962 the contract would be signed, the funding appropriated, and a superintendent hired. The Texas Maritime Academy scheduled its first classes for the fall.

On January 26 Governor Price Daniel and A&M President Earl Rudder signed the contract with the Maritime Administration. This agreement authorized the Maritime Administration to seek federal funding at last. Unfortunately, the timing was out of kilter: U.S. President John F. Kennedy had already presented the annual budget to Congress. The academy would have been out of luck for another year had it not been for the foresight of Congressman Clark Thompson. He had arranged to invite the Galveston delegation to Washington to speak on behalf of a supplemental budget request.

On March 30 Wetmore, Parker, Schwartz, Jones, and superintendent designee Captain Bennett M. Dodson testified before the U.S. House of Representatives Appropriations Committee, meeting in the Foreign Operations room. The committee posed only one question, and it was directed to John Parker: "Aren't you a member of the same Galveston Chamber of Commerce that has been sending us letters urging us to be fiscally conservative and approve no new funding?" With a deep intake

of breath, Parker replied, "Yes, but now I'm representing a different committee—a development committee." There were smiles all around. Galveston had won the day.

In an extraordinary move, the Appropriations Committee okayed federal funding. The proposed appropriation for a Texas maritime academy was the *only* item not already approved by a cabinet member and the budget director to be passed by this committee. Thompson's influence was the reason. Now the item had to be voted on by both houses of Congress. In August the Texas team of Representative Thompson, Senator Ralph A. Yarborough, and Senator John G. Tower led the successful bipartisan effort to pass the appropriation item for the Texas Maritime Academy.

Meanwhile, on February 24, the Board of Directors of the Texas Agricultural and Mechanical College System (then consisting only of the main campus and Arlington State, Prairie View A&M, and John Tarleton colleges) established the academy. This date would be celebrated ten years later as the school's official birthday. The Texas A&M System appropriated $119,740—$98,440 for repairs to Fort Crockett buildings and $21,300 for general operating expenses.

September 1 was to be the official opening day for the new Texas maritime college, according to the agreement between Governor Daniel and

The Galveston delegation enters the Foreign Operations hearing room on March 30, 1962, to appear before a subcommittee of the Appropriations Committee. Left to right: Congressman Clark Thompson, State Senator Babe Schwartz, Rear Admiral Sherman Wetmore, Judge John Parker, and Captain Bennett Dodson.

Bennett Dodson: The First Superintendent

In January of 1962 Texas A&M President Earl Rudder named retired Navy captain Bennett M. Dodson, aged fifty-two, as the first superintendent of the new Texas Maritime Academy at an annual salary of $11,400. Bennett had been chief of staff of the Service Force with the U.S. Pacific Fleet at Pearl Harbor, and he had a wealth of experience in training merchant marine officers. He had been commanding officer of the Merchant Marine Cadet School at Pass Christian in Mississippi, superintendent of the now defunct Pennsylvania Maritime Academy, executive officer of the California Maritime Academy, and head of the Nautical Science Department at the U.S. Merchant Marine Academy. Dodson was also the co-author of *Mathematics for Navigators* and the mathematics supplement to the U.S. Naval Academy's text *Dutton's Navigation*.

From his office in the College Station YMCA building, Dodson helped create Company I, 3rd Brigade—the first Aggie Marine company. He recruited the first class of cadets: they wore ROTC uniforms during their freshman year on the College Station campus and then switched to midshipman uniforms in their sophomore year at the old Fort Crockett building in Galveston.

In 1967, after five years at the helm of the Texas Maritime Academy, Dodson stepped down as superintendent. He had set the course for the first maritime academy on the Gulf Coast.

A&M College President Rudder in January, 1962. This meant that its first superintendent, Captain Bennett Dodson, had little more than seven months to set up the program on the College Station campus. Fortunately he had an additional year to get the Galveston campus ready. He needed it, and more. According to Dodson, the contrast between his Navy office at Pearl Harbor and the old Fort Crockett building in Galveston had given him second thoughts: the "building was in shambles," partly due to the ravages of Hurricane Carla. He set up his headquarters in Room 210 of the YMCA building on the College Station campus.

First things first: the school needed students. "The greatest problem of the Academy is to obtain 50 well qualified students for classes this September," said Superintendent Dodson at the first meeting of the Board of Visitors. The academy was interested in men between the ages of seventeen and twenty-two; they had to be U.S. citizens of "good repute." And they had to be single—never having been married—and remain single until graduation. Inquiries by prospective students were encouraging, Dodson said, but as late as May only six could be said to be "firm"; two of those, as it turned out, would fall away.

A recruiting brochure, handsomely produced on high-quality off-white book paper and printed with navy-blue ink, bragged that Texas ran "a close second" to New York in the quantity of its seagoing traffic. Texas, it said, "needs highly trained young men to help expand the ocean transportation and foreign commerce of the strategically located ports." A lucrative career awaited those with a bachelor's degree in marine

On April 11, 1962, A&M President Rudder appointed the inaugural Board of Visitors to advise the Texas Maritime Academy on business and industry trends and other matters. At their opening meeting, Chairman Sherman Wetmore announces the first order of business by holding up a poster designed to recruit cadets.

transportation or marine engineering and a Coast Guard license. The newly qualified third mate or third assistant engineer would have to pass the Coast Guard exam before receiving his diploma. Enrollment would be capped at two hundred students (fifty in each entering class), most of whom would be from Texas. How much would it cost the students? Estimated expenses came to $6,720, which included tuition, fees, laundry, textbooks, "slide rule and other instruments," uniforms, cruise expenses, and round trip to and from a training ship in New York City. Federal aid

The entire faculty (the superintendent) and student body (four cadets) of the upcoming Texas Maritime Academy visited the ready reserve fleet at Beaumont in June, 1962. There they toured the *State of Maine,* supposed to be the academy's future training ship. Left to right: Donnie Bilancich, Tommy Richards, Carl Haglund, Paul Hermann, and Captain Bennett Dodson.

In September, 1962, Captain Dodson was ready for the opening of the Texas Maritime Academy. Displayed near the flag in his office, room 210 in the YMCA building at the College Station campus, were photographs of his future headquarters at Fort Crockett in Galveston and of candidates for the academy's training ship.

paid for one-third of that amount; thus the total bill was only $4,470 — not for one year but for all four years!

"Historical Memorandum No. One," dated June 28 and signed by Superintendent Dodson, includes a two- by three-inch photo that "represents the faculty, student body, and floating school house of the Texas Maritime Academy." Taken on the wooden upper deck of *State of Maine* in Beaumont, the photo includes only five figures: four students plus Dodson. According to Carl Haglund, one of the pictured students, it was a big adventure. Dodson told them to wear the makeshift uniform he had designed for them out of readily available clothing—everybody could buy a white short-sleeved shirt, black tie, black shoes, and black slacks. Because of its familiar black-and-white effect, cadets came to call it their "penguin" uniform. The group took a small propeller airplane—the students' first flight—from College Station to Beaumont to go window-shopping for a training ship amid the lay-up fleet.

Pickings were slim, and fortunately the academy did not have to settle for that photographed hulk, which continued its gradual decay in Beaumont. But the junket gave Dodson free publicity that began to pique the interest of prospective students. By July 21 enrollment had crept up to fourteen. It was rough going, this recruiting business: he estimated that he had to "talk to about 200 students to get one" who qualified. Each applicant had to meet not only the entrance requirements of Texas A&M

but also the more stringent physical requirements of the Navy and Coast Guard. With little more than a month before the opening day of classes, a big question remained unanswered. Would the Texas Maritime Academy attract enough students to make the endeavor worthwhile?

The program did attract a great and generous friend in Mary Moody Northen, director of the wealthy Moody Foundation. Mrs. Northen offered the new academy a vast tract of property that would connect its Fort Crockett building to Seawall Boulevard (at the area now occupied by the San Luis Hotel). It would have made a handsome beachfront campus, but her offer was not accepted because a permanent campus for a maritime academy ought to have a harbor for its training ship. Mrs. Northen understood and promised further support. She said she hoped she would live to see such "a harbor front site with adequate facilities."

The Texas Maritime Academy was now more than an idea. It had taken four years and three months of hard work, often thankless and seemingly useless, to bring the idea to fruition. The academy had been authorized by the Federal Maritime Act of 1959 and by acts of the 56th Texas Legislature in 1959. Its state funds were appropriated by the 57th Legislature in 1961. In August of 1962 Congress appropriated its federal funds. It was now ready to start offering classes.

Texas Maritime Academy, 1962–1969
Starting from Scratch

THE sizzling sixties changed the world profoundly. Crick, Wilkins, and Watson received the Nobel Prize for decoding the structure of DNA. Houston surgeon Michael DeBakey developed the first artificial heart. It was the decade of great strides in ending racial segregation; Martin Luther King Jr. won the Nobel Peace Prize for his work in civil rights. The Beatles led the British invasion in popular music. The assassinations of John F. Kennedy, Martin Luther King Jr., and Robert F. Kennedy made the United States look like a violent country indeed, and the Vietnam conflict tore it apart. Many college campuses—but not Texas A&M—were flashpoints of demonstrations against the federal government and its war effort.

Everyone was new that fall—students, teachers, administrators, and staff. Superintendent Bennett M. Dodson enthusiastically welcomed the first class of twenty-three "saltwater Aggies" (whittled down from twenty-seven) to the start of their program in the landlocked post oak savannah region of College Station. Three cadets were sophomores transferring out of other majors; the rest were first-time freshmen. (For the record books, that was seventeen more than the six cadets in 1876, the opening year of the Agricultural and Mechanical College of Texas.)

"We've got a fine first-year group with a real Aggie gung-ho attitude," said Dodson. "Gung-ho" was no empty cliché, for Dodson had put these cadets under the guidance of Marine-trained upperclassmen. It was a new experience for A&M—the first Marine Corps company at College Station. The idea was to inspire maritime cadets with a sense of the tradition of the sea. And who better than Marines to do it? Texas A&M had been wanting to establish a Marine program for some time; the addition of maritime cadets made it possible to fill up an entire Marine company.

"I wanted my students to get Marine Corps discipline and knowledge of Naval tradition during their early college life," said Dodson. "I believe

1962

The year 1962 was on the cusp between the old and the new: it continued to feel like the conservative fifties, but as Bob Dylan sang, the times they were a-changin'. In England, the Rolling Stones began performing. It still cost four cents to mail a letter. The big hit song was "I Left My Heart in San Francisco"; also copyrighted that year was the civil rights anthem "We Shall Overcome." James Meredith, a twenty-nine-year-old African American, integrated the campus at Ole Miss. Marilyn Monroe died at age thirty-six of a drug overdose. Johnny Carson debuted as host of the *Tonight Show*. The ABC television network introduced three and a half hours of color programs each week. Gary Powers, the captured American U-2 spy pilot, was exchanged for a Soviet spy. John Glenn became the

▼

25

Texas Maritime Academy
TRAINS
OFFICERS FOR THE SEA

APPLY NOW

Offers the high school graduate an opportunity . . .

. . . to become an officer in the U. S. Merchant Marine

. . . to become an officer in the U. S. Naval Reserve

. . . to earn a Bachelor of Science degree in Marine Engineering or in Marine Transportation.

A four-year course of study with three foreign cruises aboard a training ship. One year of study (freshman year) at the A&M College of Texas at College Station - - three years of study at the Texas Maritime Academy at Galveston.

Classes commence in September 1962 at College Station, Texas.

WRITE TO:
Director of Admissions and Registrar
The A. and M. College of Texas
College Station, Texas

The first recruiting flyer, printed on a pale blue background, touts the opportunity to become an officer in the merchant marine and in the Naval Reserve. Maritime cadets would spend a year at College Station and three years at Galveston and would go on three summer cruises. This invitation to "apply now" was mailed in the summer of 1962 to high school seniors and college freshmen.

first person to orbit the earth. Telstar, the first communication satellite, was launched. The first sugar-free soft drink, Diet-Rite Cola, appeared in the market, as did aluminum cans with removable pull tabs. Two new professional baseball teams were founded: the Houston Colt 45s, later renamed the Astros, and the New York Mets. And the newest state maritime academy opened in College Station, Texas.

the best way to accomplish this is to have them train with senior Marine PLC's [Platoon Leaders Class]." The maritime cadets were assigned to Dorm 11 as Company I, 3rd Brigade, called I-3 for short. Their outfit was arguably tougher in some respects than other companies on main campus: for instance, when Saturday drill ended for everyone else, I-3 began theirs in earnest. Army companies sometimes marched across campus; the new Marine company *ran* everywhere. After the end of this spit-and-polish freshman year, Dodson promised a Navy-style corps, "a more relaxed program the latter three years at Galveston." The *Port of Houston Magazine* in 1963 described the new program in classical western terms with a nautical twist: "Seagoing cadets from the Texas A. & M. College will soon be herding ocean steeds to wharf bitt hitching posts all over the world."

By a happy coincidence, the first day of classes was also the 175th

The First-Day Class of Undergraduates

Donnie B. Bilancich	Kemah, Texas
James W. Brady	Eagle Pass, Texas
Mackay T. Conard	Everglades, Florida
John C. Connor	Kearney, New Jersey
Edward C. Davis	Houston, Texas
Richard M. Dix	Houston, Texas
John J. Gallaher	LaPorte, Texas
Carl H. Haglund	Galveston, Texas
Paul D. Hermann	Galveston, Texas
Donald R. Long	Henderson, Texas
Jimmie O. Low	Port Arthur, Texas
Daniel S. Miller	Dallas, Texas
Robert L. Mitchell	Houston, Texas
Louis M. Newman III	Bryan, Texas
Tommy R. Rasco	West Columbia, Texas
Michael E. Resner	Maplewood, New Jersey
Tommy L. Richards	Groves, Texas
Reymundo L. Rivas	New Braunfels, Texas
Richard C. Schultheis	Houston, Texas
John H. Seate Jr.	Santo Domingo, Dominican Republic
Clarence H. Shepherd	Galveston, Texas
Jack H. Smith	Galveston, Texas
John D. Weber	New Braunfels, Texas

anniversary of the signing of the U.S. Constitution at Philadelphia. Both events signaled great hope for the future. The first Texas Maritime Academy cadets began their first semester on Monday, September 17. According to the list of names in the *Galveston Daily News,* twenty of them were Texans, including six from the Galveston area and three from the City of Galveston. They enrolled in chemistry, engineering, graphics, algebra, trigonometry, English, and physical education on the College Station campus. The idea was to get most of their general education courses, plentifully available on the main campus, out of the way in the first year. The handful of students from the preceding summer were relieved and absolutely delighted to find others had joined them in this great adventure at a school as yet practically unknown. When a teacher called class roll, he said, "What is MART? There's no such major?" The students told him it stood for marine transportation, one of the two majors in the Texas Maritime Academy. "Maritime Academy? What is that? There's no such thing."

For the most part, the maritime cadets were split up. For instance, although they all took English composition, they were mixed in with the other two thousand A&M College freshmen. But, recalled one cadet from the class of 1966, "we took maritime courses in Naval ROTC together. And spherical trig—TMA deck cadets were the only ones in that class." They took classes all over campus and hung out in between classes at the

An unnamed maritime cadet does homework by his bunk in the I-3 dormitory. His study carrel contains the standard accoutrements: books (including his 1961 high school yearbook), lamp, alarm clock, transistor radio, an A&M football player figurine, a photo of his girlfriend, and a box of envelopes for letters home.

YMCA, where Dodson had his office. Another common experience was the barren Aggie social life at College Station, where dating was a challenge: the student body, of course, was all-male. As another cadet recalled, "there were about two girls on the entire College Station campus. When we could, we hitchhiked over to Sam Houston at Huntsville where the ratio was much more favorable."

The beginning of the academy almost coincided with the end of world peace. On October 22 maritime cadets, like the rest of the nation, held their breath when President Kennedy blockaded Cuba because of the recent discovery of its fully equipped missile bases. Russian ships immediately began making their way to what looked like a probable nuclear confrontation with American ships. A suspense-filled week later, Soviet Premier Khrushchev agreed to dismantle the bases, and President Kennedy agreed not to attack Cuba. The Cuban missile crisis almost precipitated a Third World War.

Ironically, just as the Texas Maritime Academy was on the way up, the Marine Research Laboratory was on the way down. Laboratory director Albert Collier, who had helped in the effort to create a maritime academy under the direction of Texas A&M, left to direct the Oceanographic Institute at Florida State University. His successor left soon afterward.

The once busy lab was now down to one professor—Sammy Ray—three assistants, and but a single research project. "The outlook," wrote Ray, "appeared very bleak." And now Ray, too, had a job offer from FSU. But Frank Hubert, dean of the College of Arts and Sciences at College Station, convinced Ray to stay on by naming him director of the laboratory.

In the spring the largest of the buildings in the Fort Crockett complex, the one that housed the A&M Marine Laboratory, was being renovated for the new undergraduate maritime program. It would be the academy's only Galveston building for the next eight years. Not surprisingly, the Fort Crockett building, which had suffered damage from Hurricane Carla in 1962, had not been kept up. Rotting floors were littered with glass from broken windows, detritus from crumbling walls and ceilings, scraps of timber, and an inch-deep layer of silt. Because broken windows allowed birds to fly in and out freely, pigeons had roosted inside, making the place a stinky mess. Sinks, stoves, and refrigerators had rusted away. Electric wires were frayed and broken. The building was hot in the summer and cold in the winter. Just about everything needed to be overhauled for the new school: windows were reglazed, ceilings and walls rebuilt, floors refinished, electric connections rewired. So much had to be done that not everything was ready in time to start classes.

These remodeling problems were received with good-natured collegiate humor: roughing it could be fun. But all of a sudden the school received devastating news. The Texas House of Representatives passed a budget from which the Texas Maritime Academy had been eliminated. The Texas A&M student newspaper, the *Battalion,* ran a photo of Fort Crockett: "This was to be maritime academy headquarters in Galveston . . . [but the] sea school may never occupy old Fort Crockett." The House Appropriations Committee said a projected shortfall in state revenues had forced its hand: according to the Texas constitution, the legislature could not okay deficit spending.

How serious was the predicament? Publicly, officials assured everyone that there was no cause for concern. State Senator Babe Schwartz termed it "just an ordinary problem" in a typical legislative battle. Dodson compared it to losing the first game before going on to win the World Series. However, in a private letter to Ralph Leavitt, president of the Maine Maritime Academy Board of Trustees, Dodson admitted, "Yes, we are in trouble." Meanwhile, as Galveston exerted pressure on the legislature to put the money back in, Dodson had no choice but to proceed "as if the appropriations are in the bag." Understandably worried and overworked, he said, "I have become a lobbyist, salesman, and campaigner and still teach classes." An editorial in the *Battalion* praised his diligence during this critical period. His cadets believed they would not lose the academy but only because Dodson had told them "that he would not let that happen to us." The editorial concluded with a stark nautical metaphor: "By no means can we say that the Academy has its head completely

1963

As the year changed, the fledgling Academy looked forward to the time when it could take up residence in Galveston, where it belonged. The year 1963 brought with it some expected problems, like renovating old Fort Crockett, recruiting the second group of cadets, arranging to take the first training cruise on another academy's ship, and planning for the formal dedication of the Texas Maritime Academy. The Academy was almost aborted by a politically motivated funding squabble. What no one expected, of course, was the way the year would end—with the assassination of a United States President.

Fort Crockett: The First Campus

Fort Crockett, the first Galveston facility used by the Texas Maritime Academy, has an interesting history. Its first structures, built in 1897, were washed away by the Great Storm of 1900. The fort was used to assemble troops and supplies for the First World War. In 1934 Lt. Col. Horace Hickam, commander of the Third Attack Group Air Corps, was killed when the plane he was piloting crashed while landing at Fort Crockett. (Hickam Field in Honolulu, named after him, would be much in the news when the Japanese attacked Pearl Harbor on December 7, 1941.) During the Second World War, Fort Crockett was equipped with shoreside artillery to guard against possible German U-boat activity; the present San Luis Hotel incorporated gun-emplacement mounds as part of its seawall landscaping. The big guns were fired only once, in practice. When it was discovered that sonic reverberation had shattered windows and crockery in nearby homes, they were never fired again. Fort Crockett also housed German prisoners of that war. By 1953, no longer needed for military purposes, the fort was decommissioned.

In 1958 the Marine Laboratory of A&M College of Texas moved to the large white stucco building there. It was joined by the Texas Maritime Academy in 1963. Over the years, that building has served A&M in many ways: equipment was stored in its basement; laboratories, offices, and classrooms filled its first floor; the second and third floors were used for laboratories, offices, and student dormitories. From the 1990s to 2002, A&M offices and labs were also housed next door in the Galveston College building. Much of the old Fort Crockett complex also houses the National Marine Fisheries Service Galveston laboratory.

above water. However we can be sure that the Academy has a Captain that will sail the ship or go down with it."

Happily, some fierce behind-the-scenes political maneuvering got the academy back into the budget. Analyzing what had happened, one observer wrote: "Politics is rough as you know and I feel that the difficulties the Academy suffered last session were punitive." The academy budget, he believed, had been deliberately sabotaged by entrenched old-time political powers in Austin. The real fight had been not over money but over racial segregation. Galveston's relatively liberal delegation, led by the outspoken Senator Schwartz, had proposed several initiatives in favor of racial equality; this was the year of Martin Luther King's "I Have a Dream" speech. The segregationist majority in the legislature had axed the academy's budget as a warning to Galveston to back off. Galveston won that battle and, despite threats, continued to be a state leader in civil rights, supporting the passage of first federal civil rights act the next year.

On February 10, the first twenty-three freshmen took part in a spectacular if ephemeral moment of shipping history when a car caravan took them from College Station to Galveston to tour the nuclear ship *Savannah*. The ship was in the Pelican Island dry dock at Todd Shipyards, the only nuclear ship service facility in the Gulf of Mexico. Cadet Mi-

In the fall of 1962, Captain Dodson teaches the first maritime cadets about spherical trigonometry so that they can understand celestial navigation. As the letters stenciled on the backs of their chairs indicate, the class was held in the YMCA building on the College Station campus. After classes, maritime cadets hung around the YMCA, treating it as their own student center.

chael Resner had arranged the visit through his father, a member of the ship's medical staff. The cadets were also officially welcomed at a luncheon at Gaido's restaurant, where a speaker read President Kennedy's Maritime Day Proclamation, noting that "in the years to come, this nuclear-powered merchant ship will demonstrate to the peoples of the world the intent of the United States of America to use the atom for peaceful purposes."

The *Savannah* would brush against the history of the academy again. It returned to Galveston on May 5, 1963, at Wharf 25. In October of 1966 Dodson testified before the Federal House Subcommittee on Maritime Education and Training that he expected "newer automated and nuclear ships" would make older ships obsolete. Because of widespread fear of nuclear energy, things did not of course turn out that way: no city wanted a radioactive ship to dock nearby. But the nuclear ship would benefit the Texas Maritime Academy in quite another practical way: its future training ship would inherit a grand piano and a gangway from the *Savannah*.

On San Jacinto Day, April 21 (also the day of Aggie Muster), the maritime cadets took their first cruise together—more of a jaunt than a cruise. They boarded *Sam Houston*, the tour boat for the Port of Houston, for an up-close look at varied ships and cargo-handling equipment in a major commercial harbor. Their own permanent training ship was still a dream.

As part of the deal that created the academy, the federal government had promised to contribute a ship on which cadets could train during the summer months. The Maritime Administration (MARAD) had assured U.S. Representative Clark Thompson that a ship would be forthcoming. But when? Every other state maritime academy had its own ship—a kind of floating laboratory for fledgling cadets. A recruiting brochure issued by Texas A&M University (renamed from A&M College of Texas in August of 1963) said: "History will record that . . . the first [ocean-related] study courses of the Texas Maritime Academy got under way; and that in the summer of 1963 some 50 A. and M. Cadets took to the high seas for a summer training cruise to Europe." Until their ship came in, those Texas tag-along cadets had to ship out with 450 New York maritime cadets aboard *Empire State IV*. A *Houston Post* editorial urged all Texans to support the Texas Maritime Academy: "Here is a constructive program out of which will come benefits not only for port cities but for all interested in trade."

That first cruise was an adventure. Twenty cadets had survived the rigors of the first academic year. Decked out in brand new midshipmen uniforms, at 9:00 P.M. on June 3 they left Houston Hobby airport, then the city's only airport. Most of them had never been outside Texas. They

Captain Dodson poses with members of the charter class of maritime cadets next to a tour boat in 1962. They wore the standard-issue Army Corps of Cadets dress uniform but were distinguished by the circular Texas Maritime Academy patch on the left sleeve.

landed at New York's Idlewild (later renamed J. F. Kennedy) airport and made their way by bus to the ship *Empire State IV.* They spent a week of orientation and sightseeing in New York City, especially enjoying Greenwich Village. Then the ship departed. After a politically expedient trip up the Hudson River to make friends with New York state legislators in Albany, they crossed the Atlantic.

Their first foreign stop was Dublin, Ireland, where President Kennedy had been enthusiastically received just a few days before. The rest of the cruise included the ports of Bremen, Germany; Antwerp, Belgium; Naples, Italy (where they had to compete with eight thousand sailors on shore leave from an American aircraft carrier); and Palma, Majorca. Texas cadets, berthed in stacked fold-up bunks below the water line, recall falling asleep to the whoosh of water and crash of waves.

In the fall semester the Texas Maritime Academy (TMA) began its eight-year-long phase of operations split between two campuses. On Monday, September 16, sophomore cadets moved 150 miles south to attend the first undergraduate courses ever offered in Galveston's Fort Crockett building. The next day they received a traditional island welcome from a minimal category 1 storm, Hurricane Cindy. The storm nicked the island with winds gusting up to seventy-four miles per hour, causing only minor inconvenience, as it went ashore on High Island.

Now Fort Crockett housed classrooms, laboratories, library, dining hall, offices, and dormitory rooms. Especially awkward were sleeping and eating accommodations. Carpenters had laid out and constructed dorm rooms, but they were empty—desks and beds had not yet arrived. Nor was there a stove; all the kitchen had was a brand new ice machine. "We can't cook," joked Dodson, "but we can make ice-cubes." For the first couple of weeks the cadets had to live in the same building as nurses at League Hall of the University of Texas Medical Branch (UTMB), Galveston. Cadet Jim Bland must have made mouths water at College Station when he wrote in a special report to the *Battalion* that maritime cadets were "forced to live among some of the sweet young coeds of our rival institution." The reality was somewhat less romantic than he implied. Cadets were segregated on a separate floor, sleeping two, three, or four to a room. A watch stander from the staff and cadet guards posted at both of the stairwells prevented any accidental wandering up to the second floor where the Filipino nurses slept.

Still, it was paradise compared to the all-male College Station campus. While cadets were eating their breakfast three blocks away in the John Sealy cafeteria, maids tidied their rooms and made their beds. A bus, furnished by the City of Galveston, carried cadets the four miles between their dormitory and Fort Crockett, where they attended class, ate lunch, attended more class, and ate supper. Then the bus carried them back to the nurses' dorms. After the long week of classes punctuated by Friday afternoon drill, said Bland, cadets had their pick of three activities: dating lovely "teasips" (the Aggie nickname for students from their rival school),

During the 1963 fall semester, the first in Galveston, maritime cadets study navigational charts in a classroom at Fort Crockett. Of the twenty sophomores, fifteen were majoring in marine transportation and five in marine engineering. Originally published on November 20, 1963, in the *Houston Post*.

sipping a "tall, cool one," or driving home "in the old joy wagon." They could walk to the beach to go swimming or surfing. Not many cadets had cars in those days; hitchhiking was the preferred means of getting around. Dating in Galveston was to prove productive for more than a few members of that first class, who ended up marrying nurses.

When equipment arrived, cadets helped carry it up the stone steps to Fort Crockett. They assembled desks and bed frames; they even moved in their own mattresses. When they finally took up permanent residence at Fort Crockett, cadets trained in rope work found cleverly maritime ways to beat curfew. On Sunday nights, a romantic cadet might sign in, make his way up to the third floor, open his window, throw out a rolled-up pilot's ladder, climb down, and visit his favorite nurse. On Monday morning he would climb up the ladder, roll it back up, and then walk calmly down the stairwell to be counted at morning muster.

Galveston, said cadets, was "like heaven" after the hard-line treatment they had experienced under their Marine Corps commander. Drilling (only once a week) was more relaxed and there were no upperclassmen to haze them. Cadets could and did still get into trouble, but instead of useless pushups, the penalties in Galveston were additional practical duties, like needed maintenance in the dorms. Sophomores assumed all the student leadership roles in Galveston's "Corps of Midshipmen of the Texas Maritime Academy": Jack H. Smith was the first corps commander; Danny S. Miller was executive officer; and the three "section" commands were awarded to Donnie B. Bilancich, Mackay T. Conard, and William W. Radican. Meanwhile, like their predecessors, the thirty-five freshman maritime cadets began their education back at the College Station campus, which had now reluctantly and for the first time admitted women students, about 150 of them. Until 1971, all TMA freshmen spent two semesters completing general education courses in College Station before moving to Galveston for their marine-related classes. Dodson was pleased with the progress: "Now that the trial year is over and we are opening our own facilities, we expect to develop one of the strongest maritime curricula in the nation."

In October the campus installed a flagpole on the south side of Fort Crockett. There the first flag-raising ceremony was held on November 1. Cadets lined up for photographs and speeches.

At Fort Crockett, meals were substantial: a newspaper reported that one cadet who had been on the Galveston campus for only three days claimed it was "the best institutional food he had eaten anywhere." Every breakfast included eggs (made to your order), bacon, ham, grits, donuts, juice, and coffee. However, when a cook caught taking food from the larder was fired, cadets had to prepare their own meals. They were immediately motivated to find a replacement. Willie Hamilton, who drove a milk-delivery truck, volunteered to cook for the cadets. They liked him and his menus so much that they convinced the administration to hire him as chef. A full course lunch and supper cost the school about two dollars per person. Typical fare might include veal cutlets with tomato gravy, simmered buttered potatoes, green beans, a salad bar, hot rolls, sugar cookies, and ice cream. Cadets ate steak once a week, shrimp once a week, and lobster once a month.

Just before the big Aggie-Longhorn football game, a group of cadets created a little ceremony of their own. They reconnoitered the movement

Maritime cadets hold their first flag-raising ceremony at the Fort Crockett campus in Galveston. The date was November 1, 1963.

of the UTMB police around the parking lot at the nurses' dorm. When the police drove off, the cadets painted "Beat the hell out of T.U." across the lot in large letters. Although they were prime suspects in the graffiti caper, the cadets were never caught.

The official dedication ceremony for the Galveston campus was scheduled for Saturday, November 23, at the Seahorse Club of the Seahorse Hotel. The price was $2.50 per person. In preparation, Texas Highway Department crews installed two directional signs, one at 53rd Street and Broadway, pointing to "Texas Maritime Academy." Everything was set, but at the last minute that ceremony, like events all over the nation, was canceled because of the assassination of an American president. On November 22, 1963, while riding in a Dallas motorcade, President John F. Kennedy had been shot and killed. Because of the difficulty of getting the word out to all those invited, Judge Peter LaValle greeted those in attendance by expressing how everyone in Galveston County and the rest of the United States was "shocked and saddened by the tragic events which occurred Friday." He offered a prayer that the new president, Lyndon Johnson, be "granted wisdom and strength in the months to come."

Galveston sophomore cadets were taking a naval history exam when they heard the news from their teacher Dr. Saville. "When he told us JFK had been killed there was complete shock. No one knew what to think. It was the first violent national event we had ever experienced," recalled

On November 16, 1963, Galveston's freshman maritime cadets march with College Station's I-3 on Main Street in downtown Houston, in preparation for the football game against Rice Institute. It was one of two Aggie victories that season.

Cadet Jack Smith. "The dedication was canceled. The City of Galveston shut down: you couldn't even buy a cup of coffee." Up at College Station, the Aggie bonfire was canceled for the first time; its stack was dismantled down to the bare centerpole.

By December, the freshman student body of thirty-five cadets at the College Station campus had shrunk to twenty-seven: three had transferred out of the program voluntarily and five had been forced to drop out because of failure to meet the strict Navy vision requirement. The remaining freshmen got into deep trouble for campus high jinks when they collaborated on setting a smoky fire in the bathroom of a neighboring dormitory: they burned some discarded rubber tires laced with sulphur. What had preceded the incident was the theft of the I-3 guidon, their company flag, by cadets living in that neighboring dormitory. The guidon had been returned, but upperclass Marines, hardened by places like Camp Lejeune, wanted payback.

The raw freshman maritime cadets went along, eagerly of course. They later said they only wanted to see the building evacuated (to enhance the drama of evacuation, they also set a doorway trip wire, though this malfunctioned). They got the desired result, but they also got caught. The incriminating evidence was an unburned page of a newspaper from a small town that was home to only one cadet on campus—a cadet in I-3. Smoke damage ruined clothing and equipment and made the neighboring dormitory uninhabitable for months. Only one saving fact stood between the maritime cadets and washing out: had the entire company been expelled, the maritime program would have suffered an irreparable loss. So the miscreants were allowed to stay, by the skin of their teeth and under close scrutiny. But their beloved company I-3 was disbanded—it was the end of Marine companies on the main campus for many years. Cadets gathered for a final solemn ceremony as they burned their company guidon. Then they were split up, most of the maritime cadets going to Company G, 3rd Brigade (G-3). Although maritime cadets back at Galveston were not surprised by the continuing shenanigans of their former company I-3, which had gathered quite a reputation, they thought the punishment severe. Many fine men came out of the old I-3. One of the more prominent, Marine Maj. Gen. M. T. "Ted" Hopgood Jr. (class of 1965), went on to serve as Texas A&M University's commandant of cadets from 1996 to 2002. Hopgood had been first sergeant of I-3.

On February 1 the postponed dedication finally took place in conjunction with the arrival of the training ship *State of Maine* from the Maine Maritime Academy. State academies were so supportive of one another that each East Coast school made its ship available to Texas: Massachusetts in 1961, to help Texans win over legislative support for their proposed program, and New York in 1963 and Maine in 1964 for regular training cruises. The original invitations, with the date corrected by hand, were mailed out once again. That Saturday was beautiful, clearing by midmorning. Festivities began with a reception at UTMB for Lieu-

1964

In 1964, the federal Civil Rights Act prohibited employers from discriminating on the basis of race, sex, national origin, or religion. The Gulf of Tonkin Resolution justified U.S. military buildup in Vietnam. The Fort Crockett campus was dedicated and Texas Maritime Academy cadets embarked on their only spring training cruise. The A&M Marine Laboratory, the other tenant at Fort Crockett, offered its first graduate course.

tenant Governor Preston Smith and Speaker of the House Byron Tunnell, followed by the formal dedication at 2:00 P.M. at Fort Crockett, complete with marches and the national anthem played by the Ball High School band. A reception at the Seahorse Hotel was followed by dinner at Gaido's restaurant.

Smith was given some speaking points to include in his keynote address. First, he was asked to sound the visionary note that the Texas Maritime Academy hoped to become the Kings Point or Annapolis of Texas. Second, he was told to mention that "the Academy will be of great assistance in getting the Texas Navy back to sea." It was an inside joke: the Texas Navy, a historical society, has had no ships at sea—or anywhere, for that matter—since the days of the Republic of Texas. The honorary organization, however, had its political uses: Texas Governor John Connally named Ralph A. Leavitt an admiral in the Texas Navy for his service to the Texas Maritime Academy.

The midnight after the dedication, the *State of Maine* departed for its two-month cruise with all forty-one Texas Maritime Academy cadets. Because Texas cadets were yanked out of Texas A&M to take their "summer" cruise in the spring of that year—the only spring cruise in the history of the Texas program—they had to make up the missed academic work during the following summer term. Freshman did it as civilian students at College Station; sophomores did it at Galveston. The ship toured the Caribbean, and afterward the cadets spent a couple of weekends in Castine, Maine. Although it was April, four feet of snow lay on the ground, much to the surprise of the Texas boys. The families of the Maine

Some five hundred people attended the February 1, 1964, dedication of Fort Crockett building 311 (left) as the campus of the Texas Maritime Academy. The dignitaries are in the reviewing stand (left); first- and second-year TMA cadets along with Maine Maritime cadets are wearing white caps (right). The view is east, past other buildings in the Fort Crockett complex toward the Gulf of Mexico. At the conclusion of the ceremony, Texas cadets would board *State of Maine* for TMA's only spring training cruise.

cadets took them in and fed them well, but the Texas cadets were happy
to return to warm, sunny weather in Texas on April 11. Ten days later,
on April 21, the Texas Maritime Academy held its first ever Aggie Muster, a ceremony honoring former students who had died in the past year.
Cadets fired a military salute and played taps. Sophomores in Galveston
completed the second part of their interrupted spring semester before going on to mandatory summer school.

After almost fading out of existence in 1962, the Marine Laboratory
in Galveston was now growing under its director Sammy Ray. In August
of 1964, A&M Chancellor Frank Hubert authorized its first graduate science course, Biology 662, the biology of mollusca. Eleven graduate students enrolled, including Donald Harper, who would later join the faculty. In subsequent summers other graduate and undergraduate biology
courses (like invertebrate zoology) listed in the College Station catalog
would be offered in Galveston. "It was a 5-week summer course that was
taught in 4 weeks," recalled Harper. It was team-taught by Drs. Harold
Harry, Sammy Ray, and J. G. Mackin—"all of them intimidating to neophyte graduate students. Lectures began at 0900 (although we were

The vessel chosen as the TMA training ship *Texas Clipper* had a distinguished twenty-year history. From 1944 to 1946, as the Navy *USS Queens* (pictured), she had carried troops and cargo. American Export Lines then converted her into a commercial passenger-cargo carrier. From 1948 to 1958 she sailed as *Excambion*, one of the celebrated "Four Aces" plying the waters between New York and the Mediterranean.

Searching for a Ship: Which *Texas Clipper?*

The federal Maritime Administration supplies each state maritime academy with a training ship. A&M President Earl Rudder had promised Texas Maritime Academy its own ship by the summer of 1965. As Superintendent Dodson and others wandered all over the country in search of a suitable Texas training ship, several candidates were mentioned. In June of 1962, rumors had circulated that Texas might get the hand-me-down ship USS *Comfort*, a World War II hospital and troop-transport vessel, from the Maine Maritime Academy. Then A&M officials said they would pick either *Alcoa Clipper* or *Alcoa Corsair*, both of which had more rooms that could be adapted for classroom use. In June of 1964 they were leaning toward *Alcoa Clipper*. But it did not work out that way. In October, 1964, the U.S. Maritime Administration announced that it would donate the American Export Lines vessel *Excalibur*, due to be taken out of service in March, 1965. Sight unseen, the eager Texas Maritime Academy named it *Texas Clipper*. But *Excalibur* was sold instead to Orient Overseas Line for trans-Pacific service.

Finally in March, the academy announced the acquisition of *Excambion*, like *Excalibur* one of the famous "Four Aces" luxury liners that ran cruises between New York and the Mediterranean. She had been inactive and laid up in the Hudson River since 1959. Built as USS *Queens* in 1944, she had been used to transport troops and cargo during the Second World War. The ship had participated in the Iwo Jima campaign. In June of 1965 she was refitted and began service as the first *Texas Clipper* training ship for the Texas Maritime Academy. She served the academy until the conclusion of her last cruise in August of 1994. In 1996 she was replaced by *Texas Clipper II*, formerly the hydrographic survey ship USNS *Chauvenet*. The first *Texas Clipper* would be sunk as an artificial reef off Port Isabel, Texas, in November of 2005.

usually glued to our microscopes by 0800) every morning and ended about noon for lunch, then sometimes continued into the afternoon. We took a break for dinner, then most of us continued working in the lab until around midnight. . . . I underwent major decompression after the course was over."

It was the first of many courses. The success of these offerings demonstrated a demand for ocean-related sciences, at least at the graduate level, in Galveston. Years down the road, when Texas A&M was looking for a place to start an undergraduate program in the marine sciences, the ongoing activities of the Marine Laboratory made Galveston the most logical site.

That same August, an international political decision in Washington would have far-reaching consequences for college-age men. The small conflict in a place called Vietnam became more serious. The tumult heated up as the Gulf of Tonkin Resolution gave President Lyndon Baines Johnson blanket authority to wage war—a move that would create a growing need for the military to draft men above the age of eighteen. The resolution also led to the country's growing need for merchant marine transportation of material for the nation's defense. His popularity bolstered by his handling of foreign troubles, LBJ easily beat challenger Senator Barry Goldwater in the November election.

However, these national and international events mattered less to cadets than the goings-on at nearby watering holes like Silver Spot, Marguerite's, and Elbow Room. Although they were under age, clean-cut cadets were usually welcome to study at their favorite tavern. Barmaids might even slip them an occasional beer and let them stay after hours to watch a risqué floor show. Or they could watch programs on the bar's TV set. That year they saw the Beatles' first appearance on the *Ed Sullivan Show* and an innovation in televised sports—the instant replay.

In January of 1965 Maritime Academy officials were trying to increase enrollment for the upcoming summer cruise on a still unidentified ship. There were forty-two cadets in Galveston, nineteen juniors and twenty-three sophomores; College Station had twenty-five freshmen cadets. National advertisements said the academy was looking for men between the ages of seventeen and twenty-two who had finished high school, were American citizens, could pass a physical exam, and were interested in taking college-level courses in English, mathematics, history, and government during a ten-week cruise to Nova Scotia, Norway, Sweden, Scotland, and New York.

1965

In 1965 the academy was consumed with anticipation over finally getting its own ship. Also memorable that year was the creation of a TMA program to fill up its staterooms with recent high school graduates.

In March the school at last announced the acquisition of its own training ship. After having been mothballed for five years as part of the National Reserve Fleet in the Hudson River, the *Excambion/Clipper* was "a bloody mess." She had been coated with a tarlike substance and left to rust just north of New York City. Even under the best of conditions—and these were not—she was an old ship with outdated equipment. She needed so much work that the $250,000 made available by the federal government was not enough.

Todd Shipyards, however, had as its personnel director Emmett O. Kirkham, a charter member of the TMA Board of Visitors. The company made the refitting possible by offering an obviously low underbid, $25,000 less than the next lowest bid, to be awarded the contract. It was more of a gift than a bid, Superintendent Dodson later recalled. The ship was towed from New York to Galveston, where she arrived on May 16, a week and a half late. Once again harbor pilot Sherman Wetmore, who had chaired the Galveston committee that helped create the academy, donated his time to help out: he drove his private automobile up to New York, where he boarded the ship and captained her as she was towed to Galveston.

Time was a critical factor. The *Clipper* was scheduled to depart for her inaugural training cruise just one month later, on June 15. Under General Manager Ralph Anselmi, Todd Shipyards sacrificed time and money to get her ready—the company even did extra work not required by the bid specifications. According to Dodson, the academy owed a great deal to the shipyard: "In three weeks we spent all of the $250,000 and the rudder and the propeller still wouldn't move. But Todd agreed to continue until the rudder and propeller were ready." The shipyard ended up donating an extra $40,000 worth of work. Still there was not enough time to do the work properly or make the ship fully functional.

The ship could sleep about 250 people; with only sixty or so cadets plus officers and crew members, she would be half empty. Why not try to fill her up with brand new high school graduates? That would kill two birds with one stone: revenue from the extra passengers would help the cash-strapped academy, and those passengers would make excellent prospects for a low-enrollment school having difficulty finding new cadets. Recruiting these passengers was a last-minute decision, just four weeks before the ship departed.

Dodson's wife drove to Galveston's Rosenberg Library to do some research: she found and copied the names and addresses of all high schools in large and midsize cities. TMA mailed each school an advertising pamphlet and took out an advertisement in school newspapers for a "special freshman summer cruise." It was billed as a "rewarding cruise study at sea." Prospective preparatory or prep cadets, as they came to be called, were told to pack swimming trunks, a jacket, a plastic rain coat, six wooden clothes hangers, a jackknife, sewing kit, toiletries, and shoeshine kit. The ship would be in port for thirty-five days; prep cadets would attend classes in two college subjects (chosen from English, history, government, and mathematics) while the ship was at sea for the other thirty-five days. They would also work about four hours a day cleaning the ship and serving food in the galley. Their total cost, includ-

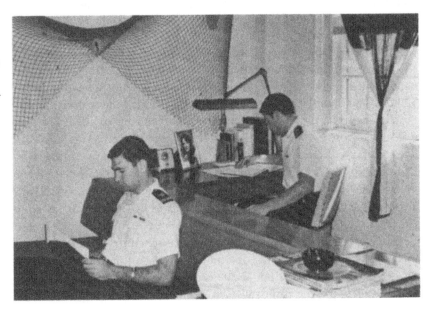

Cadets William Radican and Makay Conard study in their dormitory room in the Fort Crockett building. From their window (right), one could easily see the Gulf of Mexico.

ing tuition, uniforms, textbooks, and room and board, came to $425 for
Texas residents, plus $100 for out-of-state students—a real bargain for a
seventy-day cruise. The "suggested minimum" for spending money was
$75. The actual itinerary (changed somewhat from what had been ad-
vertised) included stops in Halifax, Nova Scotia; Southampton, England;
Copenhagen, Denmark; Edinburgh, Scotland; and Bermuda.

Lawrence Carter, who sailed aboard *Texas Clipper* as cook for more
than twenty cruises, recalled that the galley was still using oil-burning
stoves. The galley and engine rooms were very hot. Air conditioning,
a point of pride when the ship had carried passengers in the 1950s, no
longer worked. The heating had also gone out. Some ship's officers, lucky
enough to have a porthole, could not get it open for ventilation. They got
a crew member to fix it. "He came up with a sledgehammer and a crow
bar and broke out the window," recalled officer Jack Lane. That was fine

The First Cruise of the *Clipper*: A Bumpy Ride in 1965

Under the command of Captain Bennett M. Dodson, the patched-up
Clipper finally set sail with about 125 cadets, more than half of them
prep cadets. The ship was a floating hybrid: many cadets called her
"a wreck." She still had luxurious appurtenances from her liner days:
swimming pool (no longer functional); teakwood decking, railings, and
folding deck chairs; wood-paneled bar; original artwork in the dining hall
on the quarterdeck and in the afterbar; and mirrored paneling behind her
glass-and-chrome grand staircase. On the other hand, she showed the effects of half a dozen years of neglect: dirt, grime everywhere; all the decks
coated in a sticky preservative covered by a layer of canvas; crumbling
utilities; and marginally operational machinery. And some of the hastily
completed and inadequately supervised repair work proved shoddy.

As might be expected, she broke down soon after she left the pier.
The *Galveston Daily News* reported that "water pipes and air pipes, idle
seven years, went out. Pumps and circuits malfunctioned." The boilers
gave trouble, the evaporator did not work, and—no less important—
the toilets would not flush. She was towed back for two more days of repair. Then she sailed again, but did not get far from Galveston's outer bar
before she broke down a second time. She bobbed dead in the water, waiting for the delivery of a lube oil filter. Then she underwent an additional
two days of testing before she headed out to the open seas, bound for Nova
Scotia on July 1, two weeks late.

Her troubles were not yet over. At sea, the air ejector system failed,
hobbling the ship to a miserable three knots until it was fixed. Then off the
coast of Miami on the Fourth of July, she broke down a fourth time. While
engineers worked through the night to restore power, the crew on deck
enjoyed watching Miami's fireworks display. The rest of the trip was relatively smooth sailing. But the ship looked anything but shipshape. "We
only took delivery of her four weeks ago," Dodson told a newspaper reporter from the Halifax *Mail-Star*. "So you will have to excuse the mess."

while they were in the Gulf of Mexico but made them shiver when they reached Halifax with overnight lows of thirty-eight degrees.

As noted, the decks were slathered with a viscous preservative, covered by hay and canvas. That was how ships were mothballed in the Hudson River. For the rest of the summer the cadets peeled up the canvas and scraped off the glutinous mess—a process that would continue for four or five years. Rotten teak decking had to be torn up and heaved overboard. Cadets spent days and nights chipping rust, cleaning surfaces, and painting. It was miserable, dirty work. Still it was *their* ship, and that made all the difference. They took a certain pride in all the difficulties and hardships, like Mr. Allnut's affection for the chronic breakdown boiler on board the old *African Queen* in C. S. Forester's novel of the same name.

When the *Clipper* returned to her new home at Pier 19 on August 22, she received a wounded hero's welcome. After that, of course, maintenance continued: the ship needed a new small auxiliary boiler and a rectifier to convert shoreside AC current to DC current for use onboard the ship. Writing in commemoration of the twenty-fifth cruise of *Texas Clipper*, Galveston–Texas City harbor pilot Jim Coonrod, class of 1967, recalled that he and his entrepreneurial roommate had bought DC-current hair clippers to make money for college expenses. They charged fifty cents a haircut, splitting half of that and banking the other half to pay off the clippers. Remembering the countless heads of cadets needing haircuts, he said, "To this day, I can't stand cutting hair. I don't even like to go to a barber."

In the summer, while the *Clipper* was at sea, draft quotas had doubled to support the war effort in Vietnam. Draft quotas continued to rise as eighteen-year-old men increasingly questioned the rationale for the war.

From 1965 to 1970, *Texas Clipper* was berthed at Pier 19 near downtown Galveston. In this 1968 photo the tall building in the background is the Lipton Tea plant; between it and the *Clipper* is the Galveston Wharves commercial boat basin with its mosquito fleet—the shrimp boats. In April of 1997, the Ocean Star Offshore Drilling Rig museum would be installed where the *Clipper* had been berthed.

Texas maritime cadets, like college students around the nation, were exempt from the draft as long as they continued their education. After graduation, those who served in the merchant marine remained exempt because their jobs were seen as crucial to American defense. The nation desperately needed ship officers, but the Coast Guard refused to issue licenses to qualified cadets until they had also graduated (that would change the following year).

A month after the end of the cruise, classes resumed. The academy would quickly outgrow the sixty-cadet-capacity dorms at Fort Crockett and begin to house overflow four miles away on the training ship. Underclassmen fondly recalled that they "managed to keep the passageways flooded with water, the bulkheads covered with shaving cream, and the Gulf of Mexico littered with upperclassmen." But even shipboard spaces were scarce because they were occupied for other purposes, like training of seamen by the union. Academy administrators were working on a deal to get their dream campus on Pelican Island, almost entirely undeveloped except for Todd Shipyards, the AM radio station KGBC, and a bascule drawbridge to Galveston Island. Developer George Mitchell (A&M class of 1940) talked about donating land on Pelican Island to the academy. Meanwhile, junior and senior cadets were offered housing subsidies to find off-campus accommodations at places like the Driftwood Motel. Those lucky enough to have cars could plug in their eight-track tapes and cruise the seawall to observe miniskirts, both introduced that year; or they might drive up to watch the professional baseball team play their first season under the new name Houston Astros. If they smoked—and most did in those days—their cigarette packs carried the first surgeon general's warning.

Four years had passed since the first maritime cadets had started classes in College Station. It was time for graduation. They had had the vision and the faith to see the fledgling program through some difficult times. They had taken their three training cruises on three different ships: *Empire State*, *State of Maine*, and *Texas Clipper*. Now, on May 26, they attended the first ever license presentation ceremony, held in the Fellowship Hall of the Moody Memorial First Methodist Church in Galveston. That charter class included thirteen seniors: James W. Brady, Mackay T. Conard, John C. Connor, Robert B. Ellis Jr., Carl H. Haglund, Paul D. Hermann Jr., William W. Radican, Michael E. Resner, Tommy L. Richards, Joseph H. Schmidt, Richard C. Schultheis, John H. Seate Jr., and Jack H. Smith. Ten were from Texas (half of those from Galveston); the others were from Florida, California, and Maryland. A news story called TMA the "fastest growing of the five state Maritime Academies." True, it had grown 300 percent in the last four years, but that astonishing percentage was somewhat misleading: it had begun as a freshman class of twenty-three and had added a class each year since—its modest total enrollment was still fewer than a hundred students. A&M President Earl Rudder

1966

The charter class of cadets graduated in 1966, and Texas A&M was named a Sea Grant institution.

gave the keynote address for the historic event. Superintendent Dodson presided over the ceremony; Rear Admiral J. D. Craik, who would soon succeed Dodson, presented all thirteen cadets with Coast Guard licenses.

Two days later, Dodson took the eight graduating cadets—Connor, Resner, Richards, and Schmidt in Marine Engineering; Radican, Schultheis, Seate, and Smith in Marine Transportation—to College Station to receive their diplomas. Students continued to follow this back-to-back two-ceremony practice for the next nineteen years until Galveston held its own commencement ceremonies. For the first time, students from the Galveston campus appeared in an Aggie commencement; Texas Maritime Academy was the next-to-last college alphabetically, just before Veterinary Medicine, to march across the stage in G. Rollie White Coliseum. The new third mates and third assistant engineers had no difficulty finding jobs. By summer ten were sailing merchant ships, and the other three were continuing their studies. Jack Smith's experience was typical: he graduated on Saturday morning, reported to a Lykes Brothers ship on Sunday morning, and sailed out in charge of the watch that evening.

Texas Clipper's second annual ten-week cruise, from June 10 to August 16, was to European ports. She left the dock on time, and in con-

On May 26, 1966, the first licensing ceremony was held at the Fellowship Hall of Moody Memorial First Methodist Church in Galveston. The official program lists the thirteen charter cadets who made it through the four years. Presenting them with their Coast Guard licenses is James D. Craik, who would become the second TMA superintendent in 1968.

CHARTER CLASS
TEXAS MARITIME ACADEMY
OF
TEXAS A&M UNIVERSITY

*

Brady, James W. .... Eagle Pass, Texas
Conard, Mackay T. .... Everglades, Florida
Connor, John C. .... Galveston, Texas
Ellis, Robert B., Jr. .... Orinda, California
Hoglund, Carl H. .... Galveston, Texas
Hermann, Paul D., Jr. .... Galveston, Texas
Radican, William W. .... Wake Village, Texas
Resner, Michael E. .... Rockville, Maryland
Richards, Tommy L. .... Groves, Texas
Schmidt, Joseph H. .... Galveston, Texas
Schultheis, Richard C. .... Houston, Texas
Seate, John H., Jr. .... Kemah, Texas
Smith, Jack H. .... Galveston, Texas

Invocation
THE REVEREND AMOS CAREY
Lieutenant Commander (ChC) U.S.N.R.
Saint George's Episcopal Church
Texas City, Texas

★

Presiding
CAPTAIN BENNETT M. DODSON
Superintendent
Texas Maritime Academy

★

Board of Visitors Awards
REAR ADMIRAL SHERMAN B. WHITMORE, USNR (Ret.)
Chairman, Board of Visitors
Texas Maritime Academy

★

Propeller Club Award
MR. STEWART A. LE BLANC, JR.
President
The Propeller Club of the United States—Galveston

★

Navy League Award
MR. PRICE SMITH
Treasurer
Navy League of the United States
Galveston Chapter

★

Remarks
GENERAL EARL RUDDER
President
Texas A&M University System

★

Presentation of Licenses
REAR ADMIRAL J. D. CRAIK, U.S. COAST GUARD
Commandant, Eighth Coast Guard District

★

Benediction
MONSIGNOR J. J. RUDDY
Saint Patrick's Parish

trast to the previous year's cruise, this one was mechanically smooth. And profitable for seniors. It was a "senior privilege" (a traditional Aggie phrase reserving certain activities for upperclassmen) to make money from the prep cadets by selling so-called "sea stamps" for a dollar each. Preps were told they could not mail letters *at sea* unless they paid a buck to have each envelope franked with a stamp-pad marker over which a senior wrote some official-sounding gibberish. Then the envelopes were put in a coffee can and thrown overboard. Seniors could pull in about five hundred dollars before the preps got wise to the scam and began mailing all their envelopes in foreign post offices. The ship returned to a rousing welcome by well-wishers and a concert by the Ball High School band. Dodson announced that the winner of the Propeller Club's national essay contest would be given a free trip on an American ship. The academy, having completed its first cycle of operation, now was beginning its fifth year.

In those days more than half of all A&M freshman, reported the Bryan *Eagle,* dropped out in their first year. Most often, they blamed the all-male character of the College Station campus. Understandably, sophomore maritime cadets couldn't wait to switch campuses and make the "migration to Galveston, a city with real cute girls and other things foreign to College Station." That may have taken some of the sting out of being hazed as the lowest class for two consecutive years: as freshmen at College Station and as sophomores at Galveston. Cadets living on the *Clipper,* docked downtown at Pier 19, found solace at a nearby watering hole called Mike's Place, where Dotty greeted everyone with a cheery "How y'all!" Maritime freshmen at College Station described their favorite activity as "leaving for the weekend" and said they looked forward to the "more suitable male-female ratio" in Galveston.

On December 15, the Christmas Ball showed what social life on the island could offer. It was a romantic formal affair, with officers and cadets in their dress blues and ladies in cocktail dresses. That fall, the more routine entertainment for cadets was crowding around the TV to watch two series that had just debuted: *Star Trek* and *Mission Impossible.*

Meanwhile the passage of a piece of federal legislation suggested that the Galveston campus was in for some dramatic academic changes. The National Sea Grant College and Program Act of 1966 had given $475,000 to four Sea Grant institutions: Oregon State University, University of Washington, University of Rhode Island, and Texas A&M University. Founded as a Land Grant institution in 1876, A&M was now a Sea Grant institution as well and would turn its attention increasingly toward marine-related study. Texas A&M had only one campus with a seacoast—the Maritime Academy.

The Vietnam conflict, dominating nightly television news, affected campus life in very practical ways. Merchant ships were supplying the more than 500,000 American troops in Vietnam. The nation urgently needed qualified merchant marine officers to run those ships. TMA signed an

1967

In 1967, to help the nation with its war effort, TMA hosted a quick-start licensing program for outside students and allowed regular cadets to receive their licenses three months early. The first TMA superintendent stepped down. And enrollment continued to grow.

Marine Laboratory of A&M:
Science in the Background

The Marine Laboratory, established in 1952, was the first A&M program in Galveston. Oddly enough, it was set up on the campus of the Medical Branch of University of Texas. For its first six years the lab was a field station for oyster research, under the direction of A&M's Oceanography Department, in a war surplus frame building. Then in 1958 the laboratory moved a few miles southwest to the white stucco building, also surplus from World War II, at the Fort Crockett complex. During those early years its directors included Dr. John G. Mackin, Albert Collier, and Dr. Robert Stevenson. Faculty at the marine lab served as liaison between academic administrators at Texas A&M and the subcommittee of the Galveston Chamber of Commerce in their successful effort to establish the Texas Maritime Academy.

A&M's Department of Wildlife and Fisheries began funding the lab, which began offering graduate courses. Then in 1966, the laboratory offered its first undergraduate course in marine biology. Some see these courses as paving the way for all future undergraduate programs in the marine sciences; but the lab's faculty members were not aware that administrators at College Station were planning to add an undergraduate science major to the maritime academy. In 1971, the lab and its faculty were absorbed into the College of Marine Sciences and Maritime Resources, as the Department of Marine Sciences, which taught a full range of undergraduate courses leading to a bachelor of science degree.

agreement with the Masters, Mates & Pilots (MM&P) union to host an intensive ninety-day licensing program for merchant mariners, Coast Guard men, and Navy men. To qualify for admission, all they needed was a high school equivalency diploma and two years of experience standing watch in the Navy or Coast Guard. This program, known as MATES, cost students nothing and paid them a five-hundred-dollar monthly stipend. These special students lived aboard *Texas Clipper* in a "private stateroom with room steward service." The first cycle, which began in mid-January, attracted about eighty candidates; the second and third, which began in mid-March, had about sixty each. Ironically, the popularity of the union program in Texas and elsewhere may have hurt the academies politically. Some critics would come to suggest that expensively trained academy officers were overeducated and less practical than these quickly produced union-trained counterparts. Still, the nation needed more maritime officers, and TMA was happy to oblige.

The Vietnam conflict also resulted in early licensing and delayed graduation for the maritime cadets' class of 1967. Ten graduated at College Station on January 21, and eleven received their licenses at the Fellowship Hall of the Moody Memorial First Methodist Church in Galveston on Monday, February 6. If they wanted a degree, they had to return to college to make up the credits for that missing last semester. Thus their

In the spring of 1967, cadets of the Texas Maritime Academy formed the school's organized sport—baseball. The original players wore classically styled uniforms emblazoned with the team name "Maritime." The team practiced on the vast grassy area between Fort Crockett and Seawall Boulevard. Source: *Voyager,* 1968.

situation was similar to that of students during 1940s who left before graduation to serve their country in the Second World War. The early departure had been authorized because of the critical need for maritime officers to supply the American war effort in Vietnam.

In the keynote address at the licensing ceremony, Dodson noted how quickly the academy had changed: future cadets would have a different campus life, attending classes at "a multi-oceanography center on Pelican Island." In an unprecedented move, the junior class had to take over the running of the corps of cadets. In January Jim Marcontell, a senior, handed over command to William Pickavance, a junior. This marked the only time that an academy corps commander was to serve longer than one year. Pickavance served for sixteen months; he would later became the first TMA cadet to reach the rank of admiral in the U.S. Navy.

In May one lone TMA cadet, James Coonrod, went to College Station to receive his degree in marine transportation. The next month the *Clipper* departed Pier 19 with 156 cadets and a crew of 48 for a Caribbean and South American cruise, her third annual trip. Cadets continued to struggle with removing the preservative from decks: they heated the gunk with blowtorches, worked it up bit by bit with long-handled flat-blade scrapers, and tossed the mess—in those innocent days before international dumping restrictions—into the deep. Mike Cardasco recalled that because of numerous infractions, he and two other cadets had to work off so many "extra hours" that they would not get liberty in Willemstad. Cardasco secretly unscrewed the irreplaceable acorn nut from the ship's helm and held it hostage. After a futile five-hour search for the

Pelican Island: Mitchell Campus

Pelican Island, just north of Galveston Island, was a dollop-shaped sandbar with a subsoil of hard yellow clay, formed into an island by the gradual accretion of two sandbars. When the Texas Legislature gave it to the City of Galveston in 1856, the island was so inconsequential that the county clerk's office did not even bother recording the deed for sixteen years. Sometime in the middle of the nineteenth century the sternwheeler *Bardstown*, anchored on the west end of the island, broke up in a storm and sank with six hundred dollars in gold in a safe that has never been recovered. In 1880, the first quarantine station on the island began accepting immigrants from Europe. Unfortunately, the water was too shallow for passenger ships, so one of the buildings was moved across the channel to Fort Point. Dredging of the Houston Ship Channel, completed in 1914, added a clay-and-silt arm to the island's northeast edge. In 1957 a $6 million bridge—almost four years in the making—was completed; strangely enough the railroad tracks, which cost more than the roadway to build, have never been used (although some people claim one train did cross). The bridge served only fishermen, shipyard workers, and the staff of the AM radio station. Before the bridge was built, they had had to cross the Galveston ship channel by ferry.

Because it was tied up in breach-of-contract lawsuits between the Pelican Island Development Corporation and the City of Galveston, Pelican Island was unavailable for other uses. The solution to this legal quagmire came in the form of a brokered agreement to have both parties drop their lawsuits if a third party were to buy the island. In December, 1964, energy businessman and former A&M student George Mitchell bought the 2,750 acres of available land for $1.9 million. Then in March of 1965, he and the Galveston City Council donated a hundred acres of it to educational institutions: sixty acres to the Gulf Universities Research Corporation (GURC, a consortium of seven universities, including A&M, Rice, University of Houston, University of Texas, Southern Methodist University, Louisiana State University, and Florida State University), and forty acres to Texas Maritime Academy. Mitchell stipulated that if GURC did not work out, all one hundred acres would go to the maritime academy, which was what eventually happened.

"With the land and [a $1 million] Moody Foundation grant," said TMA Superintendent Dodson, "we can see light ahead." In January of 1967, the *Galveston Daily News* carried a front-page story saying that the Pelican Island acreage had been granted to TMA to replace the Fort Crockett site. The land was dedicated as Mitchell campus in 1968 and opened for classes in September of 1971.

nut, the captain declared that everyone would have shore leave. It had the desired result. Soon afterward, a bulky envelope appeared on the door to the captain's quarters with this message: "A Big Nut for a Big Wheel."

The trip south was also the academy's first chance to cross the equator and have cadets undergo the age-old initiation rite that changes pollywogs (neophyte sailors) into shellbacks (those who have "crossed the line"). The ceremony involved such things as bowing down to King Nep-

The second class of maritime cadets receive Coast Guard licenses at the fellowship hall of Galveston's Moody Memorial First Methodist Church, February 6, 1967. The only licensing ceremony ever held in February—three months early—enabled new maritime officers to fill the critical need for the American war effort in Vietnam.

tune, a shellback with a mophead wig and a trident; being slathered with galley lard; and kissing the greased belly of the "Royal Baby," a corpulent shellback dressed only in a diaper. Besides the initiation, the cruise was notable for its participation in a rescue. The *Clipper* changed its course to pick up an ill captain of a Greek crew on the Liberian-flag ship *Albino*. The captain, who had cut his hand badly, had his wound treated on the *Clipper* on the way to Rio de Janeiro. The story ended happily, for the injured captain was later able to rejoin his ship.

During the cruise, after five years as the charter superintendent of TMA, Dodson announced his retirement, to become effective November 15. He said his association with Texas A&M had been "one of the most pleasant of relations" partly because of the "splendid support" of President Rudder and others. He had actually planned to retire a year earlier, he said, but was convinced to stay on until the end of the session of the Texas Legislature. Dodson, who had first gone to sea in 1926, said that after forty-one years of sea service, he wanted to do some other things "before I'm too old." As he confessed to the *Houston Post*, he intended "to see what dry land is like." More than a dozen candidates applied to replace Dodson. The Board of Visitors passed a resolution in July expressing "the sincerest appreciation" for Dodson's having "assured the Academy an outstanding place in Maritime Education." About 250 people attended a farewell dinner held by the Galveston Propeller Club at the Jack Tar Hotel. Rudder lauded Dodson for establishing the academy on a "firm foundation." Dodson was given the key to the City of Galveston along with a plaque praising his "superior leadership, vision and unselfish service."

The academy was in serious financial difficulties that summer. As sometimes occurs in newly formed institutions, accounting practices were not as rigorous or thrifty as they should have been. For instance, faculty members recall being served lobster dinners for just seventy-five cents—much less than the cost to the school. And administrators, disregarding rules, might pay for travel out of funds earmarked for educational expenses. In June College Station sent down a business manager, Milton Abelow, to be in charge of expenditures, balance the budget, and institute reliable accounting controls. He did just that. Under his direction, the school got out of the red and into the black. According to Sammy Ray, he was single-handedly responsible for creating order out of accounting chaos. Without his unpopular tightfisted management style, the academy might have had to close operations. As the school evolved, Abelow would continue to serve as business manager, fiscal officer, and assistant to the president for budgets and planning until his retirement almost twenty-seven years later.

Captain Alfred Philbrick, who had joined the TMA in February as head of the Department of Marine Transportation, replaced Dodson as master of *Texas Clipper* for her next cruise, the first of his many. Philbrick was a 1950 graduate of Maine Maritime Academy, where he had served as executive officer for nine years. He had been executive officer aboard *State of Maine* when that ship picked up Galveston cadets in 1964. At TMA, he shared overall administrative responsibilities for the program during its early years. He was fond of telling the following story about what strange things can happen when you work with cadets, who all start out as inexperienced boys.

"We were leaving Marseilles one time and when we took departure at the breakwater, we had hard left rudder on the ship. There were shoals about a mile ahead of us and two ships were coming at us. The command came to go back to midships and the rudder wouldn't answer. Some cadet had inadvertently pulled a pin in the steering engine room that connects the steering engine to the rudder. He didn't know what he was doing—when you secure in port, which he had done, you always pull that pin so nobody can fiddle around and break anything, so when we left, he was told to secure for sailing and he just secured it like when he came in." Needless to say, his misunderstanding led to some hectic moments.

In September Rear Admiral J. D. Craik was appointed superintendent. He had been scheduled to start in November of 1967, but unforeseen circumstances delayed his actual arrival until February of 1968; Philbrick acted as superintendent in the meanwhile. Craik, born in Andover, Massachusetts, had retired as commandant of the Eighth U.S. Coast Guard District in New Orleans in 1966. When he retired he received the Distinguished Service Medal, and the Coast Guard Station in Grand Isle, Louisiana, named its entry street Rear Adm. James D. Craik Drive. In 1937, he had been the first U.S. government whaling inspector aboard a factory ship, *SS Frango*. He believed that merchant marine cadets had to

In September of 1967 Rear Admiral James Craik, U.S. Coast Guard, retired, was named the second superintendent in the history of the Texas Maritime Academy. He arrived on campus in February of 1968. Craik was the last person with the title of superintendent to be in charge of all campus programs. Source: *Voyager,* 1969.

focus on two things: professional competency to meet whatever technical challenges lay ahead; and integrity to lead others.

The fall student body of 141 cadets was the largest that Texas Maritime was ever to enroll as a stand-alone academy. Facilities were so tight in Galveston that for the first time sophomore cadets had to remain in College Station. There simply was not enough room in Galveston. This meant that the unfortunate juniors of the class of 1969 now faced their third year in a row as the lowest-ranking cadets on campus. But at least they enjoyed the luxury of spreading out in rooms no longer occupied by the sophomore class. They shifted their belongings from the ship at Pier 19 to the dorm rooms on the third floor of Fort Crockett. And they also moved their leisure-time hangout to a nearer establishment. The enterprising owner of the New Ace Lounge on 45th Street found the perfect way to attract business: he advertised free beer on Wednesday night, the only weeknight out for cadets. Cadets had their own enterprising schemes: they established a clandestine tradition involving out-of-luck homeless men they met at bars. During the cold winter weeks, cadets would feed and house next to the ship's boiler the man they had selected as the so-called "bum of the month."

Meanwhile the academy sought a long-term solution for space problems: Pelican Island was the logical place to expand facilities. Administrators worked out a two-phase plan for expansion. First, they would need room for classes and administration, possibly in a single building; another building would house a machine shop and laboratory; and they would also need outdoor recreation. The ship could continue to be used as a floating dormitory for up to 150 cadets. But old-fashioned mood lighting, a throwback to the vessel's days as a romantic passenger liner, was simply too dim for most academic uses. The second phase would include a two-hundred-student dormitory with a lounge and cafeteria facilities. Overly optimistic plans anticipated a student body of two hundred at the opening of the Pelican Island campus, increasing to six hundred, and possibly reaching as many as a thousand.

To help reach that enrollment goal, the academy signed an agreement in September allowing Galveston Junior College students to take summer training cruises and then transfer to TMA in their junior year. By November, the Board of Directors of Texas A&M University pledged more than $2 million in assets to the Galveston program, and developer George Mitchell gave TMA clear title to one hundred acres on Pelican Island.

Wetmore stepped down in December as the first chair of the academy's Board of Visitors; he was succeeded by Captain Charles H. Glenwright, marine manager for Gulf Oil Corporation in Port Arthur.

1968

Assassinations stole national headlines in 1968. Riots broke out at the Democratic National Convention in Chicago. The second TMA superintendent took office. Maritime cadets fetched a giant log from Norway for the Aggie bonfire. The first undergraduate yearbook, *Voyager*, was published. And the future Pelican Island campus was dedicated.

Craik arrived in Galveston on February 1 to assume his duties as the second superintendent of the Texas Maritime Academy. He was seen as a nice guy and a great leader. Tall and thin, he stood out in a crowd. He was easygoing and quiet when he spoke, but you knew he meant what he said. He beefed up discipline and made cadets toe the mark and pay closer attention to details like uniform inspections. Tuition that academic year in Galveston was $444 each semester and $923 for the summer cruise (out-of-state students paid an extra $150 each semester).

Cadets, like the rest of America, reeled at the violent political news in 1968. College student protests against the Vietnam War were escalating. President Johnson announced his intention not to seek reelection. Martin Luther King Jr. was assassinated at Memphis, Tennessee, on April 4. Two months later on June 6, Robert Kennedy was assassinated while campaigning for the presidency. In November Richard Nixon, who had lost narrowly to JFK in 1960, edged out Hubert Humphrey to become the new president.

Initial architectural drawings had envisioned the Pelican Island campus as looking something like Fort Apache. A two-story barracks-style building would surround an open courtyard. The ship would be berthed in a huge slip cut into the south side of the campus. Dormitories would be located on the west side of Seawolf Parkway. During a tour of Pelican Island in May, Texas A&M officials said the campus would instead build a pier for *Texas Clipper*. Any location would be preferable to the current campus—if you could call it that—split by four miles of city streets. Fort Crockett lay on the Gulf side of Galveston Island, while the ship docked at Pier 19, to the northeast on the industrial bay side. However, dorms would not be part of opening-day plans for the Pelican Island campus.

Voyager, the undergraduate yearbook, now appeared for the first time. Its founders were H. Marshall Stover and Michael Leinhart, coeditors in chief; Ronald Crook and Harry Brown, managing editors; and Leslie Dix Laughter, business manager. William McMullen was the faculty advisor. That *Voyager* established the format for subsequent yearbooks: it included photos of students, faculty, and staff, a section on activities, advertisements, and a special section on the previous summer's cruise. A&M President Rudder congratulated the students on their yearbook, which was dedicated to the first superintendent, Captain Bennett Dodson.

A month after the third graduating class received their licenses and military commissions at Moody Memorial First Methodist Church and their degrees at College Station, the *Clipper* departed on its fourth annual training cruise, this time to Europe. A recruiting brochure de-

An architect's drawing from the late 1960s depicts the Pelican Island campus as a central fort with its own heliport and a cut-out slip for berthing the training ship. This early conception envisions dormitories and athletic facilities on the other side of Seawolf Parkway. Source: *Voyager*, 1969.

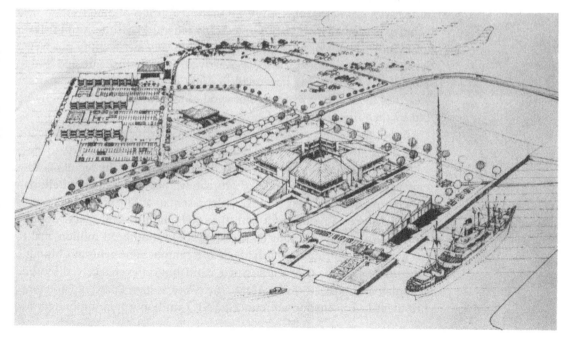

scribed work assignments for the prep cadets: they were to "serve meals in the officer and faculty dining space; make up officer and faculty cabins; clean library, lounge, smoking room, and other public spaces; assist the chefs in the galley; and operate the laundry."

A record 112 prep and 105 regular cadets departed Galveston on June 15. Greenhorns outnumbered experienced sailors, sometimes with amusing consequences. The chief mate, according to the *Houston Post,* noticed about thirty Aggie cadets at the start of the cruise chatting casually as they leaned against the taffrail around the stern of the ship. Understandably worried that a large swell or sudden change of direction might dump them overboard, he reached for the ship's microphone. His voiced boomed out over the loudspeaker, "All midshipmen will remain clear of the rail." No one moved. Taking into account their inexperience, he tried another version: "All you farmers get off the fence." They cleared the rail immediately.

At the end of the cruise, the prep cadets began a tradition of painting a shaped piece of plywood to commemorate their summer experience—the "prep plaque" would then be on permanent display in a passageway. The first plaque is entitled "Fightin' Fourth"— preps, like all cadet freshmen, are fourth-class students, whereas seniors are first-class students. Moreover, this was the fourth group of fourth-class cadets. Their plaque depicts a cartoon goat, whose name is "scapegoat," on a wooden shield.

While in New York the ship picked up a lifetime supply of free spare parts. Now that she was twenty-four years old, replacement valves, electric motors, and generators were no longer made and were growing scarcer. Al Philbrick, master of the *Clipper,* had heard that the federal government was giving away *Excalibur,* sister ship of *Excambion* (now named *Texas Clipper*), to New Jersey's Stevens Institute as a floating dormitory. Weeks before the cruise he sent up a group of engineers to inventory and label what they wanted. The federal Maritime Administration kindly removed the parts and had them ready and waiting in a New Jersey warehouse when the *Clipper* arrived. Stevens Institute and Todd Shipyards (which could have made a profit from salvaging those parts) were not too happy when they got wind of the ship having been gutted, but by then the decision had already been made.

Funding for the academy was in political jeopardy once again in 1968. The Texas Senate bill included an additional $500,000 to develop the new campus, but the House bill included only the regular academy appropriation of $461,000. Fortunately, pushed by the joint efforts of Senator Babe Schwartz and State Representative Bill Presnal (Bryan), the legislature came through with the total amount. And Mary Moody Northen directed the Moody Foundation to add another $1 million, making good on her promise to help develop a campus. The generous Moody donation was to be the largest single contribution ever received by the school. On August 20, Texas A&M University System Board of Directors President L. F. Peterson announced a $1.2 million operating budget to

Texas Clipper departed Oslo, Norway, on July 12, 1968, with a forty-two-foot log purchased for the Aggie bonfire. Cadets estimated that the log traveled about eight thousand miles by ship and by truck to reach its intended destination in the stack at College Station. Source: *Voyager,* 1969.

help develop one hundred acres on Pelican Island. Planned were docking facilities parallel to the shore for *Texas Clipper* and the 180-foot research vessel *Alaminos,* operated by the Texas A&M Oceanography Department, and other buildings to be designed by Galveston architect Raymond R. Rapp Jr. When asked how he felt about the last-minute legislative approval of the budget, Craik said, "I have only one comment to make: thank heaven."

The budget approval made the dedication of the proposed campus sweeter. On October 18, at 2:30 P.M., cadets, faculty, and dignitaries gathered to dedicate the Pelican Island campus for the use of the Texas Maritime Academy, Texas A&M Oceanography and Marine Technology Center. U.S. Representative Jack Brooks of Beaumont, the featured speaker, said that like outer space, oceans challenge our intellect and courage. The entire Mitchell family was there: Mike H. "Papa" Mitchell (the campus is dedicated to him and his late wife Katrina); George Mitchell, who donated the land; George's brothers Christie and Johnny; and their sister Maria. Also in attendance were Texas A&M President Earl Rudder and the grand dame of the Moody family, Mary Moody Northen.

How to word invitations so that guests could figure out exactly where to go proved a problem. Since the campus had not a single structure on it, the location of the ceremony had to be described topographically: "100 yards beyond north end of Pelican Island Bridge." Dignitaries were introduced, speeches were given, and finally Papa Mike, blind and in a

Norwegian Wood: From Oslo to the Aggie Bonfire

During the 1968 summer cruise, cadets aboard *Texas Clipper* proved their Aggie loyalty by passing the hat to buy a forty-foot Norwegian fir log in Oslo, Norway. A huge crane transferred it to the ship's cargo booms, which laid the log on deck. They were looking ahead to the annual pre-Thanksgiving bonfire at College Station before the football game with arch rival University of Texas. They were pretty sure theirs would be the biggest log on the stack and the one hauled the farthest. Every cadet and prep student on board carved his name on the log along with the traditional "Give 'em hell, Aggies" and "Beat the hell out of Texas." Those were the days when John Lennon of the Beatles had a hit with the song "Norwegian Wood"—cadets adopted it as the theme song of the summer cruise.

But in August the log was stuck on Pelican Island. Shipping it from Oslo to Galveston had been relatively easy, since they had their own ship. However, the campus did not own a dockside crane or truck. They borrowed a crane to set the log on the dock, but they could not find a truck big enough. Without any means of transportation to carry the log from Galveston to College Station, the academy decided to go public with their problem to see if the Aggie network could come to the rescue. "We've contacted everyone we can think of," Superintendent Craik told newspaper reporters, "but so far we've gotten no help at all. If anyone has a suggestion, we'd appreciate it." His plea had the desired result. Not only did someone have a truck; someone had an entire *fleet* of trucks. Help finally arrived from Atlas truck lines, which dispatched a semi tractor trailer to Pelican Island. The log was loaded on Friday, November 22, delivered via Highway 6 on Monday, and set on the stack that burned on Tuesday.

wheelchair, pulled the rope to unveil the construction sign. Afterward about a hundred people made their way to the Fort Crockett building, where they gathered for an enthusiastic reception.

Some faculty members of the A&M Marine Laboratory, according to a pamphlet printed by Dr. Harold W. Harry, were not nearly so excited about moving to Pelican Island: "The new marine facility of the University is to be . . . directly opposite the industrial area of Galveston Island, and across from the city garbage dump and sewage disposal plant. The garbage dump is often on fire, and the disposal plant obviously furnishes some organic enrichment to the bay. Few persons who might be expected to work in the new facility can get enthusiastic about its location."

The growing presence of Texas A&M in Galveston naturally led people to the question of identity. The college had moved so far away from its traditional agricultural origin that a managing editor for the *Galveston Daily News* wondered whether a new nickname was needed for the students of the Galveston campus: "Obviously we can't call these Aggies 'farmers.' 'Fish' would be appropriate, except that the term now applies only to freshmen." The candidates he suggested were Water Aggies, Salt Aggies, Marine Aggies, and Sea Aggies. This was the first appearance

On October 18, 1968, Mike H. "Papa" Mitchell, blind and seated in a wheelchair in front of his nurse Eunice Anderson, unveils the sign dedicating the Mitchell campus. His son George Mitchell (far right) donated the land to Texas A&M in honor of his eighty-nine-year-old father and his late mother Katrina. When Papa Mitchell arrived in America as a railroad worker at the turn of the century, he could neither read nor write in English or in his native Greek; he opened the first shoeshine parlor in Galveston.

in print of *Sea Aggies*, which has historically been the most popular nickname for campus students.

On February 13 a violent storm battered Galveston and threatened to break *Texas Clipper* loose from Pier 19. The gangway had dropped to the pier, and some lines holding the ship had broken; others were slackened. The ship, driven about twenty feet from the pier, was being buffeted by sustained winds of forty-five knots with gusts up to sixty-five knots. Tides, the worst since Hurricane Carla, were running three to nine feet high. The freak wind threatened to tear the ship from its pier. This was

1969

In 1969, Americans landed on the moon. *Texas Clipper* almost broke loose. Mary Moody Northen was named an honorary maritime cadet. And plans were announced to expand the A&M presence in Galveston dramatically.

serious, potentially life threatening. Max Blanton, class of 1969, called it "the worst thing that happened to me on the *Clipper*."

Cadets immediately alerted the crew and moved into action. A tug-boat was summoned to push the ship back to the pier so that mooring lines could be tied to pilings; having been pulled loose by the storm, the bollards (metal posts) on the pier were useless. In the Galveston area, small boats were battered, piers were washed away, and electrical service was disrupted, but the *Clipper* was saved. Cadets were commended for quick thinking and decisive action that helped maintain control of the ship under trying circumstances.

In March Sherman Wetmore's eagerly awaited history "*The Establishment of the Texas Maritime Academy, 1958–1962*" appeared. About one hundred copies of the fifty-five-page typed report were printed. As the chair of the merchant marine academy committee from 1959 to 1962, Wetmore knew the inside stories and had access to the committee's files. His well-written account, placed in the collection of the Rosenberg Library archives and the library on Pelican Island, remains the definitive story of those formative years.

Also in March, U.S. Representative William Hathaway of Maine visited TMA and praised students for being part of ocean studies. In colleges all around the country there was a great deal of student unrest because of the draft and the Vietnam conflict, but things were calm in Galveston: "I'm sure one reason there is no rioting here is because of the relevancy of the curriculum to what you want to do," said Hathaway to the cadets.

What was threatening to break loose, however, was state funding. The cost of creating the proposed new campus caused legislators to balk. The Legislative Budget Board had deleted $734,000 from the TMA budget. Craik testified that the cuts would gut essential construction on the proposed Pelican Island campus. Without full funding, he said, the campus would be comparable to "having a bathroom but no fixtures." Construction was due to start by the end of 1969. At Aggie Muster on April 21, Craik announced that *Texas Clipper* would move to Pelican Island as early as December of 1969 and that construction of the first classroom building would begin by May of 1970. When that happened, he promised, freshman and sophomore classes could finally be moved, as had been planned all along, from College Station to Galveston, and the Texas Maritime Academy would at last have all four years of its program in one place. Unfortunately, a technical difficulty in obtaining the paperwork approval from College Station for equipment money meant that no money for construction was appropriated in 1969.

In May at a ceremony aboard *Texas Clipper,* cadet Robert Thrailkill (later an instructor at the academy), on behalf of all the graduating seniors, presented Mary Moody Northen with a miniature Aggie ring, making her an honorary member of the corps of cadets; she was often called the honorary commandant. She beamed. On May 23, the licensing and commissioning ceremony was once again held at the Fellowship Hall of

Moody Memorial First Methodist Church to recognize the January, May, and upcoming August graduates: a total of twenty-seven cadets.

After a dry dock layup in Mobile, Alabama, the 1969 cruise, the fifth annual trip for *Texas Clipper,* stopped at European ports. She carried 106 cadets and 90 prep cadets. They heard music coming and going. A small shipboard band played the Aggie War Hymn as the *Clipper* left Pier 19. (The previous year, the band had been officially broken up after welcoming aboard one of their officers with the theme to "Mickey Mouse Club.") And in August a 105-piece all-girl band from Bishop Byrne High School in Port Arthur welcomed the ship back to Texas.

Craik often recounted an anecdote about this cruise to illustrate just how difficult it was to recruit seagoing cadets in a state enthralled with its landlocked heritage. A student enrolled in the summer school at sea confessed that this was not only his first ocean voyage but also his first time to see the ocean. Craik, knowing that the prep cadet was an excellent math student and therefore a promising candidate for the academy, asked how he had liked the trip and what he had planned for the future. The student said: "You know I've really enjoyed this trip and it's opened my eyes up to a lot of things about the sea. There's a closeness to nature, among others—and if I didn't have my life's vocation selected, I think I would really try this." When Craik asked what the vocation was, the student gave the classic Aggie answer: "As much as I love the sea, I love my farm more."

Artistically minded engineering cadets painted a *Texas Clipper* boiler to look like an oversized can of Schlitz beer, the first of a number of whimsically painted fixtures. The boiler became a must-see point for visitors willing to endure the high temperatures of the engine room. Under ordinary circumstances beer was not allowed aboard ship, said cadets, but this was one can of beer that officials "can't complain about." Source: *Voyager,* 1969.

While the ship had been at sea, a number of changes had taken place. On July 20 Neil Armstrong had become the first human being to set foot on the moon. Closer to home was the awarding of the contract to Houston's Brown and Root to build the academy a dock and two buildings, one an administrative and academic building, the other a technical machine shop. The Texas A&M System Board of Directors passed a five-dollars-a-month parking fee for students and faculty. And perhaps the change that had the biggest immediate impact was that Texas A&M had transformed its grading from a three-point system, used since the 1930s, to a four-point system: in simple terms, this meant that a cadet who left Galveston in June with a straight-A average of 3.0 returned in August with the same A average, only now it was worth 4.0.

In September budget woes were once again the subject of conversation as Governor Preston Smith cut $160,000 in construction costs from the State appropriation for the Texas Maritime Academy. State Representative Ed J. Harris of Galveston castigated the governor as "a hidebound landlubber." While Smith was begrudging TMA $160,000 with one hand, said Harris, with the other he was okaying $1 million for a brush control program at Texas Tech, which just happened to be located in Smith's hometown of Lubbock. Emmett O. Kirkham, acting chair of the Board of Visitors, said the cut would mean that proposed TMA buildings would be built as hollow shells because there was no longer enough money to pay for laboratory fixtures, classroom equipment, and desks. Kirkham launched a statewide public relations campaign to ask for one dollar per person in tax-deductible contributions. The first dollar came in an envelope from Rockdale, Texas, a small town near Austin. Within two weeks, more than two hundred dollars had come in; within a month, a thousand. Kirkham said the total amount of money was less important than the encouragement it represented.

Big news arrived at the end of November, when the Board of Directors of the Texas A&M University System authorized the future creation of what was then called the "Moody Marine Institute" (that working title would change before it opened) at Galveston. Named in honor of the late W. L. Moody Jr., founder of the Moody family fortune, the institute would include the Texas Maritime Academy, the Texas A&M Marine Laboratory, and Galveston-based projects conducted by the Department of Oceanography and by Sea Grant. The announcement transformed the nature of the A&M presence in Galveston. It set the stage for a new kind of student to take classes at a much more comprehensive academic institution when the proposed Pelican Island campus would open in the 1970s.

As first decades go, the sixties were tolerable. The school had survived its infancy. The Texas Maritime Academy had come into being, acquired a training ship, and fought off chronic attacks on its funding. Its institutional health could be described as satisfactory but fragile. The small size of the student body continued to be worrisome. Enrollment, which had reached its peak far short of the projected goal, showed signs of beginning to slide. Yet the school was poised for positive changes: it would soon move to a brand new campus, designed with its nautical function in mind, and there was talk of an expanded educational role.

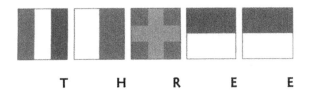

T H R E E

Campus and College, 1970–1979
The Sciences Grow

I N the 1970s, political turbulence from the late sixties became a hurricane. Many U.S. colleges made headlines for antiwar demonstrations. It was the decade when the National Guard fired on and killed students at Kent State University. Federally mandated busing to achieve racial integration was controversial. The Bakke decision outlawed racial quotas. Watergate led to the resignation of an American president. The Supreme Court's Roe v. Wade decision legalized abortion.

Oil spills from the ships *Argo Merchant* and *Amoco Cadiz* were in the news. Residents of New York's Love Canal, site of a former chemical dump, were evacuated. America extended its fishing rights two hundred miles offshore. Jim Jones ordered the mass suicide of 911 of his religious followers. First class postage rose to eight cents in 1971, ten cents in 1974, thirteen cents in 1975, and then fifteen cents in 1978. Double-digit inflation wreaked havoc with the American economy.

Students in the 1970s watched new TV fare like *The Mary Tyler Moore Show, MASH, Saturday Night Live,* and *Dallas.* And they went to movies like *Jaws, The Godfather, Star Wars, Saturday Night Fever,* and *Superman.* Pop stars Jimi Hendrix, Janis Joplin, and Jim Morrison died of drug overdoses. Baseball's Washington Senators moved to Arlington to become the Texas Rangers. Bobby Fischer became the first American to win the world chess title. The thick-and-thin bars of the Universal Product Code (UPC) began appearing on price tags. Streaking (running naked) was a well-publicized and much photographed fad on college campuses. Light beer was introduced. For the first time, soft drinks beat out coffee and then beat out milk as the most popular beverage in America.

And in the 1970s, A&M's Galveston program would show unprecedented growth.

In March of 1970, Texas A&M University started soliciting bids for the construction of the first two Mitchell campus (Pelican Island) buildings

1970

The comic strip *Doonesbury* debuted in 1970. Student demonstrations against the war closed hundreds of U.S. campuses. The berth for *Texas Clipper* was completed on Pelican Island. As enrollment at the Texas Maritime Academy was shrinking, administrators in College Station were planning to add science majors to Galveston.

as designed by Rapp, Tackett, and Fash, architects and planning consultants. Master plans envisioned a campus of about twenty buildings. As in previous artists' conceptions, dorms would be on the west side of Pelican Island Boulevard, but the ship docking facility would be off the south shore. The plans would be followed for the location of the ship but not for the dorms. The Houston firm Epco Constructors Incorporated was awarded the building contract for a low bid of $844,320, but even this was more than had been budgeted. The Don Tarpey Construction Company of Texas City got the contract to pave the campus and install utilities for $209,791.

Just as the campus was coming to fruition, Texas A&M President Earl Rudder—the man who helped make it possible—died on March 23. *Houston Post* editor Leon Hale pointed out that Rudder had changed A&M for the better, often in ways that hidebound faculty and former students resisted, by accepting women and making enrollment in the corps optional. During his eleven-year presidency enrollment doubled, the quality of students and faculty members improved, and seagoing vessels in Galveston became a new Aggie tradition. Rudder had transformed A&M from an all-male, all-military school of 7,526 students to a coed campus of 14,000, two-thirds of whom were civilians. As a measure of the high regard for him among Galveston Aggies, the Fort Crockett campus closed on March 25, so that maritime cadets could attend his funeral at College Station. Craik called Rudder a "good friend" of the maritime academy: "In the late 1950's when things were touch and go for the school, he was right there to help in its formation."

The 1970–71 Board of Visitors helps smooth the transition from Fort Crockett to Mitchell campus. Seated, left to right: Dr. Horace R. Byers; Captain C. H. Glenwright; John A. Parker; Emmett O. Kirkham, chairman; Captain Sydney Wire; James C. Craik, TMA superintendent; and Sherman Wetmore. Standing, left to right: J. C. Rudd; Captain Robert P. Walker; Captain Thurman M. Gupton; Peter J. Lavalle; Captain Ray North; Captain Wesley A. Walls; Sam D. W. Low; Captain Rober L. Jones; Captain N. S. Storter; Captain Ernest B. Hendrix; Captain Alfred R. Philbrick, TMA executive officer; and Milton H. Abelow, TMA business manager.

The first national Earth Day was honored in Galveston on April 22, with beach cleanups by volunteers from the Texas Maritime Academy. At the May 22 licensing ceremony, the keynote speaker J. T. Gilbride, president of Todd Shipyards, held out hope for a major national legislative initiative to rebuild the declining American merchant marine. Richard Nixon had promised three hundred new state-of-the-art ships under amendments to the Merchant Marine Act, but he was able to come up with only half that many before the Watergate scandal ruined his presidency.

The academy cruise (the sixth trip for *Texas Clipper*) visited Europe that year. The crew included 105 maritime cadets and 81 Texas high school graduates, who could get room, board, transportation, and two college classes for $650 ($800 for residents of other states). The *Galveston Daily News* reported that as the strains of the Aggie War Hymn faded when *Texas Clipper* pulled away from the dock, one cadet yelled out so that everyone on land could hear: "I've changed my mind!" According to the *News,* he remained aboard. About two dozen cadets making up the first official Texas Maritime Academy band (there had been unofficial pickup bands in the past) played the Aggie War Hymn. The editors of the yearbook joked that the band's "enthusiastic play and captive audience made up for any lack of ability." That summer, the band played at parades and at the arrival and departure of the ship. The band had a joyous occasion at which to make music in Plymouth, England, where the *Clipper* helped celebrate the 350th anniversary of the departure of the *Mayflower.*

During the summer, France offered pleasant diversions. A number of cadets traveled on an overnight tour to Paris, where they got an eyeful: "We got to go into a nightclub called Lido's Follies—it was quite a place. It's kind of like a topless Ed Sullivan" show, said a freshman. The ship made news for its flexible onboard utilities. It carried its own gas supply while under way, reported the October issue of *Southern Union News* magazine, but Southern Union Gas was pleased to supply natural gas while the ship was tethered to land.

Clipper Stowaway: A Man without a Country

The 1970 summer cruise was notable for a stowaway incident. On June 28, a boy of about sixteen years of age had been caught trying to break into lockers while *Texas Clipper* was docked in Le Havre, France. He had been put ashore but somehow made his way back onboard, where he was found hiding behind a lifeboat after the ship had set sail. He had no papers and would not admit his identity. The ship's officers billeted him fairly comfortably in the hospital room. It was a great topic of discussion among cadets—the whole thing seemed like fun. At the next port,

▼

Hamburg, Germany, he was handed over to police. They grabbed him roughly and were about to take him away. The ship's officers breathed a sigh of relief that the problem had been taken off their hands. But then the German officials asked when the *Clipper* was scheduled to depart so that they could return the boy. They did.

It was no longer fun. The ship faced potential fines plus court costs and transportation costs if the stowaway were carried to America. They had to get the boy to identify his country. The kid-glove treatment came to an end. Captain Philbrick cleaned out the ship's brig, which had previously been used only for storing paint and supplies, and placed the boy there under ship's arrest. He was fed minimal meals—little more than bread and water—and awakened every hour to be escorted to the bathroom. Hungry and sleep-deprived, the boy finally broke down. He admitted to a cadet who spoke French that he was the son of a dock worker from Oran, Algeria; this was his fourth attempt to get to America.

Philbrick contacted the Marine Nationale of France, who sent out a pilot boat from Le Havre on June 30 to pick up the youth. The *Clipper*, not wanting to enter the port officially for fear of the legal implications involved in harboring a stowaway, circled outside the breakwater. Plied by an expedient gift of a couple cartons of American cigarettes, the French police removed the boy from the ship permanently. Had his nationality gone unknown, the *Clipper* might have been forced to keep him in the brig for more than a month until he could be handed over to immigration officials in America. Philbrick said, "We almost had a case of 'a man without a country.'"

Mitchell campus was a campus in name only in July of 1970. A bare sandy wasteland, its only structure was the newly completed docking facility for the training ship *Texas Clipper*. The only way to get there was via a temporary construction road. Workers filled in the area above the dock to raise the ground level prior to laying foundations for the first buildings.

While the ship was away on its summer cruise, work had been completed on the *Clipper's* new docking facility—the only structure on the Pelican Island campus. Dump trucks were still hauling in fill to raise the ground, getting it ready for the foundations of the first buildings. In August, the ship had to dodge Hurricane Celia out in the Gulf before making it back to her permanent home at the Pelican Island pier for the first time. Out of respect for the hurricane, the ship was secured with new extra-heavy cable, and her engine plant was kept running all night just in case.

Luckily for the campus, Celia made landfall near Aransas Pass, about two hundred miles southwest of Galveston, on August 3. But the hurricane's exceptionally strong wind gusts made the Galveston ship channel choppy, and squall bands soaked the campus under construction. Paving fell behind schedule: heavy rains transformed Mitchell campus into a quagmire of mosquito-breeding mud, and it turned out that even more fill was needed to raise the land before concrete could be poured.

As physical construction proceeded, administrators at College Station were also constructing a bold new plan for the campus, a broadened role that would forever change undergraduate education in Galveston. Rudder's successor, Dr. Jack K. Williams, proved to be another first-rate friend of the maritime academy. In November he was officially named president. A month later, he and Clyde Wells, president of the Texas A&M Board of Directors, toured the classrooms and administrative offices at Fort Crockett and the student dormitories aboard *Texas Clipper*.

Back at College Station John Calhoun, vice president for academic affairs, convinced Williams that what A&M needed was a place to concentrate ocean-related programs. As Calhoun recalled, "The maritime program had been established in Galveston. The A&M marine biology field program was located in Galveston. There was a National Fisheries Laboratory in Galveston. George Mitchell, a strong A&M supporter had land in Galveston which he was willing to donate to the institution." The choice was obvious: Galveston. Williams liked the idea. Williams and Calhoun groomed William H. Clayton, Calhoun's associate dean for research in the College of Geosciences, to head up the whole operation.

Declining enrollment caused worry for the Texas Maritime Academy. Since the high enrollment point of fall 1967, the program had lost momentum. It had stayed about the same for a few years and then in the fall of 1970 enrollment dropped from 137 to 116 students. A drop of twenty-one students may not sound like much, but when it represents more than 15 percent of the total enrollment, brows begin to furrow. On the positive side there was now more room for cadets in Galveston. During the previous two years, sophomores had had to remain behind on the main campus. Now they were able to rejoin juniors and seniors on the coast. Sophomores, finally in residence on the Galveston campus, were ecstatic. As a tongue-in-cheek yearbook editor wrote, "we left College Station in our rear view mirrors, crying all the way."

In 1970, the founding fathers
came up with the idea for
the sciences program for
undergraduates in Galves-
ton—the College of Marine
Sciences and Maritime Re-
sources. Left to right: Jack
Williams, Texas A&M president; William Clayton, associate dean, College of Geosciences; and John Calhoun,
A&M vice president for academic affairs. They created
the new expanded college
that included the Texas Maritime Academy. The photo
was taken in 1977 when
the institution was named
Moody College, and Clayton
was its provost.

Williams formally announced in March of 1971 that the Texas Maritime Academy would soon be part of a bigger and grander institution, the
proposed College of Marine Sciences and Maritime Resources (called
the Moody Marine Institute in earlier discussion). The Texas Legislature had passed a bill introduced by Senator Babe Schwartz and Representative Bill Presnal authorizing the creation of the new college. That
key term *college* meant that the educational program in Galveston was
now on equal academic footing with programs in the College of Liberal
Arts, the College of Engineering, and all the other colleges that made up
Texas A&M University. It would be a separate-but-equal college of the
university, the only one located off the main campus.

Initial plans also called for the Galveston campus to "serve as a coastal
focus" for the ocean programs of Texas A&M. After all, it made sense to
study the ocean near the water's edge in Galveston rather than 150 miles
inland in College Station. It was hoped that research and extension services in oceanography would follow the successful model that had already been established in agriculture and engineering. However, as
Calhoun noted, "the necessary campus cooperation among established
programs at Texas A&M did not materialize." Opportunities were lost.
For example, A&M's fifteen-story oceanography building would be constructed in College Station, not in Galveston.

1971

In 1971, radio and television dropped all cigarette
ads. Students would be
politically enfranchised for
the first time when the
passage of the 26th
Amendment lowered the
voting age from twenty-
one to eighteen. A&M's
undergraduate program in
Galveston was renamed.
All four years of its program moved to the new
campus on Pelican Island.

The president of the University of Texas Medical Branch was delighted that the A&M presence on the island was growing: "The higher the academic population in Galveston, the better we like it!" Dr. William H. Clayton was appointed the first dean of the newly created college. Clayton brought with him impressive academic credentials in oceanography and the complete support of administrators at College Station. The *News* saw his appointment as "concrete proof that all systems are go for full development of the Texas A&M campus on Pelican Island."

Reality, however, was less pleasant than public relations announcements let on. As noted, enrollment at Texas Maritime Academy had been slipping, and College Station believed that finances were shaky. Clayton recalled that during his first day on campus he asked the business manager Milton Abelow, "How much money do we have?" Clayton, pleasantly surprised by the answer, credited Abelow's "aggressive accounting" and money-saving habits. The campus may not have been rolling in money, but it was no longer in the red. Also arriving on campus that year was James McCloy, a geographer and assistant dean of academic affairs. At the time of writing, McCloy was associate vice president for research and academic affairs and was the longest serving faculty member in the history of the A&M undergraduate program at Galveston.

The new Mitchell campus received favorable regional publicity. On June 6, headlines of a Sunday supplement in the *Dallas Morning News* asked: "Have you heard about the Aggie Navy? It's no joke!" Newspapers loved the idea of a college campus with ships. On May 9, the *Houston Chronicle* featured a full-page photograph of the stern of *Texas Clipper* in its Sunday supplement "Texas Magazine." The nine-page cover story took a look at the Texas A&M fleet docked at Pelican Island, including the 186-foot *Alaminos*, the 100-foot *Orca*, and the 82-foot *Leprechaun* (a converted Navy PT boat). The *Clipper*, the paper noted, was being used as a laboratory, dormitory, and dining hall for the maritime cadets. The *Houston Post* gave the campus and its fleet similar pictorial coverage four months later.

On June 7 *Texas Clipper* left on its summer cruise with seventy maritime cadets, eighty-nine prep cadets, and forty crew members. For the first time the ship sailed with a state-of-the-art onboard system for treating sewage. In this respect the *Clipper* was a leader in reducing pollution, reported the *Battalion,* for most ships in the world at that time simply dumped raw sewage at sea. The innovative system used bacteria to break down waste. It was maintenance free but not goof proof, as the ship's personnel had to learn the hard way. Just before an inspection of living quarters aboard the ship, cadets used lots of bleach, as they always had in the past, to clean their toilets. When all those toilets were flushed at about the same time, the deluge of bleach killed the bacteria in the tank, rendering the system useless. But what Aggies break, they can also fix. After analyzing what had happened, ship's officers agreed not to inspect all cabins on the same day, thus cutting down on the sudden overwhelming

International Ping-Pong Diplomacy, *Clipper* Style

While *Texas Clipper* was in Las Palmas in the Canary Islands, it was berthed next to *Prilib,* a Russian oceanographic ship. Cultural-exchange ping-pong matches between players from America and Communist China had been much in the news. Hence, in the spirit of "ping-pong diplomacy," a friendly match was arranged informally between the captains of the respective vessels. Captain Al Philbrick of the *Clipper* lost "diplomatically or otherwise," it was reported. Afterward, the *Clipper* received a Russian flag and invited about fifty Russian crew members aboard to watch a couple of movies (*Texas across the River* and *The Great Race*) and listen to the ship's band play several songs, including the Aggie War Hymn. The two ships parted the best of international friends.

impact of bacteria killers. And they declared bleach off limits for the ship's head; instead, they stocked a weaker cleaning solution. Problem solved. But future generations of cadets would grow to hate Bippy powdered chlorinated cleaner (made by prison inmates at Sugar Land), the weaker biodegradable cleanser that doesn't quite make bathroom porcelain shine.

That summer saw the largest enrollment ever in graduate classes in the A&M Marine Laboratory: seventy students in the first summer session; forty in the second. About 60 percent of those students were undergraduates, getting a leg up on their education. Faculty members at the laboratory did not yet know it, but they would become the first science teachers two years later when the marine sciences program began.

In August, when she tied up on Pelican Island, the *Clipper* signaled the beginning of the full four-year program in Galveston. No longer would cadets have to spend their first year or two taking general courses at College Station before moving to Galveston for sea-related courses. The Texas Maritime Academy officially closed its office in the YMCA building and shifted all activities 150 miles south to the new Mitchell campus on Pelican Island. During the last weekend of October, the academy completed its move from the white stucco building at Fort Crockett, which it had occupied since 1963, to two new buildings on Pelican Island. The academic building included science and navigation labs, classrooms, offices, and a library, while the engineering building had steam and diesel labs, welding facilities, and a machine shop. The Marine Laboratory remained at Fort Crockett.

On September 1, A&M President Jack Williams announced the official start of the Galveston-based College of Marine Sciences and Maritime Resources (the acronym CMSMR never caught on). As approved by the Board of Directors of the Texas A&M University System on July 27, the college would incorporate the Texas Maritime Academy, the new Moody Marine Institute—including the existing Marine Laboratory, headed by Sammy Ray and teaching units "for such fields as marine life sciences and marine economics"—and the Coastal Zone Laboratory. The *Galveston Daily News* called it "the best news Galveston has had in many months." There had been considerable behind-the-scenes competition between Galveston and Corpus Christi over which city would get the new college. The *News* gloated: "It is apparent that the Galveston forces can be credited with a significant victory." Eddie Schreiber, a charter member of the committee to establish the academy and Galveston's mayor when George Mitchell donated a hundred acres of Pelican Island to the school, believed that the new campus had helped persuade Texas A&M officials to locate the college in Galveston. Indeed it had.

In the fall semester, twenty-two full-time faculty members, of whom only six had doctoral degrees, were instructing seventy cadets in the Texas Maritime Academy and twenty-four graduate students in the Marine Laboratory. Pelican Island had its own unique traffic problems: the new Mitchell campus could be reached only by a bridge that always seemed to be in the up position when anyone was in a hurry to reach or leave the campus. Unfortunately, not too many cadets were trying to get there. The academy continued its enrollment slide with 21 percent fewer students than in the previous fall.

In November, after a four-year stint as superintendent of the maritime academy, Retired Coast Guard Rear Admiral J. D. Craik stepped down. He was to be the last superintendent in charge of the entire Galveston campus. Now that the maritime academy was part of a larger academic program, future superintendents would no longer run the show.

An austere Mitchell campus was ready for occupancy in 1971. Patches of greenish brown brush were the only growing things. A paved road can be seen leading from Pelican Island Boulevard to a main parking lot and to the docking area with additional parking. The two structures surrounded by shell fill and sand are the engineering building (left) and the academic building (called admin and, later, Kirkham Hall).

The year ended with an unpleasant incident. In December the Galveston County Crime Squad and FBI agents, as part of a marijuana crackdown, searched *Texas Clipper* with drug-sniffing dogs. They turned up very little. All that was found on the ship was a tiny bit of hashish, reported to be "about the size of an aspirin." Students complained about the lack of search warrants, but the administration, which had authorized the search, said it was legal because dormitories were owned by the state.

The nuclear-powered merchant marine ship *Savannah* left in January on its final voyage from Todd Shipyards, just east of the campus, to the scrapyards in Savannah, Georgia. The ship had proved that nuclear power worked, but it was expensive and was perceived by the public as scary. Ports did not want to berth the ship, passengers did not want to sail on it, and stevedores did not want to work on it.

1972

MASH debuted on network TV and HBO became available on cable TV in 1972. Burglars were caught breaking into Democratic headquarters at the Watergate Hotel. The Texas Maritime Academy turned ten and enrollment bottomed out. The college was renamed for the second consecutive year. Students began publishing their first newsletter, the *Channel Chatter.*

Mutiny on the *Clipper?*

Texas Clipper for the first time in its history was the subject of negative publicity. Two instructors had questioned its safety in a twenty-nine-page report, "The Texas Maritime Academy: A Study in Frustration," which they mailed to the parents of every cadet, to President Richard Nixon, and to consumer advocate Ralph Nader. As enrollment had dropped, the report said, so had students' morale. The report called the *Clipper* unseaworthy, fearing that during rough weather the ship "would roll heavily, causing injuries, or possibly capsize." There were also lesser charges about poor lighting and ventilation, overcrowded living conditions, and unsanitary eating facilities. The academy administration called the report "a bunch of exaggerations" and said that one of its authors had "encouraged the crew to mutiny, telling them their human rights had been infringed."

The episode stemmed from a routine inspection during the summer cruise. A substance later identified by the ship's doctor as marijuana was discovered in a prep cadet's locker. The stuff was thrown overboard, and at the next port (Ireland) the cadet was put off the ship. Some cadets, unhappy with the handling of the incident, threatened a hunger strike. It never happened, and the rest of the cruise continued without further difficulties.

Administrators said that although she showed the wear expected of a thirty-three-year-old vessel, the *Clipper* was fundamentally sound and seaworthy, as evidenced by annual Coast Guard inspections. Work had already been under way to improve lighting. Old, unused cargo booms were later placed in the bottom of hatches and covered with tons of concrete to lower the ship's center of gravity and reduce her rolling.

The brouhaha was covered by *Houston Chronicle* reporter Chase Untermeyer, who would go on to become the assistant secretary of the navy for manpower and reserve affairs; he would be the commencement speaker for TAMUG in May of 1986. At the end of the story, he predicted accurately that the "confusion of claim and denial, of personalities, of staff firings, and of student opinion may, like a squall, die down quickly."

The Texas Maritime Academy marked its tenth birthday on February 24, the anniversary of the Texas Legislature's appropriation of funds to start the program. In preparation for the expanding program, the enabling legislation had been amended in 1970 to "provide general instruction for all students in educational programs related to the general field of marine resources." In its first ten years, the academy had graduated 135 men, reported the *Port of Houston Magazine*. Most were now officers onboard ships plying the waters of all the seas of the world.

In February Texas A&M President Jack Williams presented Galveston Mayor M. L. Ross with a model of the Pelican Island campus and with coral specimens from the Gulf of Mexico, as an exhibit of the university's activities in Galveston. Williams praised Galveston for its invaluable community support. On February 29, the A&M Board of Directors authorized the creation of a "general academic department" that would offer courses other than those in transportation or engineering. The function of the department would be to offer those supplemental courses required for a student to graduate with a bachelor's degree. And its faculty, although not merchant marine officers, would stand weekend watches on the docked *Texas Clipper*.

In the spring semester the campus began a long-standing tradition of holding senior picnics, mostly at Carbide Park in Hitchcock. The proceedings involved beer, barbecue, softball, volleyball, Frisbee, and football and lasted all day for a dollar (later raised to two). Seniors were the stars of this event, but underclassmen also participated happily. As a student editor wrote, "Don't think that this will be like the one you went to in high school where all you had was punch, chips, and cookies. This senior picnic will have good food and cold beer (both in large quantities). Also present will be cokes and chips for those of you who still cling to those high school memories. Fine with us; more beer for the rest of us."

At the licensing ceremony on May 5 for the sixteen members of the graduating class, the Pelican Island buildings—the academic building (also called admin, and later Kirkham Hall) and the engineering building—were dedicated. Dean Clayton presided over his first licensing ceremony, the inaugural ceremony on campus, and Mary Moody Northen commissioned the new cadet officers. This was the only ceremony held under the institution's shortest-lived name, College of Marine Sciences and Maritime Resources. The chair of the federal Maritime Commission, Helen Bentley, congratulated the citizens of Galveston and all of Texas on being the home of one of the leaders in ocean studies. A&M President Jack Williams pledged that these buildings, "the first of more than 20 to be built on this campus," would be used "to develop maritime leaders in this nation."

In June the school engaged in what now seemed like a routine every two years: battling the legislature to get biennial funding. Although the campus had requested additional money, Governor Preston Smith wanted to cut funding. The increase was needed to fund all the functions of the proposed new college, including the Coastal Zone Laboratory, the Moody Marine Institute, and a research complex. The compromise budget finally approved, a little over $1 million, was expected to increase to $3.4 million in the next year.

The summer cruise went to Europe that year. For the first time the ship carried a woman, Diane Denman. The first academic counselor for the college, she had previously served as an English teacher and counselor at Galveston's Ball High School. Students onboard included sixty-three TMA cadets and sixty-five prep cadets. Women students, said the administration, would soon be coming to Galveston. And soon, as at College Station, students would be able to live off campus and would not be obliged to join the corps of cadets. Such students would ready themselves for land-based careers in maritime industries that do not require a U.S. Coast Guard license. "Soon" did not arrive exactly as predicted in the fall of 1972; it would be delayed another year.

Since the Second World War, no U.S. maritime academy ship had docked behind the so-called Iron Curtain that isolated the Soviet Union from the West: *Texas Clipper* became the first. Two cadets made a personal kind of political history when the ship was docked in Las Palmas. They made friends with five crew members of another ship docked nearby, the *Yuri Gagarin,* a Russian missile tracker. Russian crew members told the American cadets that if they concealed the TMA insignia on their blazers (the official shore-leave uniform of cadets in those days), they could take a guided tour of the Russian ship. It happened. The cadets covered their insignia and got an early taste of détente.

In July, the campus program was renamed Moody College of Marine Sciences and Maritime Resources in recognition of the generous support of Galveston's Moody Foundation. The new longer acronym MCMSMR was pronounced "mick-MISS-muhr." The three-syllable tag was not a thing of beauty, but it did have the advantage of brevity over the seventeen-syllable full name.

A mimeographed sheet of campus news with the working title "Pre-Newsletter Newsletter" made its first appearance on September 13. The writer of the first issue, academic counselor Diane Denman, announced a contest to name the newsletter. Two weeks later it reappeared under the name "Moody College Newsletter." Finally on October 4, it received its permanent name *Channel Chatter,* courtesy of Cadet Tony Brochtrup. His naming ability won him a pizza and a pitcher of iced tea. The newsletter was full of information about parties at the Falstaff hospitality room (where pitchers contained beverages other than iced tea), administrative matters, cafeteria menus, parking regulations, Aggie football, and intramural sports like flag football. The college entered the local YMCA basketball league and played its first game against the American National Insurance team on November 16.

In the fall nine Iranian nationals, the first foreign students ever in the Galveston undergraduate program enrolled in the maritime academy.

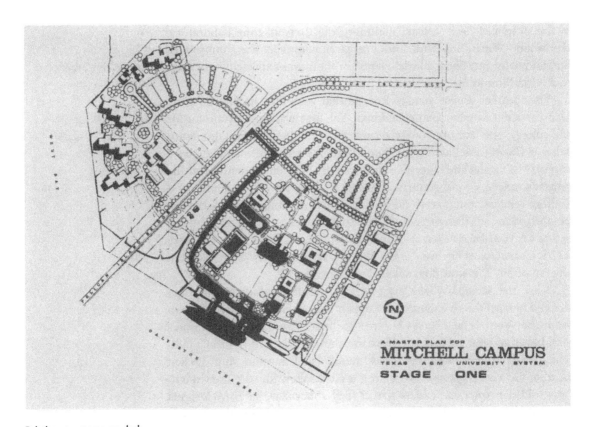

A MASTER PLAN FOR
MITCHELL CAMPUS
TEXAS A&M UNIVERSITY SYSTEM
STAGE ONE

Existing structures are darkened on the 1972 master plan for Mitchell campus, now including extant sewage treatment facilities and the small oceanography building. Had this plan been followed, it would have resulted in a lushly landscaped campus divided into two sections: academic buildings on the east side of Pelican Island Boulevard and dormitories on the west. The two sides were to be connected by a road under the bridge. As with so many predictions, this master plan would prove unrealistic.

Their stay was brief. When Assistant Dean James McCloy called the regional Iranian embassy to complain about the students' behavior, including blatant scholastic dishonesty, they were summarily transferred to Maine Maritime. The Galveston program needed all the warm bodies it could get. Even counting these international students, total enrollment had decreased yet again, although this time by only two cadets.

An internal committee set up to review the curricula of the Texas Maritime Academy attributed declining enrollment to a weak job market. Because of automation and a dwindling U.S. flag fleet, the demand for ship officers was far less than the supply. The committee, however, predicted growth in shoreside jobs. That semester marked the end of enrollment decline for the campus. Although the academy would continue to shrink slightly, the addition of civilian students the following fall would more than make up the loss.

Up until the fall semester of 1972, the only two undergraduate programs in Galveston had been marine transportation and marine engineering, designed for merchant marine cadets. On October 13, Sammy Ray was appointed chairman of the Department of Marine Sciences, the first department outside the merchant marine field. The faculty included David V. Aldrich, E. L. Beckman, Ernest L. Kistler, James M. McCloy, Tai Soo Park, and W. B. Wilson. They had to plan three separate options for the new department: Ray took the lead on developing the curriculum that would become marine biology; McCloy, marine sciences; and Kistler, maritime systems engineering. Ray later recalled that Texas A&M had deliberately sought no official legislative authorization for the new programs—that would probably have stirred up opposition; instead they "just expanded" the maritime program. Since no one objected, the strategy worked.

On the national scene the year ended with President Nixon's reelection. However, his victory was tainted by unfolding revelations about a White House–sponsored burglary at the National Democratic Headquarters at the Watergate complex in Washington. Some suspected that the president had known about it and ordered a cover-up.

Pelican Island became a snow capitol in the winter of 1973. On Thursday morning, January 11, cadets woke up to the heaviest snowfall in Galveston since 1895, which had been the second heaviest ever recorded. By the time flakes stopped falling, the ground and the deck of the *Clipper* were powdered with two and a half inches of snow. Many area schools and businesses closed or sent their employees home early. Cadets and faculty built snowmen and held impromptu snowball fights. By Saturday, only a few rapidly melting patches of snow remained. A second snowfall on February 9 reprised the scene with another inch and a half of snow. Higher temperatures melted that snow by evening. Two snowfalls on the Gulf Coast in two months: astonishing! The next measurable snowfall in Galveston would not occur for another fifteen years.

In keeping with the academy's broadening mission, in January the maritime library announced a forthcoming loose-leaf book listing its collection; there was no card catalog yet. The library occupied a single classroom on the second floor of the admin building on Pelican Island, and the librarian's office was inside a closet.

If its library was unimpressive, the building itself created an architectural stir. In February the admin building won the 1973 Honor Award for design from the Texas Society of Architects. Assistant Dean McCloy accepted the award on behalf of the campus at a luncheon in San Antonio. An article in *Texas Architect* said the building stood "in harmony both with the flat open sea and the treeless plains of the mainland." The structure was designed around a breezeway "affording ample visual access" to the dock and vessels. The award cited "the open corridor system, favorable orientation to both sun and breeze, and the possibilities for future modification of educational space."

On February 28, John "Jack" Webster Smith received his commission as rear admiral in the U.S. Maritime Services and was appointed the third superintendent of the Texas Maritime Academy. Smith, a retired captain in the U.S. Navy, was former director of instruction at the National War College. The new subsidiary role of the academy made the superintendent's office less important. Beginning with Smith's appointment, the

1973

In 1973, scandal plagued the federal government. Gerald Ford replaced Vice President Spiro Agnew, who was forced to resign over a tax evasion case. Watergate hearings were broadcast live on TV. The World Trade Center, the world's tallest building, opened in New York City. Galveston's A&M program accepted its first civilian students into its first science major. The first women and the first African American started classes. And overall enrollment started its most dramatic period of growth ever.

office of the superintendent would run only the maritime academy and would report to a higher-level academic officer in charge of the entire campus—at that time a dean, William Clayton.

Moody College of Marine Sciences and Maritime Resources was expecting about fifteen hundred high school students on March 28 for the first ever "Sea Day." The event, held at the Moody Civic Center on Galveston's seawall, was designed to educate students about the potential for sea-related careers. More than twenty-one hundred showed up. Because the extra six hundred could not fit into the Hotel Galvez for lunch, they were sent to other nearby restaurants. Speakers painted a rosy picture for jobs in the maritime industry and in the sciences. During the ceremonies there was a moment of silence in thanks for the recent release of American prisoners of war in Vietnam.

The next day Galveston hosted the first ever gathering of officials from all six state maritime academies: the State University of New York Maritime College in Fort Schuyler; Massachusetts Maritime Academy, Buzzards Bay; California Maritime Academy, Vallejo; Maine Maritime Academy, Castine; Texas Maritime Academy; and the newest one, established in 1969, the Great Lakes Maritime Academy in Traverse City, Michigan.

In April, A&M President Jack Williams spoke in Galveston about his commitment to the Mitchell campus programs: "We want to build the kind of curriculum inventory to attract students from everywhere, and we are trying to make the Texas legislature know that this is a campus of the state university system and it deserves financing." He focused on the continuing effort to obtain the $7.5 million needed for construction. Friday, April 13, turned out to be a lucky day for MCMSMR: the Texas Higher Education Coordinating Board approved the first degree outside the Texas Maritime Academy. The bachelor of science degree in marine sciences would join those in marine transportation and marine engineering. No other similar program existed anywhere else in the state. The Mitchell campus was now ready to accept for the first time undergraduate students not in the corps of cadets. No housing was available on campus; cadets could live on the ship, but aside from a few rooms on the third floor of Fort Crockett (more than two miles south), there were no dorm rooms for anyone else.

The annual ceremony for presenting licenses and awards was held in May in Galveston's Holiday Inn, next to Port Holiday Mall near UTMB. Fourteen cadets graduated the next day at College Station. Soon afterward the U.S. Coast Guard relaxed its vision standards for license recipients. Now a transportation cadet needed only 20–100 vision in each eye, correctable to 20–20 in one eye and 20–40 in the other; revised standards were even less stringent for engineering cadets. These more reasonable standards made it easier to attract qualified students.

At just about the same time as the cadets received their Coast Guard licenses, the dean of Moody College of Marine Sciences and Maritime Resources received a house, donated by George Mitchell and the Mitch-

The start of the summer
training cruise in June of
1973 had to wait until *Texas*
Clipper was lowered from the
dry dock at Todd Shipyards
on Pelican Island. While
workmen were checking her
plating and rivets, the *Clipper*
gave everyone a rare opportunity to see her exposed
hull and propeller.

ell Energy and Development Corporation. The new one-story home at
54 Adler Circle became the "official and required residence" of present
and future leaders of the Galveston campus.

Summer was eventful. The *Clipper's* departure was delayed one week
to the second week in June while the ship was put into dry dock in neighboring Todd Shipyards. The year's student body of fifty-eight cadets and
seventy-eight high school students set sail for another European cruise.
On June 19, the first satellite message ever sent by *Texas Clipper* was
bounced from Tenerife to a telephone at the Goddard Space Center and
then relayed to Galveston. The ship sent greetings to the mayor of Galveston, the governor of Texas, and the president of Texas A&M Univer-

sity. Later, stationed near the Cape Verde Islands, the ship allowed scientists including Dr. Elizabeth Kampa of Scripps to study fish movement during what would be the longest eclipse for the next 177 years. They almost missed the eclipse because of cloudy conditions, but the sky cleared in time. And the *Clipper* became the first ocean vessel to transmit voice and photographic communications during an eclipse—fittingly enough, a recording of the Aggie War Hymn was played as background to that first voice transmission. While the ship was at sea, an additional seventy-one students, more than half of them graduate students, were enrolled in the largest ever shoreside summer school program for the campus.

When the *Clipper* arrived home on Sunday, August 12, Pelican Island was cut off from Galveston Island. The bridge was out. The night before, underpowered tugs had lost control of a sulphur barge they were trying to turn; the runaway barge slammed into the span, knocking it three feet out of kilter. *Texas Clipper* had to tie up at Pier 35 on Galveston Island. A single-lane wooden ramp that temporarily patched the Pelican Island bridge was replaced by a steel ramp fashioned at Todd Shipyards. The bridge would not open for vessel traffic until repairs were completed a month later. After investigating the incident, the U. S. Coast Guard laid down new rules that forced ships to turn a good distance *before* they reached the sulphur docks.

That fall the campus received national attention over the arrival of the academy's first woman cadet (although news releases claimed she was the first woman merchant marine cadet ever, SUNY Maritime had broken the gender line the previous year). Susan Jean "Sudi" Carter, aged twenty-four, already had a master's license for small boat operation, but she wanted to ship commercially on larger vessels. Having transferred from another university, Carter began at TMA as a sophomore. Breaking the sex barrier was fraught with unexpected difficulties. No merchant marine cadet uniform was designed to fit a woman; special uniforms had to be ordered from the Navy. As pioneer women throughout the nation were beginning to make themselves known in fields previously reserved solely for men, the *Galveston Daily News* reported that Carter was "neither a libber nor a lubber." A higher profile woman, U.S. Representative Leonor Sullivan of Missouri, chair of the House Committee on Merchant Marine and Fisheries, visited the campus that semester. Sullivan noted two pressing problems: convincing exporters to ship their goods on U.S. ships and making sure that those ships sailed on schedule.

A new day was dawning at Pelican Island's Mitchell campus as a whole as well as within the academy: the first twenty-three undergraduates in the marine sciences, including six women, started attending classes on the Galveston campus. It was no longer, as the enabling legislation had described it, just a "Nautical School for . . . boys." In the blink of an eye, women had advanced from 0 percent to 6 percent of the total enrollment (College Station, having been begrudgingly admitting women

In the fall of 1973 Galveston admitted its first seven women undergraduates. Susan Jean "Sudi" Carter (pictured) made headlines as the only woman in the Texas Maritime Academy corps of eighty-six cadets. Source: *Voyager,* 1974.

since 1963, had finally declared itself coeducational in 1971). The Galveston college also accepted its first African-American student, Joe Sybille, a cadet studying marine transportation. In all 109 students (86 cadets and 23 marine sciences students) attended class that semester. This was the last academic year in which cadets would make up the majority of undergraduates.

Classes were small, often only seven or eight students; the school had to request waivers from the state-mandated minimum of ten students per class. This meant undergraduates had an extraordinary opportunity to strike up relationships with faculty members. In many ways, that fall marked the second start of undergraduate education in Galveston. For the first time, cadets with close-cropped hair and dressed in khaki uniforms were joined by "non-regs," civilian students dressed in blue jeans and flip-flops and sporting the long hair of the hippie era. The contrast was obvious during the day. But after hours, when the cadets traded in their uniforms for casual clothing, little but their hair distinguished them from others.

The new bachelor of science degree in marine sciences was actually a complex of three separate curricula: marine biology (life sciences), marine sciences (physical sciences), or maritime systems engineering (civil engineering for ocean-related structures). Civilian students got to pick one. The administration referred to students by their four-letter acronym as MARE (marine engineering), MART (marine transportation), or

Students hung out between classes on the second floor of the academic building. In the fall of 1973, the renamed Moody College of Marine Sciences and Maritime Resources admitted its first undergraduates other than cadets. The twenty-three new marine sciences majors made up about 20 percent of the undergraduate population. Source: *Voyager,* 1974.

MARS (marine sciences), said a yearbook editor, "but your fellow students classified you as a snipe, decky or fish freak."

Life on campus had also changed for other reasons. The Texas Legislature had lowered the minimum legal drinking age from twenty-one to eighteen. Previously only seniors had been "legal," but now school-sponsored functions could serve beer to just about everyone on campus. A student lounge, newly painted and equipped with vending machines and furniture, opened in the easternmost room on the second floor of Fort Crockett. Intramural volleyball and basketball were rescued when the First Lutheran Church let students use their gym at 22nd Street and Winnie: four teams competed, one each from cadet companies A, B, and C, and one MARS team. A rowing club was also founded that semester.

As usual, classes started on Labor Day (never a holiday for Aggies). Students bought all their textbooks from the store on the quarterdeck of the *Clipper,* for there was as yet no bookstore in the student union building and, of course, no student union building. Classes on the second day, however, were canceled when Tropical Storm Delia buffeted the campus that Tuesday with winds of sixty-eight miles per hour; the storm, nicknamed "Devious Delia," returned on Thursday with gusts at fifty-two miles per hour. Galveston suffered downed trees and power lines and street flooding, but the major annoyance on Pelican Island was taping windows, removing the tape, and then having to repeat the process two days later. On September 23, about fifty-five students from twenty-six colleges and universities attended the second national student conference on marine affairs. The first such conference had been hosted in College Station; this year's two-day affair was hosted in the Galvez Hotel with the Galveston campus as local sponsor.

On October 31, after an eight-month political struggle led by Senator Babe Schwartz, the legislature finally authorized tuition revenue bonds it had promised for campus construction. Now plans could begin in earnest for a 250-student dormitory, a student center with a cafeteria, the extension of utilities, a sewage treatment plant, and paved roadways. The administration did not waste any time. Plans for Galveston's proposed dormitories were presented to the Board of Visitors of the Texas Maritime Academy in November.

The Research Vessel *Gyre,* a new Navy oceanographic ship, docked in its Galveston campus homeport for the first time during November of 1973. The $1.8 million ship was 174 feet long and was classified by the Navy as an auxiliary general oceanographic research or AGOR ship. Designed to carry ten crew members and eleven scientists, the ship had an automated engine room that could be run by a single engineer on watch.

In December *Texas Clipper* got its own piece of specialized equipment —one that received much enthusiastic use. A foosball table donated by the local Aggie Moms' club was installed in the ship's afterbar. Talk about a home-field advantage. Under ordinary circumstances, playing foosball requires good eye-hand coordination, but while the *Clipper* was under

Jacques Cousteau, famous
undersea explorer, author,
and inventor, laughs with
maritime cadets. Flanking
Cousteau are cadet execu-
tive officer Pat Titus (left)
and cadet commander
William Ricker (right). In
December, 1974, these two
students would die in a car
accident; scholarship and
loan funds were established
in their memory.

Cousteau and the *Calypso* on Pelican Island

World famous underwater explorer Jacques Cousteau called the Mitchell campus home for more than a year. In May of 1973 he tied up the 140-foot wooden ship *Calypso* on the outboard side of the 465-foot *Texas Clipper*. Students remarked that *Calypso* looked much smaller in real life than on *National Geographic* television specials. Although his vessel badly needed repairs, Cousteau was as usual short on cash. He jumped at A&M's offer of free dockage. In November at the College Station dedication of A&M's new fifteen-story oceanography building, Cousteau mentioned the quality and generosity of the Galveston campus. Because *Calypso* crew members had to cross the quarterdeck of the *Clipper* to reach their own vessel, they became friends with cadets, going so far as to exchange paperback books. Some of those French titles had lurid covers that became collector's items. Cousteau was there in June to wish cadets and crew aboard *Texas Clipper* bon voyage.

When his fully repaired *Calypso* departed the MCMSMR Pelican Island dock for a research cruise in October of 1974, Cousteau left behind fond memories. The two ships paid each other compliments in February of 1975: *Texas Clipper* master Jack Lane served as the *Calypso's* second officer, and Jacques Cousteau was named honorary commandant of the Texas Maritime Academy Corps of Cadets.

way, the game became fiendishly challenging. Veteran players learned to time their moves to the roll of the ship so they could beat next summer's prep cadets and earn some extra spending cash.

1974

In 1974, a U.S. president was forced to resign. Atari released the first home-computer game, Pong. Word processors were introduced. Enrollment on the Mitchell campus doubled. And Galveston's first science undergraduate received his diploma without ever having set foot in Galveston.

A bus shuttled students back and forth between Fort Crockett and Pelican Island daily, beginning at 7:45 A.M. "But the bridge was up," said students, their favorite excuse for being late to class. Beginning in February, controversy flared when it was proposed that the bridge not be lifted for boats and ships during peak automobile traffic hours. Shrimpers claimed that detouring around the island would add an hour to their runs, prohibitively costly in terms of fuel, labor, and shrimp. The issue was settled in August, when the U.S. Coast Guard decided that the bridge would remain closed to boat traffic for three and a half hours a day during morning, lunch, and quitting-time peak hours. The moratorium helped students and faculty get to their classes on time and weakened a time-honored excuse for lateness.

In the absence of any sports facilities, athletic activity on campus was almost nonexistent. You could toss a baseball or a football around, but you could not run safely on the uneven ground of the campus, pitted with shallow divots and strewn with loose oyster shell. About the only intramural activity that year occurred when a team of cadets challenged the naval science faculty to a basketball game. But where to play? Once again, First Lutheran Church in Galveston helped out by offering their hall, where cadets won bragging rights over faculty members. That was about it for sports that year.

On February 12, A&M's Galveston campus received a double boost. The A&M System Board of Directors appropriated $120,000 to design two new buildings: a dormitory and a student center with a cafeteria. And they elevated Clayton from dean to provost, a strategic move that placed him above the deans of the colleges at Texas A&M University and on a level with the presidents of Tarleton State and Prairie View A&M University. Because of the change in rank, Moody College of Marine Sciences and Maritime Resources was now viewed as a part of both Texas A&M University and the Texas A&M System. The move also made it easier politically for the campus to compete for direct funding from the state.

At their April 30 meeting, the Board of Regents authorized "a new instructional degree program" of maritime systems engineering (MASE), a civil engineering program that focused on the design of offshore structures. Since 1973 MASE had been one of three curricula for students enrolled in the marine sciences program. In other words, your degree would say marine sciences; but your transcript would reflect that your curriculum had emphasized maritime systems engineering. Now a MASE degree had its own name, although for a time it would continue to be offered through its parent Department of Marine Sciences. Ernest Kistler, who designed the program, had argued that it was more accurately a *marine* degree, but *maritime* systems engineering won out. Within the MASE degree, students could focus their studies on ocean engineering, hydro-mechanics, or coastal structures. Because engineering facilities on campus were slight, Kistler carpooled his students to the University of Houston's ninety-four-foot-long wave tank. In those days, students got hands-on education wherever they could find it.

Graduating seniors were recognized in May at Galveston's last ceremony devoted solely to "licensing, commissioning, and awards"; the following year's ceremony would include non-reg students. Times were changing. Maritime cadets had attended classes at College Station from 1962 to 1971, but only three years after the last of those cadet had left the main campus, an article in the *Battalion* said that "to the typical College Station Ag, Texas Maritime Academy in Galveston is a stranger." That same month, Sammy Ray became the first faculty member on the Galveston campus ever to receive the university-level faculty distinguished achievement award in research from the Association of Former Students of Texas A&M University.

Nationwide gasoline shortages and long lines at filling stations hurt attendance at the second annual Sea Day in Galveston. The event had attracted an overflow crowd in 1973; only about five hundred people—a drop of about 75 percent—showed up in May of 1974. The cause was obvious. Many school districts said they had to cancel so that they could save their gas supplies for daily bus pickups.

The national energy crisis also affected the *Texas Clipper* training cruise. Because of rising prices and decreased availability of fuel, the ship shortened its miles traveled by switching from European to nearer Caribbean ports. To publicize the summer school at sea program for prep cadets, a free trip aboard *Texas Clipper* was offered to the winner of the outstanding marine or maritime-related exhibit at the annual Houston

Rattlesnake sightings on campus in 1974 made people nervous. An ominous handwritten notice was taped to the outside wall of a toilet stall in the men's room on the first floor of the academic building. Source: *Voyager*, 1975.

Rattlesnake in the Men's Room

MCMSMR Assistant Dean Dr. Henry Pope and others took part in a rattlesnake hunt on Pelican Island in February, 1974, to determine population density. They turned up four rattlers, from two to three feet long, and also found nine king snakes, the natural enemy of rattlesnakes. During the semester a rattlesnake worked its way up through a floor drain that was not screwed down in the men's room on the first floor of the admin building. After the snake was caught, maintenance people fastened the drain tightly with screws, and someone posted an ominous warning sign on the bathroom stall: "One rattlesnake already killed here. Watch out." It made going to that men's room an uneasy experience.

Science and Engineering Fair. When the first winner turned out to be Lynn Bell, an eighteen-year-old female student from Westchester High School in Houston, unprepared administrators scurried around to recruit four other female high school students so that a shipboard veranda (a suite of cabins) could be devoted entirely to women residents. Those intentionally isolated freshman plus sophomore cadet Susan Carter made a total of six women shipping out with 146 male students. Carter said that after spending the last nine months on land at the academy, she was just "one of the boys" when it came to doing all the work onboard the ship. Bell went on to become the coordinator of ship supply and fleet services and supply for ARCO Marine Incorporated. The cruise got quite a sendoff when Jacques Cousteau came aboard to wish the crew bon voyage. He made a special effort in his remarks to encourage women to seek sea-related careers.

On June 20, Texas Governor Dolph Briscoe spoke by satellite to the ship, naming the lieutenant governor of the Netherland Antilles to the honorary rank of admiral in the Texas Navy, a historical organization. On the way to Cuba an even more welcome announcement came to a crew member onboard. Sidney Perrett was informed that he had become the father of a five-pound, nine-ounce girl, Stacey Ann. Perrett was congratulated and asked if he had anything to say. "Just tell them I love them," he said. Mom and baby did fine and were waiting for him when the ship returned in August.

Growth was on the way. The design contract for two new buildings was awarded in July: a $2.2 million classroom and laboratory building with faculty and administrative offices, and an 8,500-square-foot central services building for utilities, maintenance, and campus police. In the fall, Texas A&M enrollment was 21,463, an increase of almost 16 percent; MCMSMR enrollment was 220, an increase of more than 100 percent—the largest increase in the A&M System. Almost 10 percent of the new Galveston students were women. Although it was only the second year that the campus had admitted them, civilian students already outnumbered cadets 112 to 108. Tuition was $850 a year for Texas residents; $1,225 for cadets (plus $858 for the summer cruise); and $2,100 for non-Texans. In other words, a typical science major from Texas could earn a four-year degree for about $3,400.

An undergraduate-written newsletter called "Super Copepod" was surreptitiously printed and circulated. It parodied in detail what was going on in school politics. Students loved it, faculty members quietly passed it around, and administrators hated it. The underground news-

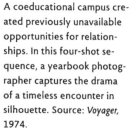

A coeducational campus created previously unavailable opportunities for relationships. In this four-shot sequence, a yearbook photographer captures the drama of a timeless encounter in silhouette. Source: *Voyager,* 1974.

Practical Jokes in Fort Crockett Dorms

Now that cadets had moved onto the ship, science students moved into the dormitory rooms they had vacated at Fort Crockett. But calling them dormitory rooms was stretching the truth. They were really unsupervised apartments. The men lived on the second and third floors of the east side, the women on the third floor of the west side of the building. At night the doors to the women's side were locked, but students learned that all they had to do was climb up into the attic to walk freely from one side to the other. In those days, access to both sides was vital: the only pay phone was in the women's side; the only laundry machines were in the men's side—inside the men's bathroom.

The men's dorm soon became split into two rival camps, one on the north, and the other on the south side of the hallway. Practical jokes began innocently enough with water balloons but soon escalated to waves of water surging from twenty-gallon trash cans (on concrete floors, the water could not hurt much). At the start of one episode, the perpetrator threw a dead mullet in the crawl space above the ceiling tiles over his victim's room. The victim smelled something odiferous but did not know where the odor came from. Then one night, after the stench had dissipated, maggots hit him in the head. Furious, he figured out an elaborate revenge. He caught a feral cat in the swamps of Beaumont and put it with food above the ceiling of the perpetrator. Where was the meow coming from? While everyone gathered to watch, the new victim stood on a chair, lifted up a ceiling tile, and found himself face to face with the cat, arched in an attack position. Both screamed. The cat jumped onto the student's head, ran down his body, then bounced up and down the dorm halls, ran down to the library (the marine biology library was then on the second floor at Fort Crockett), and threw itself against windows trying to get out. When the door opened, the cat bolted and never returned.

letter was especially inclined toward spreading the latest coded gossip about rivalries between academic departments and college administration, between fish freaks (marine sciences students) and corps turds (cadets), between the Galveston and College Station campuses. A typical issue was entitled something like "Super Copepod Meets the Sinister Provost." Its main storyline recounted in overwrought prose the continuing saga of a heroic marine biologist, known as Super Copepod, in his never-ending battle against evil administrators for the good of science and intellectual freedom on Guano Island, berth of the famous ship *Texas Cuspidor* and home of "Muddy College."

The underground newsletter ceased publication when its founding author graduated. Its appearance was probably attributable to the broadening of the college community beyond a cadets-only student population, and there was a another development also reflecting this. The college established its first elected form of student governance, the Student Advisory Committee. Forerunner of the Student Senate, the SAC advised campus administrators about student concerns. James Dodson, majoring in marine sciences, was elected its first chairman.

Issues of governance were in sharp focus at the time. Along with the rest of the nation, members of the college community watched in disbelief as the executive office unraveled. On August 9, Richard Nixon had become the first American president to resign. His action came after televised hearings, damaging revelations, the release of taped conversations in the Oval Office, and the vote of the House Judiciary Committee to approve impeachment. In September the new president, Gerald Ford, pardoned Nixon and offered amnesty to draft evaders and military deserters.

The first person to receive a degree in marine sciences, oddly enough, turned out to be someone who had never set foot on the Galveston campus. As an undergraduate at College Station, he had decided to major in marine sciences as soon as the new degree plan had been announced. But when he discovered that some required courses were not yet available in Galveston, he stayed on the main campus, where they *were* being offered. There he remained until he fulfilled every single course requirement. The academic administration on the Mitchell campus, not exactly pleased with these circumstances, had no choice but to certify his degree.

Graduating seniors in those days were exempt from having to take final exams in their last semester; they graduated before regular classes ended. On December 14 Sammy Ray walked up to the microphone on the dais in the G. Rollie White Coliseum at College Station during commencement exercises. He asked for the recipients of the bachelor of science degree in marine sciences please to come forward. One person, Alan Bunn, stood and climbed the steps. He and diploma-hander Ray had the whole stage to themselves. Having witnessed dozens of students cross the stage for each degree, the crowd enjoyed the droll moment. After he graduated, Bunn worked for NOAA's National Ocean Service, officed with the Texas Sea Grant College Program in College Station.

Tragedy struck the campus during final exam week. Early on Friday morning, December 20, two cadets died in an automobile accident. William P. Ricker, aged twenty-one, commander of the corps of cadets, and Patrick Allen Titus, twenty-two, the corps executive officer, were driving toward campus when their car collided with the rear end of a truck on the middle of the Pelican Island bridge. The car was immediately engulfed in flames; the two men were pronounced dead at the scene of the accident. They had been distinguished students majoring in marine transportation and planning on sea-going careers. The Galveston campus held its first Silver Taps, a poignant Aggie tradition, in their memory. All lights, including car headlights, were extinguished as students, faculty, staff, family, and friends gathered around the flag, flying at half mast. A bugler played taps three times, to the North, West, and South, but not to the East because the sun would never rise again for the Aggie being remembered.

Afterward, the families of the deceased expressed their appreciation in a way that would benefit future Aggies. The Titus family established a loan fund for needy students. Ricker's father willed 25 percent of his total holdings to the Galveston campus. Some of those holdings—in oil wells—turned out to be worth a great deal of money. The resulting William Paul Ricker Memorial Endowment Fund established numerous undergraduate scholarships and annual distinguished service awards for faculty and staff.

1975

In 1975, personal computers made their debut. American involvement in Vietnam ended. Marine biology and maritime systems engineering degrees were added, and the college graduated its first science students, its first African American student, and its first women.

During the spring semester the *Galveston Daily News* began carrying the regular column "Moody College Memos" by Barbara MacLeod, the first public relations director for the campus. One of the stories that semester was about a student vote to see if the campus colors ought to remain maroon and white. Students said the unique nature of the Galveston program justified an independent decision on school colors. The administration agreed and gave them the go-ahead. When the vote was tabulated, the nautical combination of blue and white was the clear favorite. But the administration balked and told frustrated students they had to keep maroon and white because they were Aggies.

On February 7, tugboats lost control of the fifty-thousand-ton British ship *Shackleford* on its way to the Duval Company sulphur docks. The ship knocked down power lines to Pelican Island and came within six feet of colliding with the Pelican Island bridge. Even though underwater backup cables restored power to the campus within a half hour, classes after 3:00 P.M. were canceled—"good news for those who skipped anyway," said the *Channel Chatter*. In a moment of creative punning, the story was published under the headline: "Where Were You when the Ship Hit the Span?"

Sea Day in March attracted almost seven hundred high school students, up from the previous year but still well behind the record twenty-one hundred students who had attended two years before. On April 4 the campus inaugurated an oil-spill control school, the first ever run by a university. The school, part of the Texas Engineering Extension Service, offered a five-day course on how to limit the damage done by oil spills. Like the famous fire-fighting school at the main campus, the oil-spill control school fit the mission of the Galveston campus well. Afterward, any time an oil tanker accident occurred, the news media would come to Galveston for authoritative interviews about what could be done to clean up the spill.

The campus was strapped for room. MCMSMR sought $10 million in bonds to expand facilities. With an enrollment of about 225, the campus had insufficient classroom space and was forced to improvise. Students attended classes in the admin building, in a lounge on the training ship, and at Fort Crockett (a four-mile roundtrip). Physical education classes were held in the YMCA on 23rd Street (an eight-mile roundtrip) until the campus outgrew those facilities and had to discontinue physical education the next year. Under a special waiver, Galveston students then became the only undergraduates of Texas A&M University who did not have to take P.E. to graduate.

Students did get some physical activity in intramural sports. That spring a new softball team was born under the name Staff Infections;

faculty-staff intramural teams were still using the name when this book
was being written. Meanwhile the campus began to plan for its own
gymnasium, the first of many aborted plans. It was the start of a mind-
boggling eight-year set of maneuvers around financial, administrative,
and political roadblocks before a gym would at last open its doors in 1993.

The fragmented library collections were finally consolidated in a
single place. As noted, the marine biology holdings had been in a room
on the second floor at Fort Crockett, and the undergraduate collection
had been in a classroom on the second floor of the admin building. Both
were moved to the windowless engineering building. The people at Fort
Crockett did not like losing their journals, but the consolidation certainly made the entire collection more immediately accessible to those
on Pelican Island. Because the library shared the building with a noisy
machine shop, even signs saying "Quiet" could not insulate readers from
the dull roar from grinding lathes or welding operations. For the next
eleven years the machine shop and the library would continue their uneasy marriage.

On May 9, MCMSMR held its first college convocation (previously
called the licensing, commissioning, and awards ceremony) in the Grecian Room of the Hotel Galvez—the very room where the idea for a
Texas Maritime Academy had been hatched back in 1958. The Honorable
Bill Presnal, state representative for District 28, was the keynote speaker.
Graduating cadets received Coast Guard licenses and Naval Reserve commissions; and underclassmen took their place as the new commanding
officers of the corps of cadets. The first four Galveston-educated marine
sciences students were recognized: Scott Davison, Nancy Lippincott,
William McNutt, and Margaret Whinnery. Awards were given out to students in all three majors—marine transportation, marine engineering,
and marine sciences.

Tuition for two summer classes on shore that summer was twenty-
five dollars for Texas residents. In addition, students paid fifty dollars per
five-week summer session to stay in the dorm. Captain Jack Lane, an
assistant professor on the campus since 1969, replaced Al Philbrick as
ship's master. Philbrick, who left to take a job in industry, had been
the master of *Texas Clipper* during her first ten years as a training vessel. The summer cruise once again followed a Caribbean itinerary to
conserve fuel. But there were some unusual events. At the last minute,
on the advice of the U.S. Maritime Administration, the ship was diverted
to Ponce, Puerto Rico, because of civil unrest in the planned stop at
Kingston, Jamaica. As the ship was sailing into Santo Domingo, a shipboard band played the Aggie War Hymn, reported the *Galveston Daily
News*. After a few seconds of silence, the crew of the nearby HMS *Canopia*
from Northampton "turned up its loudspeakers, and replied to the War
Hymn" with a skirl of bagpipe music. The *Houston Chronicle* described
summer school at sea as "an undulating lecture hall" and reported that
after some unsettling wave action, one student asked the history teacher,
"May we have a barf break?" Senior cadet Susan Carter noted that now

the presence of women at sea was routine. As more freshman women had entered the academy as cadets, the previous year's bizarre 85 to 1 female-male ratio was reduced to a more comfortable 15 to 1.

On July 25 the Texas Higher Education Coordinating Board approved a new bachelor of science program in marine biology to start the following fall. Marine biology, previously one of three curricula for marine sciences students, now became a degree program on its own. It focused on the life sciences; the marine sciences degree focused on the physical sciences. The total enrollment for MCMSMR in the fall semester was 332 students, more than 54 percent of them enrolled in the sciences. Most of the growth in the 1970s would continue to be in the sciences, primarily in marine biology.

This new reality meant that it was time to reevaluate the role of the Board of Visitors, which had served as an advisory committee for the Texas Maritime Academy since it began in 1962. The federal Maritime Administration no longer required the presence of such a board on the campuses of maritime academies. However, Galveston valued the advice given by board members, experts in sea-related business and industry. Provost William Clayton praised the old Board of Visitors, which included such members as founders Emmett O. Kirkham and Sherman Wetmore, for selfless "dedication and vision" during the formative years of the academy. The new board, reduced from fifteen to nine members, would now advise academic administrators about all programs at the college. The campus was saddened when sixty-four-year-old Rear Admiral James Craik, the second superintendent of the Texas Maritime Academy, died on October 8 at the U.S. Public Health Hospital in Galveston. Craik had served for four years, from 1967 until 1971.

In 1975 three important new buildings were under construction. The student center (foreground) would allow students to eat in a cafeteria instead of in the galley of *Texas Clipper.* Cadets had been living aboard the ship, but noncadets had no on-campus housing. The new two-section dorms—the three-story A-dorm and two-story B-dorm—would change that. The third building, a physical plant (far right, above the oceanography building), would house campus police, maintenance staff, and utilities. Photo taken on January 22, 1976.

Sailors have been complaining about food at least since the beginning of the age of sail, and probably before that. In December a self-appointed group of cadets (unbeknownst to their corps commander) took it upon themselves to declare a boycott of the noon meal. Their protest had some positive impact. The next year they were given representation on a committee looking at ways to improve the food service. That semester the editor of the *Channel Chatter* said most students had to admit that cafeteria food had improved: "I haven't yet found cockroaches on my plate," he wrote. Heady praise, indeed.

In those days, August and December graduates left the Galveston campus with no fanfare. There was no local ceremony to mark their success; they simply drove up to College Station to receive their diplomas. Of course, they were eligible to receive awards at the next annual convocation in May, but most were too busy working by then to attend. Two pioneer women graduated on December 13, 1975. Susan Carter, from Overland Park, Kansas, became the first female graduate of the Texas Maritime Academy and the second in the nation (SUNY Maritime had graduated a woman in 1974). She earned a U.S. Coast Guard license as third mate and a bachelor of science in marine transportation. She would return to campus for the May convocation to receive a commission as ensign in the U.S. Navy. "This is the occupation I wanted," she told the *Galveston Daily News,* "and it just opened up to women in time for me." Andrey Elizabeth "Bonnie" Cockrell from Rosenberg, Texas, became the first African American to earn a Galveston degree, a bachelor of science in marine sciences. She had been the president of the marine sciences club in her senior year.

On Valentine's Day, February 14, the campus fielded its first intercollegiate baseball team under faculty coach Mark Gentine. Unfortunately they were outscored as Lamar University swept the doubleheader 16–1 and 12–0 at Cardinal Stadium in Beaumont. In the midst of this debacle the college nine found some cause for hope in the second game's first three innings. Lamar was held scoreless. Dreams of "an upset or even a close game" were dashed, however, in the next inning. The match went as expected for the MCMSMR walk-on team facing a well-coached team of scholarship players from Beaumont. The school also fielded a soccer team, the Texas A&M Mariners, in the Galveston Amateur Soccer Association. In October of 1977 the Mariners would tie Sam Houston State University 2–2.

The campus continued growing. More than 376 students were enrolled in its five degree programs in the spring of 1976. Three important buildings were under construction: a student activities center, a dormitory building, and a utilities building. Meanwhile George Mitchell donated property on Eckert's Bayou for use as a marine research station. And the campus was given the okay to begin planning athletic facilities.

1976

In 1976 Jimmy Carter became the thirty-ninth U.S. president. Apple Computer company was founded. U.S. spacecraft broadcast live TV images from Mars. Campus life improved immeasurably with the addition of a real dormitory and a student union building.

In April about 160 former students of the Texas Maritime Academy held a reunion, organized by Robert Thrailkill, in Seawolf Park. On May 7, the national Sea Grant Program director Robert Abel told graduating seniors at the convocation ceremony, held in the auditorium of the ANICO building in Galveston, that they had been trained to find significant careers related to the sea. Recently injured, Abel had to lean on the lectern to stand up. He was obviously in some discomfort, but he refused to let pain keep him from addressing the students. The following weekend at College Station, Moody College of Marine Sciences and Maritime Resources graduated twenty-six students. Among them were John Cleary, Dennis McLaughlin, Steven Schropp, and Ralph Stahl, who received the first bachelor of science degrees in marine biology. Marine biology was no longer merely an option open to those pursuing a degree in marine sciences.

In honor of the nation's bicentennial, the *Clipper* scheduled a North American cruise with stops in Boston; Halifax, Nova Scotia; Alexandria, Virginia; New York City; Charleston, South Carolina; and New Orleans. In every U.S. port the ship became part of the nation's two hundredth birthday celebration. As an added bonus, all summer the *Clipper* passed old square-rigged sailing vessels on their way to or from New York harbor for the Fourth of July parade of tall ships from around the world. It was breathtaking to watch ship after ship under full canvas appear on the horizon.

By the fall semester the results of the construction push had changed campus life. Three buildings more than doubled the interior square footage on campus. A two-wing dormitory building opened, the A-dorm wing two stories tall and the B-dorm wing three stories. Students could finally live on the Mitchell campus. Up until then, as described, cadets had lived on *Texas Clipper* and a few other undergraduates had occupied rooms in the old Fort Crockett building. The new dormitory could sleep 240 students. At the same time a student union building opened, complete with a cafeteria, darkroom, bookstore, lounge, and gameroom with ping-pong and pool tables. The cafeteria meant that students no longer had to jam up in the narrow passageway of the ship's galley to eat, and the bookstore replaced the cramped ship's store on the *Clipper* quarterdeck. The third building, for central services, housed the chillers and boilers needed to air-condition and heat all campus buildings, and it provided offices for the campus police and office and work spaces for the physical maintenance staff.

For those interested in exploring the ocean depths, the campus offered its first continuing education course in SCUBA diving, which attracted fourteen students. The inaugural issue of the college's first literary magazine *Sea Spray*, a collection of original poetry and prose, was published that semester. It was edited by undergraduates Paul M. Brissette and D. J. Doss (with me as its faculty advisor). Athletic facilities being planned for the following year were an Olympic-sized swimming

pool, four tennis courts, a baseball field, and a football/soccer field surrounded by a 440-yard shell track—depending upon funding. Meanwhile, city facilities cut special deals for students. The YMCA at 23rd
Street and Avenue L offered membership for a special rate of fifty-five
dollars a year. To make sure students had excess pounds to exercise off,
the Paladin Club on 50th Street at Broadway enticed them with Friday-
night beer for $1.25 a pitcher and mixed drinks for seventy-five cents.
Chips and dip were provided free.

Merchant marine education now expanded beyond the two standard
degree programs in marine transportation and marine engineering. Two
other degree programs, marine sciences and then marine biology, began
offering undergraduates the options of taking additional courses in marine transportation and of sailing on training cruises so that they could
qualify for a Coast Guard license as third mate upon graduation. This
"license option" became known by the suffix -LO added to the name of
the degree, hence the acronyms MARS-LO (pronounced "marzlow") and
MARB-LO ("marblow") were born. The LO students had a substantial
academic load, 15 to 20 percent heavier than that of their counterparts
in degrees without a license option.

On October 4, the hundredth anniversary of the founding of Texas
A&M passed in Galveston with a whimper. Galveston Aggies complained
that unlike their fellow students on the main campus, they were not
given the day as a holiday. "Maybe the situation will be remedied by October 4, 2076," said a letter to *Channel Chatter*.

About 460 students registered for the spring semester. In recognition
of his contribution in helping to establish the Texas Maritime Academy,
Rear Admiral Sherman Wetmore was presented a TMA plaque and the
rear admiral's two-star flag that *Texas Clipper* had flown during her bicentennial cruise. Attending the ceremony were Galvestonians Edward
Schreiber, John Parker, and Hugh K. Jones, all of whom had helped make
the academy possible in 1962.

Students looked for new ways and places to satisfy their need for
sports. Both men's volleyball and basketball moved about fifteen miles
north to the gymnasium at College of the Mainland in Texas City. The
volleyball team went undefeated during the regular season in a citywide
league but lost in the finals. An intramural slate of five basketball teams
played an entire season in a month. Perhaps most interesting was the
start of women's basketball. Two teams, unimaginatively named Team A
and Team B, played each other all semester at the Galveston Seaman's
Center. Team A won all but two games. The soccer club traveled to play
the College Station club on the field next to the football players' dorms.
Soccer players had to dodge bottle rockets shot at them by those who evidently disapproved of this game. The club also played in a three-team
Galveston soccer league against the Latin American Aztecas and the
European American Islanders.

1977

In 1977, the movie *Star
Wars* became an instant
cult classic. Just before
the start of the fall semester, Elvis died—or at least
that was what the news
media reported. The
Northen Student Center
was dedicated. The name
of the school was short-
ened to Moody College.
Enrollment passed five
hundred for the first time,
and a two-term summer
school was authorized on
campus.

The fifth annual Sea Day on March 30 included tours of Sea-Arama Marineworld in Galveston. About forty cadets aboard the Danish training ship *Danmark*, docked in Houston, visited the Galveston campus to see what the Texas Maritime Academy was like. It was an opportunity for TMA cadets to welcome foreign cadets as they themselves had often been welcomed overseas by host countries.

The age-of-exploration mural on the lobby wall of the student union was dedicated in April. The Houston Propeller Club had donated the six-thousand-dollar bas-relief map depicting lines of travel around the world by epochal maritime explorers like Balboa and Columbus. (The mural, showing its age, was replaced by a photographic display in the 1990s.) In May the first science undergraduates who had spent all four years at the Mitchell campus received their diplomas.

At the third annual college convocation of MCMSMR it was announced that Dr. David Aldrich, of the Department of Marine Sciences, had received the Minnie Stevens Piper Foundation award for outstanding achievement in the teaching profession. Aldrich was the first faculty member from the Galveston campus to win the Piper, Texas' most prestigious statewide teaching award. Among the graduates were the first two to receive degrees in maritime systems engineering: Roderick Pinkett and Kyle Roberson.

A full-fledged summer school program was born in Galveston that year. For the first time the school offered a full slate of two consecutive five-week summer sessions on the Mitchell campus. The expanded shoreside summer offerings included English, chemistry, computer science, economics, mathematics, physics, and marine-related courses. All unmarried undergraduates were required to live in the dormitory and eat in the cafeteria. A Texas resident taking two courses in one session paid $34 in tuition and fees plus $315 for room and board.

The summer cruise returned to Europe for the first time in four years, a hopeful sign that the effects of the oil crisis might be lessening. A week out, on June 16, while the ship was south of Bermuda, mate Tim Nelick flashed "Gig 'em, Aggies" to the passing Research Vessel *Gyre*, usually docked on Pelican Island but now on its way back from the Mid-Atlantic Ridge with a collection of rock samples. The sign was returned by the *Gyre*'s second officer James Nelick, Tim's brother—both were former students of Texas Maritime Academy. Too much distance separated the two vessels that night to make blinker lights clearly visible, but radio contact made the communication Aggie-clear.

On June 10, the Texas Higher Education Coordinating Board okayed a significant name change and reorganization. The unwieldy name Moody College of Marine Sciences and Maritime Resources was shortened simply to Moody College. Provost William Clayton had called the old longer title "cumbersome and somewhat redundant." Students preferred the new name because "it was easier to say." The reorganized college was made up of three parts. First was the newly created School of Marine

Technology, which included the departments of marine sciences, marine biology, maritime systems engineering, and general academics. The Coastal Zone Laboratory and the Texas Maritime Academy, the other two parts of the college, remained the same. The name change raised some eyebrows among those who thought that dropping the words *marine* and *maritime* from the institution's name might signal the beginning of covert aspirations to move away from marine-related degrees toward more general majors, but such suspicions proved unfounded.

The day after the name change, the student union building was officially dedicated as the Mary Moody Northen Student Center. Mrs. Northen, chair of the Moody Foundation, had enthusiastically supported the creation of the Texas Maritime Academy and helped fund scholarships, library purchases, and construction on the campus. In the mid-1960s she had begun hosting an annual breakfast sendoff on the morning of the departure of *Texas Clipper* on its summer cruise. She always said she loved the polite uniformed cadets, who would often call on weekends to take her out for an ice cream sundae. The college, of course, was named after her family, whose fortune was amassed by her father W. L. Moody Jr. To mark the occasion of the student center dedication, a larger-than-life-sized photo portrait of Miss Mary or Aunt Mary, as she was affectionately known, was installed in the building's lobby. And more construction was in the works. Before June was out the Texas Legislature authorized a new two-story classroom building and a facility for berthing small boats.

Student life was varied. What was to have been a barber shop in the student union building became instead the office of the Student Advisory

The entrance sign in 1977 reflects the new shortened name of Moody College. Notice that it proclaims administrative allegiance not to Texas A&M University but to the Texas A&M University *System.* The sign may look permanent, but institutional name changes were so frequent in the 1970s that when it rained, wet stone revealed the ghostly remnants of former names.

Committee (the order for barber chairs was canceled before the building opened). Students often hung around the student center to play pool, foosball (relocated from the sloping deck of *Texas Clipper*), or ping-pong. The most popular outdoor recreation was surfing or simply going to the beach. One of the more exotic part-time jobs for students was working at Sea-Arama Marineworld. Some scraped and cleaned tanks, some put on shows as divers in the large observation aquarium or as water-skiers in the show, and some cared for animals in the park. Thus a number of fledgling scientists got their first taste of working with live marine mammals.

If you did not have a car, said students, there was not much to do on campus in the evening, especially since no outdoor lighting had been installed. When the sun went down, the campus turned pitch black unless there was a full moon. Students relied on "goofing around" in the dorms and making their own fun. One moonless Friday night after a college party at Seawolf Park, someone proposed a game of volleyball. Points were easy to come by in total darkness. Throwing glow-in-the-dark Frisbees was also popular. Students discovered that if light bulbs in the dorm were loosened, the game could be brought inside: a dark hallway made a perfectly straight flyway for a glowing Frisbee. Some said that not being able to see at night actually improved the campus. In the harsh reality of daylight, the almost treeless sand-and-shell campus looked so bleak that students dubbed it Mos Eisley, after the wasteland spaceport from which Hans Solo and Luke Skywalker escaped in the popular 1977 movie *Star Wars*.

In July stalwart Galveston supporter Jack Williams stepped down from the presidency of Texas A&M for health reasons but became an active chancellor of the Texas A&M University System. The reorganization meant that the Galveston campus lost political allies in the office of the presidency for a number of years. Dr. Jarvis Miller, the new president of Texas A&M University, took a brief trick at the wheel as the *Clipper* made its way from Corpus Christi to Galveston on the homeward-bound leg of the summer training cruise. One skeptic commented that was the only helpful thing Miller ever did for Galveston programs. According to Senator Babe Schwartz, Miller's presidency was a hindrance.

The number thirteen proved lucky repeatedly that summer. *Texas Clipper* returned successfully from her thirteenth annual cruise; after a week of routine maintenance in dry dock at Todd Shipyards, she resumed her berth on the south edge of the campus. Thirteen Moody College students graduated from College Station on August 13. Among them was Joseph Sybille, the first African American cadet to graduate from the Maritime Academy. He received a bachelor of science degree in marine engineering and a U.S. Coast Guard license as a third assistant engineer.

An absent-minded math professor became a campus legend for a clumsily dramatic move. It happened one class period at Fort Crockett, where undergraduates were still taking classes because of overcrowded

conditions in the sole classroom building on the Mitchell campus. The professor was so busy writing an equation on the blackboard that he lost all sense of where he was. Students gasped as he stepped off the teaching platform and into a trashcan. Thrown off balance, he lurched toward the board to right himself, in the process bursting his chalk into a dozen dusty pieces that went flying everywhere. Now, teetering in the opposite direction, he bumped into the lectern, which toppled over with a crash. Finally he regained his balance. He looked first up at the students and then down at his foot, still jammed into the trashcan. Slowly and deliberately, he bent down to extricate his foot. Although few students recalled the calculus problem being worked that day, they never forgot the lesson in professorial physics. More than twenty years later, the story having been passed from one generation to another, students still hoped for the repeat performance that never came.

1978

On March 1, Admiral Jack Smith retired after six years as superintendent, the third and longest serving in the history of the Texas Maritime Academy. In his farewell address he said his years at the academy had been a source of satisfaction that had added vitality to his life, and he expressed faith in the quality of students: "We have been shipmates for a little while—you and I—in this ship, at this Academy. Now the helm must be put hard over."

In April students finally had some regulation playing areas. The Pelican Island campus officially opened its outdoor athletic facilities: a

TMA Cadets Appear in B-Movie

In July of 1975, Texas A&M University had expressed tentative interest in acquiring Galveston's former U.S. Customs House, on the Strand between 17th and 18th Streets, as classroom and laboratory space for MCMSMR. The application fell through, but by quirky circumstance about forty cadets did get to use the building in March of 1978, albeit briefly, as extras in a wretched B-movie called *The Bermuda Triangle*, released in 1979. Short on cash, the production company figured they could hire a bunch of college students for almost no money. They needed sailors in the U.S. Navy. What made maritime cadets so desirable was that their dress blue uniforms looked close enough to Navy uniforms to fool moviegoers. Sunn Classic Pictures, producers of the television series *Grizzly Adams*, would not have to pay anything for costumes.

Set the scene: another ship has mysteriously fallen prey to the dark powers of the so-called Bermuda Triangle. An alarm sounds at a naval base somewhere near Bermuda. Out of the front door of headquarters (otherwise known as the Customs House) come spilling an ever-alert group of naval officers (portrayed by TMA cadets) to man the fleet in pursuit of—whatever. The movie made them look more like junior high students escaping the confines of school for afternoon recess than military personnel on their way to save the nation from peril. The uniformed cadets had to run down the long flight of steps and climb back slowly for several takes until the director finally shouted "Print!" That was it. The rest of the movie was shot elsewhere and its scenes were cobbled together awkwardly. College Station has its *We've Never Been Licked*; Galveston has its *Bermuda Triangle*. No one ever believed that either movie ought to be nominated for an award, but they are fun to watch if you can manage to find a copy.

twenty-five-meter swimming pool with low and high diving boards, four tennis courts, a track around the soccer/football field, a baseball diamond (soon to be moved to make way for the small boat basin), and an area for playing basketball and volleyball. The pool was especially welcome. It had been a long time coming, delayed by the red tape of budget approval and slow construction due to inclement weather. The delays made anticipation intense. After the rounded concrete bottom was laid and before it was filled with water, the pool had a brief but popular history as a clandestine skateboard park. At night, students watched for the campus police car to drive off Pelican Island bound for the Fort Crockett campus. Then they gave the signal and skateboarders came out in full force, hanging ten in the deep end. Formal opening as a pool for swimming was delayed a few days by rain that washed debris into the pool. Finally, the pool was all cleaned up, and "Splash Day" arrived. Unfortunately a cold front had just pushed through Galveston, lowering temperatures. When Moody College Provost Clayton gave his ribbon-cutting speech, only a few shivering swimmers were brave enough to take the opening-day plunge. After that, though, the swimming pool became one of the most popular outdoor spots on campus.

The men's volleyball team advanced to the tougher division at College of the Mainland. Women's basketball also moved up to College of the Mainland with a field of four teams. The women got into the spirit of things by coming up with clever team names: Wild Bill's Babes defeated Sweet Young Things in the finals. Coed volleyball started its inaugural season on a court between the student center and the classroom laboratory building. The rules demanded that each team have at least one woman on the court at all times. It proved popular enough to convince eight teams to brave mosquitoes near the often muddy playing surface. Coed volleyball had come to stay. Students of Moody College on the Pelican Island campus considered themselves part of the Spirit of Aggieland: "We try to participate in as many of A&M's traditions as possible, as shown by our Bonfire, Aggie Muster, Corps March-Ins, and yell practices for the football season," wrote *Voyager* yearbook editors.

At the May convocation the first Edwin Eikel Outstanding Student Award was given to marine sciences graduate Wayne Stolz. The legend behind the award has often been told. While visiting the Pelican Island campus Eikel, president of the Intracoastal Towing and Transportation Company, had been impressed by the politeness and eagerness to please of an undergraduate student who volunteered to give him a campus tour. The student was never identified, but Eikel's will endowed the annual award, which became the most prestigious student award offered on the Galveston campus. However, the legend does not hold water. The real origin of the award was more prosaic: Eikel's successor liked A&M and was a good friend of President Clayton. Eikel family members wanted to

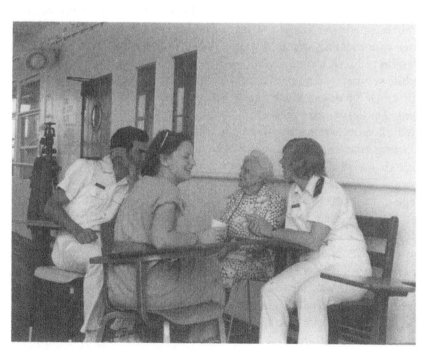

Mary Moody Northen (wearing the print dress) enjoys a conversation on the portside promenade deck of *Texas Clipper.* Each year, she sponsored a formal breakfast just before the start of the training cruise.

donate money to A&M; they followed Clayton's advice in endowing an award. "The legend of the anonymous friendly student makes a good story," said Clayton, "but it's not true. Edwin Eikel's widow Virginia did visit the campus afterward on numerous occasions and loved meeting students."

Summer tuition had risen to $125 for each five-week session plus $190 for a seven-day meal plan. The *Clipper* cruise for the summer included the program's first ever Panama Canal passage and a stop at Callao, Peru. Marine transportation cadet Charmaine Walter of Berkeley, California, became the first woman to serve as a company commander in the Texas Maritime Academy (some claimed she was the first in any state maritime academy). Texas governor Dolph Briscoe spoke at the annual Mary Moody Northen breakfast, wishing the ship smooth sailing. During the cruise the ship stopped at the equator for an especially elaborate ceremony. King Neptune and Davy Jones (crew members wearing dyed mops for wigs) were empowered to initiate pollywogs into shellbacks. All first-timers, pollywogs, had to plead guilty to a slew of trumped-up charges, including polluting the ocean with Bippy cleanser; visit the Royal Doctor for internal cleansing with foul-tasting throat spray; appear before Royal Barbers for hair sliming with cooking lard; greet the Royal Baby by kissing his belly; and then be washed down with fire hoses for external cleansing. Those few overconfident pollywogs who maintained their innocence had to go through the ceremony twice. Afterward the initiated received their shellback certificates (suitable for framing) and a wallet-sized card to show the next time they crossed the line, exempting them from having to repeat the initiation.

On July 1, retired Navy Rear Admiral Kenneth G. Haynes became the fourth superintendent of the Texas Maritime Academy. Haynes was former commanding officer of the USS *Providence* and a recipient of the Legion of Merit award for his work with satellite transmission systems while serving as deputy director for operations of the Defense Communications Agency in Washington, D.C. He had also served as head of the language department at the U.S. Naval Academy in Annapolis. He inherited a healthy maritime academy. According to an article in the *Battalion*, starting salaries for third mates graduating from TMA averaged twenty-five thousand dollars a year. Both campuses announced record enrollments: for the first time, TAMU topped 30,000 (30,255) and Moody College topped 600 (614).

Undergraduate Tom Schatz, writing for the *Channel Chatter*, vividly described the atmosphere at the start of a typical semester: "Well, the second week is over and we're entering into week three. This is known as the transition state. Parties will begin to dissipate slowly and books will begin to open for the first time (even if it's just to look at the pictures). Freshmen will begin to wonder if there is anything to this school besides beer, broads, and bathing suits. They begin to hear the common passage, 'Wait till the first test!' and most, those already into the party

fever, will shrug it off. Wait till the first test!! At this time juniors and
seniors have seen just about everyone and are beginning to wonder what
on earth they're going to do for subject matter on any of their seven papers. . . . New students will wonder if the food will ever become digest-
ible or at least tolerable to glance at. Old students know all too well. . . .
All in all the third week means things are beginning to settle down. The
rain will keep more and more students inside and little by little school
will finally become a reality for everyone."

The Texas A&M Board of Regents, in an intriguingly worded minute
order, reorganized the administrative chain of command for the college. Previously, Moody College had reported directly to the president
of Texas A&M University. Starting in October, Moody College would report directly to the chancellor of the Texas A&M University System "by
way of the president of Texas A&M University." The change was more
than cosmetic; it meant that the Galveston campus had climbed another
rung in the academic hierarchy. This set the stage for further progress the
following year. Some also saw it as a strategy designed to reduce the un-
friendly influence of A&M President Miller and to increase the friendly
influence of Chancellor Williams.

The second floor of B-dorm, known as B-2, sponsored Cleanup Day
on campus on October 15. Litter pickers were treated to "all the cokes
and ice cream they can down," wrote the *Channel Chatter.* On other occasions, dorm residents added to certain kinds of litter. One popular
prank was to fill an LP record album cover with shaving cream, take it
out into the hallway, stick the open end under someone's door, and then
knock. When the victim came to answer the door, the prankster stomped
on the album cover, shooting shaving cream all over the victim. The
tricky part was to make sure you had a well-constructed, sturdy album cover—otherwise the cream could backfire. Another traditional
and messy prank was stuffing a room with crumpled newspaper. All you
had to do was save a semester's worth of old copies of the *Battalion*
or *Galveston Daily News,* convince the dormitory resident advisor (RA)
to lend you a key, wait until the victim was off campus, and then stuff
the room. Aficionados of this prank were usually male students who
picked on "a cute girl." Once when the victim's room got overstuffed,
black newsprint smeared the walls and ceiling; the RA was forced to re-
paint the room.

On October 27 the Texas Higher Education Coordinating Board authorized a new degree program in maritime administration, focusing on
the business of the sea. The MARA degree, previously offered as a mar-
keting and management option for those pursuing the degree of marine
transportation, covered both business and transportation. It became the
sixth bachelor of science program on the Galveston campus, joining marine biology, marine engineering, marine sciences, marine transportation, and maritime systems engineering. The number of departments also
increased: marine biology and maritime systems engineering, previously

In November of 1978 the shell of the classroom laboratory building was complete. When ready, the building would more than double classroom space and provide needed offices and laboratories. Photo originally appeared November 23, 1978.

part of the Department of Marine Sciences, now separated into independent departments.

The annual Halloween party included pumpkin carving, costume judging, and cockroach racing. A dorm council was set up to govern the lives of residence halls and to sponsor parties. The dorm council sponsored the first casino night at the Islander. Ernie's was the "in" place for students to relax over a beer.

Construction on the two-story classroom and laboratory building, begun in June, was now well under way. The straight-line pathway between the original classroom building and the Northen Student Center had been obliterated by the huge construction site, bordered by cyclone fencing. Students had to detour around the site, which was muddy during rains and a source of dust on dry days. It was especially hard on cadets, who needed to keep their shoes shiny for inspection. In November the construction site expanded to include the area that would become a parking lot for the new building.

1979

It was a year for changes. In 1979 the school became Texas A&M University at Galveston. Its provost became a president. And students began attending classes in the new classroom laboratory building.

Students Adrian Corbett, Tom Schatz, and Ray Reis painted a mural of underwater life on the east wall of the cafeteria. The mural depicted a diver, fish, plants, coral, and an octopus (by the 1990s, it had faded and was painted over). Mathematics instructor Carol Congleton—not the person who had stumbled into the trashcan—had had difficulty finding a textbook for spherical trigonometry; so she wrote her own and had it published by Cornell Maritime Press in June of 1979. The textbook was still in classroom use more than twenty years later.

Energy problems remained in the news that spring. In February President Carter sought congressional permission to ration gas and to enact other energy conservation measures in response to moves by Kuwait and Venezuela to curtail oil production and raise oil prices. In Galveston and elsewhere there were long lines at the gas pumps. To help reduce the wait, drivers were allowed to buy gasoline only when the day matched their license plates—those with odd-numbered plates could fill up on odd-numbered dates only. As they walked around campus, some students listened through an earplug to the newly introduced miniature cassette player called the Sony Walkman. On March 28, the Three Mile Island nuclear reactor near Harrisburg, Pennsylvania, narrowly avoided a meltdown in the worst nuclear accident in American history. And, more relevant to an institution of higher education, America created a new arm of federal bureaucracy, the Department of Education.

In May A&M Chancellor Jack Williams delivered the address at the Moody College Convocation. The next day, the students graduated at main campus, College Station. As usual, Moody College was one of the last colleges to be recognized. The small contingent let out a traditional Aggie "Whoop!" as they marched across the stage to receive their diplomas. Jean McLaughlin became the first woman to receive the MASE degree.

Tropical Storm Claudette visited Galveston in the last week of July, setting a new national record for rainfall in a single day: forty-six inches of rain recorded in northern Galveston County. Many members of the TAMUG community were stranded as streets ran with water as deep as three feet. Some unfortunate car owners had their engines ruined by rising water.

In the summer the $2.4 million classroom laboratory building was completed. And in August, the Mitchell campus got a significant name change: on July 26, the A&M System Board of Regents said that from now on Moody College would be called Texas A&M University at Galveston (its acronym TAMUG was either spelled out letter by letter or, more commonly, pronounced as "*Tah*-mug"). As a full-fledged university it contained its own colleges: the School of Marine Technology was renamed the Moody College of Marine Technology; the Texas Maritime Academy was renamed the Texas Maritime College. TAMUG also included the Coastal Zone Laboratory, which kept its name unchanged. Clyde Wells, chairman of the Board of Regents said: "This action will not change the classification nor the role and scope of the institution, but it is our intention to give every support possible to the development of additional curricula." The announcement predicted that enrollment would rise to twenty-five hundred by 1985.

In keeping with the restructuring of the campus, Clayton, elevated from the rank of provost, was named the first president of TAMUG, and Rear Admiral Haynes had his title changed from superintendent to dean of the Texas Maritime College. By and large, present and former cadets were unhappy with the loss of the term *academy*—they believed that *college* conveyed no sense of the historic connection with the sea. Regardless of its name on official brochures, many people would persist in referring to the maritime program as the academy.

In the fall, undergraduates reached a new record of 640. They began attending classes in the new classroom and laboratory building. It had been completed in the spring and was stocked with furniture and equipment just in time for the start of fall classes. A wonderfully pleasant addition was long-time benefactor George Mitchell's donation of palm trees to be planted around campus. Landscaping before this consisted of a lonely row of palm trees lining the east side of the road from the campus entrance to the *Clipper*. TAMUG's maintenance crew pulled up a volunteer hackberry tree (which seemed to be the only kind of tree that could grow naturally on Pelican Island) from the other side of Seawolf Parkway, dragged it over to the new building, and set it in the planter by the building's entrance.

Students, of course, loved being part of a school that could now wave a banner including the beloved words *Texas A&M*. Many, accepted as students at College Station where there were no available dorm rooms, switched to the Galveston campus where there was plenty of dorm space. They always felt like Aggies, regardless of the name on the campus entrance. For many students on campus, this third name change in two years cemented the continuing relationship to Aggieland: "As long as I get my diploma from A&M," one said, "it doesn't matter what they call us." The editors of the *Channel Chatter* saw it as a sea change: "Well, we're no longer Moody Aggies but bona fide Aggies at Galveston. . . . The main significance of the name change is recognition of an increasing importance of marine education to Texans, and the need to meet the growing potential for higher education in the marine field."

The *Channel Chatter* also reprinted a story from Galveston's *In-Between* magazine about nuclear waste storage a little east of the campus on Pelican Island. When the nuclear-powered merchant ship *Savannah* departed Galveston for the last time in January, 1972, it left behind 122 pounds of highly radioactive uranium 235 at Todd Shipyards, which had serviced the ship since 1963. The material was stored there for about five years. The facility, which had also accepted from other sources hospital waste and irradiated water, was called "the largest halfway house for nuclear garbage in the state of Texas." Back in 1963, recruiting brochures had touted the advantage of attending a maritime academy in the same town as the shipyard that regularly serviced the first atomic-powered merchant vessel in the world. At that stage people had been pleased Galveston promised "to become an important center for commercial nuclear propulsion." Now it was seen as a liability, a cause for worry. Eventually, the federal government cleaned up the waste facility. In 1992, the Texas Health Department's Bureau of Radiation Control would certify Todd Shipyards as radiation free so that it could be sold.

Several popular pastimes, described by the *Channel Chatter*, captured the madcap spirit of college life in those days: unscrewing and flipping plastic "EXIT" signs to read "TIXE"; holding water fights on dorm balconies; using masking tape and pennies to make doors inoperable; blockading doors with water-filled trashcans; and rearranging the letters on dorm door nameboards "to spell out funny names or sly innuendos about the people that live there." The newsletter politely declined to give examples of the innuendos. Under cover of night, cadets painted a "For Sale" sign on the smokestack of *Texas Clipper*. Another time they painted the stack with the words "Blinko's Bait Camp." Both times the stack was quickly repainted the next morning.

From the second-floor balconies of B-dorm hung bed sheets protesting the quality of cafeteria food. One sheet asked a popular Houston TV consumer advocate for help: "Save us, Marvin Zindler!" Students had some cause for the food protests—or at least they believed they had. One weekend, the campus was served repeatedly thawed and refrozen tamales. Almost everyone came down with food poisoning except the soccer team, who had missed dinner because of an all-day tournament. One student who had slept through the meal awoke to take a shower but was surprised by the low water pressure, which he later discovered was due to chronic toilet flushing. The food item became infamous in campus lore as the "ptomaine tamales."

On November 1, the *Burmah Agate* ran into the freighter *Mimosa* southeast of Galveston: smoke from the resulting fire was visible for miles. The accident spilled 2.6 million gallons of oil offshore. Students enrolled in Texas A&M's oil-spill control school witnessed a real-life example of what could happen right on their doorstep. As part of their education, some cadets toured Todd Shipyards where the ships had been towed. One cadet said: "The collision had carved a cut in the bow

Students attend a flag-raising ceremony in front of the new classroom laboratory building. Left to right: Roger Young, Melinda Beltz, Steve Newsom, Mary Beth O'Brien, Ken Irving, and Marty Paul. On November 10, 1979, the A&M System Board of Regents formally presented the building to the campus, now known as Texas A&M University at Galveston.

of *Burmah Agate* that looked for all the world like a big smile. It was a haunting sight."

On November 10 the chairman of the TAMU System, Clyde H. Wells, formally presented the new classroom laboratory building to the campus. Former TMA student Joe H. Moore, chairman of the Board of Visitors, and Mark S. Sanders, chairman of the Student Advisory Committee, made remarks. The building was accepted by John R. Schwarz, vice president for academic affairs. Bishop John McCarthy of the Galveston-Houston Catholic Diocese gave the invocation.

The event came soon after the Iran hostage crisis had begun. On November 4 Iranian students had taken over the American embassy in Teheran. President Carter responded by freezing Iranian assets in American banks and stopping the purchase of Iranian oil; the trouble would not dissipate until early 1981, after the shah had died of natural causes and the United States agreed to unfreeze Iranian assets. On December 19, the federal government provided a $1.5 billion loan to bail out Chrysler Corporation, poster child for the crisis in confidence over American-made cars.

The decade of the seventies was the school's adolescence, still slightly awkward but full of promise. The struggling Texas Maritime Academy became a strong, integral part of a broader institution of ocean studies. The effects of growth during the single decade were staggering. The school moved to a new campus with an aggressive construction program. The institution was called by five different names. Finally, it got what it had always wanted, a name incorporating the prestigious A&M. Its chief executive officer rose in the ranks from superintendent to dean, to provost, and finally to president. Degree programs tripled. Course offerings increased exponentially. Enrollment swelled by more than 450 percent. TAMUG was surely pleased with itself. But this adolescent still had a tough young adulthood to face.

TAMUG, 1980–1989
Survival and Resurgence

THE 1980s were a decade of hostile corporate takeovers and in-your-face billionaires like Donald Trump and Leona Helmsley. A new disease called AIDS made frightening headlines. Millions watched in horror as the space shuttle *Challenger* exploded, killing the entire crew including a schoolteacher. Designer labels were all the rage, even for children's clothing. Communism and the Berlin Wall fell. The Vietnam Veterans Memorial was dedicated in Washington, D.C. The first woman was appointed to the Supreme Court. Cabbage Patch dolls, re-tailing at less than twenty dollars, were so effectively promoted in lim-ited editions that some sold for hundreds of dollars. It was the decade of MTV, CDs, Madonna, slam dancing, punk, and rap. The blockbuster movies included *E.T., Platoon,* and *Star Trek.* Among the most popular television shows were the *Cosby Show* and *Cheers.*

TAMUG would face an unnerving roller coaster ride in the 1980s. Undergraduate enrollment began an eight-year decline, and the school was threatened with legislative closure. Then toward the end of the de-cade enrollment began to surge, and the school was rated as academi-cally superior by two prominent national magazines.

The decade began with a bang. Financial news was scary or happy, de-pending on where your money was. Inflation during the preceding year was the highest it had been in thirty-three years. Gold prices peaked at $802 an ounce on January 18, a 25 percent increase in a single week. Oil prices skyrocketed, too. Salaries took off and jobs were plentiful. Mother Nature stole the front page with the volcanic eruption of the century. On May 18, members of the TAMUG community watched television in fascinated horror as Mount St. Helens blew its top in Washington State. Twenty-six people were killed in the explosion, estimated to pack the punch of five hundred atomic bombs of the kind dropped on Hiroshima in the Second World War.

1980

Classes began to increase in size in 1980; some grew to have sixty students. Tuition cost more than two thousand dollars a year. TAMUG suffered adverse publicity as it accepted and then rejected its old-est student ever.

Walking around campus, now made larger by the addition of new buildings on the outskirts, became inconvenient. As Ralph Waldo Emerson wrote, "they say the cows laid out Boston. Well, there are worse surveyors." At TAMUG, students laid out many of the paved walkways on campus. After students tromped their own dirt paths between the Northen Student Center and the new classroom laboratory building, concrete walkways were floated on the exact routes of the paths. The result helped define that area as the new geographical center of campus, the quad, as it came to be called. Its focal point where five walkways converged was a dirt-filled concrete circle, occasionally decorated with plants. The circle would be paved in the 1990s to receive the *Texas Clipper* anchor, which was later replaced by the clock tower. The campus flagpole was moved from the south side of the classroom lab building to a spot west of the circle.

That semester the library purchased its first photocopy machine for public use. In the last week in March, students could visit the Norwegian Maritime Academy training vessel, the sailing ship *Christian Radich*, docked at Pier 15 in Galveston. The square-rigger had participated in the 1976 bicentennial tall ship review in New York City. Norwegian cadets, invited to a Texas-style dance party at the Northen Student center, adeptly two-stepped their way through the Cotton-eyed Joe. They had learned all the steps, they said, at discos in Norway.

TAMUG added its first relatively large classes because it now had a room large enough to hold more than sixty students—the auditorium in the classroom lab building. An amusing story about that classroom in-

TAMUG students treat Norwegian cadets to a Texas-style dance party at the Northen Student Center, Aggies and Scandinavians linking arms to pick out the steps to the Cotton-eyed Joe. The Norwegians arrived on the tall ship *Christian Radich*, which paid a three-day visit to Galveston in March of 1980. Source: *Voyager*, 1980.

volves its swivel blackboard. Before the start of a biology class taught by a particularly shy professor, students had prepared the board. The side facing the class was crammed with intricate mathematical formulas and bore the message: "Do not erase!" So the professor, chalk in hand, swiveled the board to write on the other side. What he revealed to the class was an anatomically correct drawing of a naked woman. In vain, he looked for the eraser; students had taken care to hide it. He could not allow the image to remain and started frantically wiping it with his bare hand. But when he realized just where his hand was in relation to the image, he became even more embarrassed. Although the prank was never repeated, the professor began to carry his own eraser with him to every classroom.

In May, three-term Speaker of the Texas House of Representatives Bill Clayton (no relation to TAMUG President William H. Clayton) delivered the first convocation address under the new name Texas A&M University at Galveston. The summer cruise spent most of its time in the Caribbean and Gulf of Mexico. At College Station, A&M President Jarvis Miller got into trouble when he refused to shake the hand of graduating cadet Melanie Zentgraf, who had led a class action suit that would eventually (in 1984, when it was settled) force corps organizations like the Aggie band to admit women. In response to criticism over his ungentlemanly behavior, A&M reassigned Miller and named an acting president. TAMUG hoped that his permanent replacement would be more supportive of Galveston programs.

The campus was saddened by the violent death of a popular teaching assistant in biology. On July 27 Jeffery Giles, a graduate student at TAMUG, was murdered while working part-time as a security guard. He had tried to stop two men from burglarizing a car in the garage of the By-the-Sea Condominium. One of the men killed him, stole his car, drove to Austin, and murdered another person the same day. The murderer was caught, convicted, and sentenced to death in 1982. Giles was a soft-spoken teacher, a gentle person who had helped found the nationally respected *Mother Jones* magazine, known for its investigative reporting on issues of social justice. An annual award was named in his honor for marine biology students who also excel in the humanities.

In August Galveston suffered an ordered evacuation for a storm that never lived up to its prepublicity. When Hurricane Allen reached category 5 status, officials ordered coastal evacuation. The result was the densest traffic jam in the history of Galveston and Harris counties. Allen, weakened to a category 3 storm, finally made landfall on August 9 in a sparsely populated section of South Texas. Galveston endured high tides, heavy waves, and sustained winds of only twenty-six miles per hour—hardly cause for concern. About the only problem on campus was the week-long closure of the swimming pool for cleanup due to heavy rain. Galvestonians who had been frightened into evacuating returned angry with officials who had alarmed them for no reason. Officials, in turn,

Sammy Ray (left), who began working at the Texas A&M marine lab in 1960, examines oysters with Judy Wern (center) and another unidentified student at a local reef. Ray taught the first marine biology courses in Galveston: a graduate class in 1964 and an undergraduate class in 1966. He helped set up both the marine sciences and the marine biology departments. He is a leading authority on oysters.

were worried that this false alarm might jeopardize any future effort to get residents to evacuate.

In the fall, tuition (including room, board, and fees) was $2,100 a year for Texas residents; cadets paid the same amount plus $1,200 for a summer training cruise; nonresidents paid about $3,200 a year. This meant that a Texas resident majoring in the sciences could earn a four-year degree for as little as $8,400. Even the out-of-state rate was such a bargain ($12,400 for four years) that many found it cheaper than tuition in their home state. TAMUG's specialized sea-related programs attracted undergraduates from far afield. Students could major in history, engineering, or biology just about anywhere; if they wanted to major in marine transportation, maritime systems engineering, or marine biology, they came to Galveston.

That semester the Galveston campus received unwanted publicity nationwide—even national radio newscaster Paul Harvey picked it up —for its oldest almost-student ever. James H. Petrie, aged seventy-one, of Kirkland, Washington, had retired from the Southern Pacific Railroad in 1961, earned an aeronautical engineering degree in 1966, then worked for Boeing. Petrie said he had worked on a ship as a teenager, "but I took a different route and I want to find out what I missed." At first he was accepted into the marine transportation program, received a federal education loan of twenty-four hundred dollars, went through orientation, and purchased his uniform. But then he was told that because of his unemployability in the maritime industry, he could not participate in the federally subsidized Coast Guard licensing program. By the time he would be eligible for graduation, he would be seventy-six and, he was told, "the potential is virtually zero that companies hiring . . . graduates of this institution would employ a man of your age."

The university offered him a compromise: he could attend classes but without the possibility of obtaining a merchant marine license. Petrie found that unacceptable. He cited federal initiatives to do away with forced retirement at age sixty-five so that people could work longer: "That's what I'm trying to do." Forced to change his mind, he went in another direction. If he could not get a Coast Guard license, Petrie said, he would apply to the University of Washington law school to get a law degree. (Two years later, the U.S. Maritime Administration would bar anyone older than twenty-five from admission to licensing programs.)

In November, Ronald Reagan defeated Jimmy Carter in a landslide victory to become the fortieth president of the United States. The day he was sworn into office, on January 20, 1981, Iran released the remaining fifty-two American hostages held in Teheran. But TAMUG was more concerned with an election result on the state level: State Senator Babe Schwartz, who had shepherded the school from its founding and protected it from budget slashing by the legislature, had been defeated in his bid for reelection. The school had lost its champion in Austin.

The institution had come a long way since admitting its first women students in 1973. An article in the *Channel Chatter* compared the ratio of females to males during 1981 in all the state maritime academies. Texas Maritime came way out ahead with 12.5 percent of its cadets female; New York Maritime and California Maritime both had 5.6 percent; Massachusetts Maritime and Maine Maritime both had 3.7 percent. The reporter, Mary Hancock, said that "spending three cruises and close to 150 credit hours" together changes one's image about the opposite sex. And though women in 1981 were "not always accepted as full fledged members of the maritime community," they no longer had to fight to enter academies or to board ships. Being outnumbered had some advantages. As one student remembered, it meant that if she were on a tight budget, she did not have to worry about paying for dinner or drinks— there were always men eager to take her out and pick up the tab. For the men, having few women on campus made it tough to find dates. Some tried to meet nursing students at UTMB. Upperclassmen would stick around on campus for freshman orientation so that they could get a jump on dating the new women students. However unbalanced the male-female ratio, lasting relationships developed: a number of former students ended up marrying each other.

In January a break in the pipe supplying water to Pelican Island made Houston TV news. Being without water for a few days was certainly inconvenient, said the editor of the *Channel Chatter,* "but the most irritating thing about the whole matter is that Channel 2 [NBC] mentioned that no one lives on Pelican Island except a bunch of A&M Cadets." That casual remark raised hackles: "Well, even A&M Cadets use water, and so do their non-Corps counterparts." The editor said she felt like driving up

1981

In 1981 the first U.S. space shuttle was launched. The Texas Legislature got around to giving the official nod to the institutional name of Texas A&M University at Galveston, a name that had been in common use for the past two years. The Mitchell campus celebrated its tenth birthday. The marine fisheries major was added.

and down the streets of Galveston with a loudspeaker blaring, "There *are* people on Pelican Island."

In April, fourteen maritime cadets ran 150 miles from *Texas Clipper* to the Brazos River as part of the annual March of Dimes fund-raising Aggie Corps March to the Brazos. During the trip, a lone student would run about thirteen nine-minute miles while the others rode in a university-owned van. Then he would hand off the baton to the runner for the next leg. The longest leg was twenty-two miles. The trip was full of adventure: runners lost their way on the Katy-Hockley exit, were heckled by some rude motorists, and had to use their baton to fend off barking dogs. They reached the Brazos at 10:15 on Saturday morning, reported the *Battalion*,

TAMUG Name-Change Finally Becomes Official

The A&M Board of Regents had adopted the name Texas A&M University at Galveston in the fall of 1979. That was standard practice: all previous name changes had been enacted internally by the Board of Regents without seeking legislative action. Thus the campus had been using the new name on its letterhead and in communications with the regional accrediting association and the federal Department of Education. However, this time political opposition—coming largely from old-school members of the Texas A&M Association of Former Students and disgruntled members the Board of Regents—demanded that the change be formally ratified by the Legislature. The renaming effort had died in committee several times over the past session.

But on April 30, 1981, the Senate Finance Committee voted 8–0 to change the name *officially* from Moody College to Texas A&M University at Galveston. State Senator Carl Parker of Port Arthur had argued that although the institution might be called Moody in the appropriations bill, when graduates got their degrees, the certificates said A&M. The Moody family understood the advantages in changing from a college to a university under the name A&M. A life-sized portrait of William Lewis Moody Jr., founder of the Moody Foundation, was hanging on the wall of the committee room. After the unanimous vote, reported the *Houston Post*, State Senator Ray Farabee of Wichita Falls said he thought he saw the portrait smile.

The same day the Texas House of Representatives also voted unanimously to change the name. On May 31, 1981, the State Senate passed the name-change bill. It became law when Governor William Clements signed it. A great deal of the credit for pushing through the name change goes to Marilyn Schwartz, wife of former State Senator Babe Schwartz. She lobbied the Senate and House tirelessly. Afterward, the campus bookstore held a big sale on Moody College paraphernalia—pencils, pens, T-shirts, baseball caps, and sweatshirts went at a deep discount. The Moody family name remained an integral part of the university: undergraduate degrees in marine sciences, marine biology, and maritime system engineering were administered by the Moody College of Marine Technology; and the liveliest building on campus was the Mary Moody Northen Student Center.

twenty-five hours after they had left the ship and an hour before the College Station corps arrived. Karl Haupt, a senior cadet and marine sciences major (and future master of the *Clipper*), said no one was there to greet them: "It was a very unglamorous entrance." The disappointed group left the grounds, showered, then luckily returned just in time to glimpse the Dallas Cowboy cheerleaders. It was the third year the cadets had made the run; only eight of about eighteen finished the run the first year. Afterward the cadets met some of their College Station friends and socialized.

Texas Attorney General Mark White spoke at the Galveston convocation ceremony in May. Amid rumors that he might run for governor (which would prove true), White gave what sounded very much like a campaign speech. He addressed lawsuits, prison reform, and the challenges of citizenship. When asked about his political aspirations, White said only, "I have aspirations to be a good attorney general."

The Research Vessel *Gyre,* docked on the campus, took part in an effort to find the sunken *Titanic* in the summer of 1981. The venture was sponsored by oilman Jack Grimm of Abilene. Grimm gave up in 1983; *Titanic* would be found by another team led by Bob Ballard in 1985. *Texas Clipper* embarked on a European training cruise but had to make two last-minute itinerary switches. Unexpectedly high fuel costs forced the ship to forgo a scheduled visit to Copenhagen in favor of Southampton, England, which was closer. And miscommunication in docking reservations forced another quick switch from Bermuda to Nassau, in the Bahamas. Consequently the 1981 cruise was dubbed the "mystery cruise." On the shoreside campus, TAMUG held its first summer camp for gifted children in elementary school. The initial program proved so successful that it continued and grew over subsequent summers and would give birth to the Sea Camp program.

TAMUG announced that two of its faculty members had received recognition for their teaching and service. Sammy Ray was named Minnie Stevens Piper Professor for his excellence in teaching. Professor of biology and wildlife and fisheries, he had been the first department head of marine sciences, the department that gave birth to marine biology and maritime systems engineering. He was only the second faculty member in the history of the school to receive that prestigious statewide award, biologist David Aldrich having received it in 1977. Ray's career illustrated that it is possible to teach and publish: the A&M Association of Former Students had honored him in 1974 for his research.

Francis Tormollan became the first Galveston campus teacher to be named *emeritus*—a title reserved for the few faculty members whose service to their institution is truly distinguished. After he retired, he became associate professor emeritus of marine engineering. In August, Frank Vandiver was named the nineteenth president of Texas A&M University. According to Babe Schwartz, Vandiver viewed Galveston programs slightly more favorably than had his predecessor Jarvis Miller.

A chart prepared as part of
the reaccreditation process
for TAMUG shows dramatic
growth over a decade. More
important than the raw
numbers was the phenome-
nal percentage increase in
money, faculty, staff, students, equipment, acreage,
library books, and buildings.
Source: Institutional Self-
Study Report, 1982.

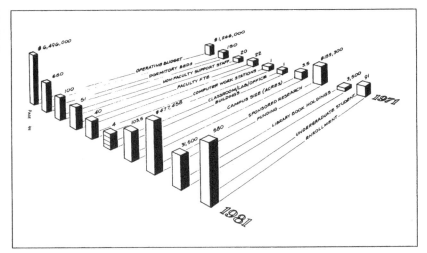

At the start of the fall semester the Texas Legislature had raised the minimum legal drinking age from eighteen to nineteen. Since most freshmen could no longer drink legally, serving beer at university functions had to be strictly supervised. As one might imagine, the new law was not popular with college students. But the impact of the restriction may have been somewhat lessened by a brand new diversion for many students: MTV started broadcasting.

In October TAMUG celebrated the tenth anniversary of the opening of the Pelican Island campus and the simultaneous founding of the College of Marine Sciences and Maritime Resources (absorbing the Texas Maritime Academy that had existed since 1962). The *Galveston Daily News* published a twenty-four-page insert on the history and future plans of the institution. As part of the festivities, A&M President Vandiver made his first visit to the campus. The Galveston Chamber of Commerce hosted a dinner reception at the Moody Center, the Aggie Singing Cadets performed, and an all-university picnic was held at Carbide Park.

During those ten formative years the operating budget had risen from approximately $1.3 to $6.5 million. Curricula had expanded from two to seven degree programs; buildings had multiplied from three to nine; undergraduate enrollment had more than quintupled from 91 to 575 (580 in some reports); faculty had more than doubled from 22 to 51; and the library book collection had increased almost tenfold from 3,500 to 31,500. And of course the physical campus had come a long way, as President Clayton noted: "The rattlesnakes are gone, and shrubs, trees and grassy areas have largely replaced the mud expanse." Still the campus was no country club—an editorial cartoon in the *Channel Chatter* claimed that the official island bird was the mosquito; the island flower was weeds; and its official tree was the telephone pole.

Other changes occurred that year. The Department of Marine Biology began offering its students the opportunity to major either in marine bi-

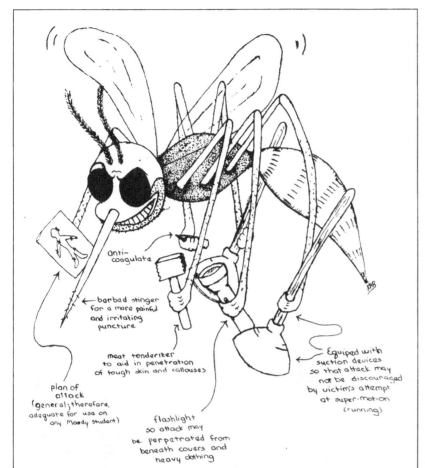

Anti-
coagulate

← barbed stinger
for a more painful
and irritating
puncture

meat tenderizer
to aid in penetration
of tough skin and callouses

Equiped with
suction devices
so that attack may
not be discouraged
by victim's attempt
at super-motion
(running)

plan of
attack
(general; therefore,
adequate for use on
any Moody student)

flashlight
so attack may
be perpetrated from
beneath covers and
heavy clothing

An editorial cartoon drawn and labeled by an anonymous undergraduate for the campus newspaper focuses imaginatively on a favorite subject—mosquitoes. The original caption reads: "All points bulletin: The enemy has been reported 'at large' (and boy are they big!) on Pelican Island. Enemy is described as armed and dangerous." Source: *Channel Chatter,* September 21, 1981.

ology or in the new curriculum of marine fisheries. And the Department of Maritime Systems Engineering was transferred from the Moody College of Maritime Technology to the Texas Maritime College, which included the Department of Marine Engineering. The latter was a practical move designed to help both engineering programs retain their professional accreditation. Within the same college, they could share resources more efficiently and cooperate more closely.

In November, the campus was abuzz with the news that a senior TAMU member of the Aggie corps of cadets had been suspended for six weeks because of what he did when Southern Methodist University cheerleaders ran out onto the playing area of Kyle Field in College Station. According to Aggie tradition, only players are allowed on the field. A number of Galveston Aggies at the football game had watched as the cadet, in full uniform as befitting his responsibility as officer of the day, caught up with the cheerleaders and then "brandished his saber and thrust it" threateningly at one of them. An Aggie football player who was on the field waiting to receive the kickoff helped restrain the saber-wielding cadet. After the cadet was removed from the stadium, SMU went on to outscore the Aggies 27–7. The suspension delayed the senior's graduation a semester. Carrying ceremonial sabers on the College Station campus was banned for the next year.

1982

The first successful transplant of a mechanical heart occurred in 1982. *Cheers* debuted on TV. TAMUG unveiled the carved wooden triptych in front of the entrance to the auditorium. A maritime cadet posed for the figurehead on the sailing ship *Elissa*. The undergraduate newspaper changed its name to *Nautilus*. And police chased a murder suspect across the Mitchell campus.

Three eight-foot by five-foot mahogany panels, each weighing about seven hundred pounds, were installed in February of 1982 on the hallway wall between the two entrances to the auditorium in the classroom laboratory building. Pittsburgh artist William Pochiol had sculpted them. He titled the work "The Tempest." Two and a half years in the making, it is arguably the finest piece of art on the campus. Some students wondered at the time why the cash-strapped and facilities-poor school had not used the money for more practical purposes, but state law required

A carved triptych entitled "The Tempest" is installed at the entrance to the auditorium in the classroom laboratory building, February, 1982. Between classes, students often sit and study in the artistic space in front of the eight-foot-tall mahogany panels.

that a certain percentage of the cost of new buildings be dedicated to artwork.

Pochiol chose four-inch-thick slabs to provide the depth necessary for his bas-relief carvings. He spent five months designing the panels, considering more than fifty plans. A TAMUG student, marveling at the complex interweaving of mermaidlike figures on the left panel, asked Pochiol how he had managed to make their mouths look so much like fish mouths. The artist said, "Well, actually, I'm not very good at carving mouths. That's the best I could do at the time." The right panel depicts sea, land, and sky creatures. The dramatic center panel features a single imposing godlike figure emerging from an uncarved surface.

Inclement weather, equipment problems, material holdups, and faulty design of the balcony supports delayed construction of the new four-story dormitory building, C-dorm. The layout of the dormitory was modified from existing architectural plans for the construction of a La Quinta Inn motel; the school saved money by not having to pay for original plans. C-dorm was certainly needed to accommodate rising enrollment. Cadets who had paid for dormitory rooms continued to live on the training ship because no rooms were available.

In March, Arthur G. Hansen was named chancellor of the Texas A&M University System, succeeding Frank Hubert. Lieutenant Governor William P. Hobby Jr., a legend in Texas politics, spoke at the convocation ceremony in May. He emphasized how essential TAMUG was to the present and future welfare of the citizens of Texas. "There is an obvious demand for your services," he told graduating students, "and that in itself illustrates a significant need to expand." The most critical need at the time was a library.

Cadet Poses for Figurehead on Tall Ship

TAMUG cadet Amy McAllister was immortalized in decorative art by posing for the figurehead of Galveston's square-rigger *Elissa*, open for public tours beginning on July 4, 1982. McAllister was hoisted up and strapped to the bow of the ship, where she was photographed by sculptor Eli Kuslansky. Suspended by hemp ropes tied around her ankles and waist, she held a flower gracefully to her bosom. The artist selected the cadet because of her resemblance to the young Mary Moody Northen, whose generous donations had helped obtain and refurbish the vessel.

"When I was asked to model for the figurehead, I felt quite honored," said McAllister. "Someday, it will be a story I'll tell my grandchildren." The life-size figurehead, carved from Honduras mahogany, was painted white and fastened to four carved trail boards attached to the ship's bow. McAllister had to be flown home from the *Texas Clipper* training cruise by the Galveston Historical Foundation so that she could take part in the dedication ceremonies for *Elissa*. After Mary Moody Northen unveiled the statue, she took one look at the figurehead and remarked, "It looks nothing like me."

To create a figurehead for the 1877 sailing barque *Elissa,* a sculptor searched for someone who looked like a young Mary Moody Northen, the ship's benefactor. He found her in twenty-year-old TAMUG cadet Amy McAllister, who volunteered to be tied to the ship's bow and photographed from all angles. The white wooden figurehead, unveiled on July 4, 1982, is modeled on those photos. Source: Texas Seaport Museum. Used with permission.

A former student who had been injured on the field while playing an intramural sport filed a lawsuit against TAMUG. He said that the surface of the field was too uneven for safe play and that his injury resulted from the school's negligence. The intramural field was plowed, rolled, smoothed, and reseeded in the fall. Administrators denied any connection between the lawsuit and the resurfacing. The suit was settled. Everyone agreed that the field, at any rate, was much improved.

Women cadets at Texas Maritime had now become an integral part of the school. By the summer, thirty-five of the 250 maritime cadets were female. Women were especially attracted to the license option program offered to majors in marine biology or marine sciences.

The Student Advisory Committee voted to change the name of the campus newsletter from *Channel Chatter* to *Nautilus.* The impetus behind the change was that the broadened curricula and growing reputation of the school merited a more professional-sounding name on its newsletter masthead. The name *Nautilus* was suggested by Oliver Wendell Holmes's famous 1858 poem "The Chambered Nautilus," employing the "growing shell" of the sea creature as a metaphor for human development.

Indeed, the school had its share of growing pains. An editorial took a dispirited look at what was keeping TAMUG from becoming a world-class university: "The antiquated bridge and engine room of *Texas Clipper,* the inadequate library facility, the lack of a real student government,

Finishing work was under way in 1982 on the four-story dormitory building, the largest structure on campus until the 2004 engineering building went up. After design and construction delays, C-dorm was ready for occupancy in the fall of 1982. It was built to accommodate a burgeoning student population, but by the time it opened, the growth trend had flattened out and C-dorm proved difficult to fill. Source: *Voyager,* 1982.

the controversial cafeteria food, and the unpopular weekend training program." Yet, said the *Nautilus* editorial, "Acting as if world class designation could someday be a reality is the first step toward making it a reality."

Name changes continued to confuse people, and no wonder. In about a decade, the school had operated under five different titles. Even the *Galveston Daily News* got mixed up, variously calling the school Moody College, Texas Maritime Academy, or Texas A&M University. Name jumbling got so bad that John Merritt, public affairs officer for the campus, photocopied in bold large letters on an eight-by-ten-inch sheet of paper, "There is no Moody College. Only cadets are in the Texas Maritime Academy. Texas A&M University is in College Station. The name of the school is Texas A&M University at Galveston." He drove out to the newspaper building and placed copies of that piece of paper on every single desk, from secretary to publisher. That pretty much solved the name problem in the *News*. But a number of local people still used the wrong names and continued to believe that the campus taught only upperclassmen, as it had up until 1971.

In October the dean of the Texas Maritime College, Admiral Kenneth Haynes, stepped down. He had been appointed the fourth superintendent of the Texas Maritime Academy in 1978. His title was changed to dean when the program switched from an academy to a college. However, just as the maritime program would continue to be informally called the academy, its head would continue to be called superintendent. After he left, the position was filled largely by academic administrators rather than retired Navy and Coast Guard officers, as had been the former practice. William Clayton, president of TAMUG, for the time being also assumed the function of superintendent.

That fall, the campus was the site of a chase scene that looked as though it had come straight from a crime movie. On November 30 a Houston man murdered a woman security guard in Galveston. The murderer fled to Pelican Island, where he tried to run campus police off the road. He wrecked his getaway truck, ran across a field to some oil storage tanks on the Mitchell campus, and vanished in a marshy area. Students were told to lock their doors, close their balcony sliding doors, and stay inside as the entire campus was put on alert. The lockdown proved frighteningly effective: afterward, bloody handprints were discovered on C-dorm doors. The murderer eluded local police and left the campus. He evidently swam across the channel from Pelican Island to Galveston Island. Then he hitchhiked to Houston and caught a flight to Queens, New York, where he was finally arrested two weeks later.

1983

In 1983, CDs were introduced as a new way to store music, and cell phones were now available to civilians. About 50 million people watched the last *MASH* episode on TV. Hurricane Alicia battered the campus, causing extensive damage. And TAMUG began planning its first library building.

In January, ten years after the campus had begun enrolling women, Jane Bedessem became the first woman commander of the maritime corps of cadets. The previous year, she had served as corps executive officer. At that time the ratio of men to women in the corps was about 7 to 1. What she remembered as her biggest contribution to the corps occurred when she was an underclassman. "I was the squeaky wheel who got the order of cruise duties changed from Watch-Training-Maintenance to Watch-Maintenance-Training." It does not sound like much of a change, but it was a big deal for cadets. Under the old schedule, after losing sleep during the midnight-to-4:00 A.M. watch (during their Watch day), they then had to attend 8:00 A.M. classes and take exams (during their Training day). "We were just too exhausted to prepare for one of Commander William T. McMullen's excruciatingly difficult tests four hours after we got off watch," said Bedessem. "But we were told, at first, that the schedule could not be changed because the acronym for Watch-Training-Maintenance—WTM—also happened to be the initials of William T. McMullen." Persistence paid off, and the desired change went through.

TAMUG bade a sad farewell to one of its more popular teachers, chemistry professor Charles D. Mickey, who died unexpectedly on January 30, just after the first week of the spring semester. Mickey had been named an outstanding chemistry teacher by the Texas Chemical Council and the Manufacturing Chemists Association in 1965–67 and was voted Most Effective Teacher in 1976–77 by TAMUG students.

In the spring semester, TAMUG hosted the first Galveston Science and Engineering Fair. Gerald Hite, a physicist in the marine sciences department, founded the annual event. The Kempner Fund underwrote the first fair and TAMUG supplied the venue. A few years later the fair would be expanded to include all of Galveston County. But students were more excited by the reopening of Streater's tavern on 14th Street: all day on Thursday and Friday, you could buy any of eight different brands of beer for just two dollars a pitcher.

In April, a TAMUG student was swept out to sea while windsurfing. R. Troy Swetnam, aged twenty-one, was a marine sciences major from San Antonio. His windsurfing board was recovered sixty miles east of where he had last been seen. Swetnam was declared dead in May when his tattered wetsuit and one tennis shoe washed up; his initials were written on the inside of the suit. It was impossible to determine whether he had drowned or been killed by a shark. The award to the outstanding Sail Club member is named in Swetnam's honor, and the Swetnam endowment supports an annual scholarship.

Hurricane Alicia, an extraordinarily destructive category 3 storm, struck Galveston on August 17–18. Winds gusted up to 102 mph as the storm dumped almost eight inches of rain on Galveston. Damage in the Galveston-Houston area was estimated at $3 billion. Eight persons, including three cadets, stayed on board *Texas Clipper* as two tugboats under full power kept her from being blown away from the campus dock. Just before dawn on August 18, after one of the tugs had to leave to stop a runaway barge from slamming into the Pelican Island bridge, the 175-foot seismic research vessel *Arctic Seal* was ripped from mooring at Pier 41 across the Galveston channel. Her captain fired up engines but was unable to prevent being forced underneath the lines and smashing into the stern of the *Clipper*. It was a life-threatening situation for the sixteen people, mostly scientists, on the *Seal*. Potential danger from wind-whipped antennas on board the *Clipper* delayed their rescue. Finally *Clipper* crew members Tom Cromer and Bob Nation were able to rig a Jacob's ladder connecting the two vessels and a guide rope along the deck of the *Clipper*. One by one, in blinding rain, the *Seal* crew climbed up the ladder and followed the guide rope to safety. Just before noon, the storm abated down somewhat, allowing a tug to help *Seal* return to Pier 41. Some of the rain-soaked refugees were so shaken that they refused to reboard *Seal* for the short trip back across the channel; they took a bus instead. *Arctic Seal* suffered extensive damage, said her manager afterward, but because of "help from the people aboard *Texas Clipper,* no one even received a scratch!"

High winds, horizontal rain, and flying objects shattered windows, collapsed roofs, and soaked carpets, sheetrock, and furniture. In C-dorm the rain soaked all floors on the west side of the building. Fifteen rooms in A- and B-dorms were torn up by shattered patio-door glass. Hallways, classrooms, and laboratories were damaged at Fort Crockett, and the small boat basin was also damaged. Because the campus had been evacuated, no one was hurt. The campus needed a major cleanup in the storm's aftermath but was open for business on August 25, 1983, when students began to check into their dormitory rooms. The paperback collection in the campus library, still located in the engineering building, was ruined by wind-driven water leaking through a few spots in the roof. Carpeting in the library's reading lounge loft wrinkled and shrank from leaking water, and had to be replaced. Luckily the hardbound book and journal collection suffered no losses. Because the library space was so small about several thousand volumes were safely in storage, most of them at Fort Crockett. The C-dorm roof suffered the most expensive damage, allowing water to seep into walls, which led to chronic mildew problems. New guttering was installed after the storm. It took a year and a half and $550,000 to repair roofs, sheet metal, and structural damage to buildings on campus.

The big budgetary news was a $4.5 million appropriation for a library building, 26,667 square feet of space to house a hundred thousand volumes. The collection would no longer need to be split between the engi-

When the day was pleasant, students could play volleyball on the sand court near C-dorm and the swimming pool. At night and during inclement weather, their only choice on campus was to play in the makeshift gym in a cargo hold of *Texas Clipper*.

Exercising inside a Cargo Hold

The only indoor exercise area on campus was in the number three cargo hold (originally an area for storage) inside *Texas Clipper*. Recognizing how difficult it was to find one's way through the labyrinthine passageways of the ship, the *Nautilus* editor said: "If you don't know how to get there, ask the watch." It was a quiet area below the water line. Like the surrounding ship channel, it was cool in the winter and warm in the summer. So you bundled up from November through March, and sweated all the other months. The number three hold offered a meager collection of equipment: a weight machine, free weights and benches, a climbing rope, and a dozen workout mats used to soften old wooden decking that looked as if it were made from railroad ties. Two caged light bulbs illuminated the hold. One basketball hoop (later there would be two) on a backboard was affixed to the ship's bulkhead. This "gym" had only one way in and out: a steep twenty-foot metal staircase. Crew members opened up an emergency fire exit, up a vertical ladder to the old baggage room and from there to a stairway leading to B-deck; once again, you might need to ask the watch for directions. Basketball players had to be prepared for startling bounces caused by the rough-hewn decking planks. Volleyball players had to keep the ball lower than the ten-foot overhead, which ricocheted shots back at your head. With all its drawbacks, it was the campus's only nighttime playing area. Students used it almost every evening for games or exercise.

During summer cruises, the movement of the ship added a peculiar element to playing in the cargo hold. If you jumped during a ship's roll, the decking was unexpectedly closer or farther away when you landed. Students said dribbling a basketball during rolls required finesse and imagination.

neering building and storage at Fort Crockett. The proposed building would more than double the current space, get the library away from the noise made by the machine shop, and finally include space for comfortable sitting and studying. The architects named for the new library building would be Rapp Partners of Galveston. The company had already designed the master plan for the Pelican Island campus and its first two buildings, the admin building and the engineering lab.

After students had left on their winter break, an extraordinarily frigid arctic cold front swept over Galveston in the last week of December. The thermometer dipped to 14 degrees F on Christmas morning, the coldest temperature recorded in Galveston since 1930. The campus had to deal with frozen or burst water pipes.

Mary Moody Northen celebrated her ninety-second birthday on February 11, 1984. Legal moves were under way to place her estate under limited guardianship, on the basis that she had become incompetent. She continued to be a great friend of the maritime academy.

On March 30, TAMUG held its first annual Maritime Ball in the ballroom of the 1859 Ashton Villa, Galveston's finest antebellum mansion.

1984

In 1984 the campus opened a snack bar. Apple introduced the Macintosh computer. *The Cosby Show* debuted on TV. Best-selling American novelist James Michener took a trip on *Texas Clipper*. The campus was in the middle of an eight-year struggle to escape the doldrums of a flat or declining enrollment. TAMUG advertised itself as the "best kept secret in Galveston Island," but even this did not help enrollment much.

The ball was conceived as a dress-up occasion, an opportunity for students to don stylish evening gowns, elegant tuxedos, and sharp full-dress uniforms. It worked beautifully. Students said they had difficulty identifying one another in formal attire. Live music, soft lights, and dancing made it a memorable evening, appropriately captured by many flash cameras. After this promising start, the Maritime Ball became one of the most anticipated social events every year.

Student life improved some with additions to the campus. In March the Student Advisory Committee approved collecting a ten-dollar fee each semester: the funds would go toward improving the student center complex. The Northen Student Center increased its services, especially in the evening when the cafeteria was closed. A snack bar near the east entrance to the cafeteria now satisfied the after-hours need for munchies. It contained a soft drink vending machine, a sandwich-and-fruit machine, and a microwave; students could chat while sitting at tables with tablecloths. Operating hours were 6:30 A.M. to 11:30 P.M. daily. In the spring the gym in the cargo hold of *Texas Clipper* was updated with two basketball backboards, hoops, and nets, setups for volleyball, and ping-pong tables. It also became safer. Protection pads softened metal support beams in the middle of the play area, plywood covered uneven planking on the gym floor, and all protruding metal hooks were removed from the surrounding bulkheads (walls).

Despite these improvements, Mitchell campus remained austere. New generations of students took the changes for granted and complained about other things. Some coined the name "Pelicatraz" to describe what they saw as its prison-yard atmosphere. The eight squat buildings scattered over the hundred-acre campus, said the *Battalion,* "could hardly be called eye-catching. What a visitor does notice is the scant amount of landscaping. Trees and shrubbery are hard to find and the groundcover seems to be more marsh grass than St. Augustine." The remarks made the TAMUG community wince, but they were too true to deny. The failure of landscaping, however, had a great deal to do with the difficulty of planting on an island made from salty dredge spoil (public relations people prefer to call it "opportunity reclamation land"). In the early days of Mitchell campus, hoping for recommendations on which plants would thrive on the island, administrators sent samples to the soil lab at College Station. They received this terse reply: "If you have anything growing on this island, guard it with your lives."

The Mitchell campus received one of its defining landmarks in March. Dow Chemical Company donated a twelve-foot-diameter propeller from *Point Sur,* a seagoing tug of the V-4 class that had participated in the D-Day invasion of Normandy during the Second World War. Mike Tavary (TMA, marine engineering, class of 1971) arranged for the donation. Eventually the six-ton propeller would be permanently mounted on a massive granite base outside the northeast corner of the proposed library building.

In April, State Senator Chet Books sponsored a bill to expand the role of TAMUG by allowing it to offer undergraduate degrees in programs unrelated to the sea. The proposal created immediate political opposition from nearby junior colleges; College of the Mainland and Galveston College worried that expanded offerings from a general-purpose TAMUG could hurt their enrollment. On the other side, friends of TAMUG expressed concern that such expansion would undercut its unique mission of educating undergraduates about the ocean and would make it just like any other school. The issue was eventually settled in favor of keeping TAMUG focused exclusively on the sea.

The City of Galveston now began work on constructing a modern bypass for Port Industrial Boulevard, later renamed Harborside Drive, which was grooved with railroad tracks, pitted by pot holes, and patched with wobbly concrete slabs. Driving over the surface ensured that cars needed frequent front-end alignments. The project would result in a smooth, multilane road that connected 25th Street with Interstate 45. At an overpass called the Judge Charles B. Smith Viaduct, the new road would intersect with the road to the Mitchell campus, 51st Street or Seawolf Parkway. It made commuting much easier and faster, except on days of heavy rain, when low-lying stretches beyond the east and west ends of the overpass filled with impassably deep water.

World-famous author James Michener stands by to board *Texas Clipper* in June of 1984, headed for the site of the New Orleans World's Fair; the run was the first leg of the training cruise. Left to right: Frank Kemery, TAMUG corps commander; Frank Vandiver, Texas A&M president; John Caple, chair, TAMUG Board of Visitors; author James Michener; William Clayton, TAMUG president; and William J. Briggs, ship's captain.

Famous Novelist Ships out on *Clipper*

Every year, just before the ship departed, a guest speaker would address the cadets at the Northen breakfast. In 1984 the dignitary was novelist James A. Michener, then author of thirty-two books, including the novel *Hawaii* and the Pulitzer Prize–winning *Tales of the South Pacific*, which became one of the most successful musicals of all time both on Broadway and in the movies. In recognition of his cultural contribution, he was the 1977 recipient of the Presidential Medal of Freedom, the highest civilian award in the United States. His novels sold so well that it was said a forest had to be cut down each time he published a new book. At the breakfast he admitted to a TAMUG administrator that he had never before sailed the Gulf, and he wanted to do it while he was researching a novel about the history of Texas, eventually published, of course, under the title *Texas*. He got an invitation on the spot.

"I've sailed on all the oceans of the world, but have never sailed the Gulf of Mexico," Michener told the newspaper. "I'm going on the journey to fulfill that obligation, one I've had a very long time." Michener boarded *Texas Clipper* for the first leg of the trip to New Orleans. On June 4, while the ship was under way, he spoke about writing to a composition class of freshmen. Michener told students that the best path to success is possession of a wide vocabulary, and that the higher you go, the more your success depends upon your ability to communicate. "I'm a lousy writer," he said, "but one of the world's best re-writers." By way of illustration, he pointed to a passage in his most recent novel *Poland:* "It took 22 drafts to get right." He also graciously spent time in the afterbar of the ship signing books and talking with people about his writing. The ship docked inside the World's Fair grounds at New Orleans.

Cadets splash onboard *Texas Clipper* in a makeshift swimming pool. Before disposing of a worn-out rubber survival raft, enterprising cadets inflated it, cut off its overhead cowling, and filled it with seawater from fire hoses. The pool lasted for about a week. Source: *Voyager,* 1985.

On July 30, the British-flag tanker *Alvenus* ran aground off the coast of Louisiana. It cracked, dumping 2.8 million gallons of Venezuelan crude oil into the Gulf of Mexico. Four days later the murky oil washed ashore on Galveston Island beaches. Still reeling from Hurricane Alicia, Galveston had had a difficult time attracting tourists back to its beaches. Now it was faced with an ugly oil spill. Bad luck continued as a rainout on Labor Day, usually one of the most profitable beach days of the year, reduced the small number of beachgoers to near zero.

That fall, Ronald Reagan and George Bush beat Democratic hopefuls Walter Mondale and Geraldine Ferraro, the first woman ever nominated by a major political party to run for the White House. The student hangouts were the Interurban Queen, where Santos Cruz served up his famous margarita (which, he said with some claim to authenticity, he had invented in 1948 for pop singer Peggy Lee); and the club bar at the Holiday Inn at Port Holiday Mall, which sold drinks for a dollar to the sound of live music on Thursday nights. Students swore to teachers that you went there "only if you didn't have Friday classes." To celebrate the spring and fall equinoxes, many students gathered for an all-day blues bash at somebody's house, an all-day party with beverages, music, and barbecue. And of course students continued to look forward to the annual senior picnic at Carbide Park.

The contract for the new library was awarded to S&S Contracting in December. That same month, the Southern Association of Colleges and Schools reaccredited TAMUG. The action followed publication of a four-hundred-page self-study report (a book-length analysis of conditions by faculty and staff of the university) and an investigative campus visit by association members. Institutions of higher education undergo such a reaccreditation process every ten years. A chart in the report boasts that in 1981 the campus had all of forty computer work stations; this represented a vast improvement over the single computer—a broken Hewlett Packard the size of a washing machine—on campus in 1971.

In January, the maritime administration degree received approval from the Texas A&M Board of Regents to split off from the Department of Marine Transportation. The new Department of Maritime Administration, after a dramatic rise in enrollment to about seventy-five students, would have its own budget. The school now offered eight degree programs; two of them, MARB and MARS, offered students the option of taking additional course work and training to earn a Coast Guard license.

Unstable weather on February 10 caused winds to gust to fifty-four miles per hour and to spawn tornadoes and hailstorms on Pelican Island. The building at the old Todd Shipyards to the east suffered damage, but the campus remained unscathed. By the next weekend the weather turned pleasant, encouraging participation in a brand new citywide event in Galveston. On February 16, students made their way through crowds

1985

In 1985, laser videodiscs were introduced and video revenue for the first time exceeded theatrical-release revenue for movies. The TAMUG Sail Club won the coveted Kennedy Cup. TAMUG held its own graduation ceremony in Galveston, the first Aggie commencement ever authorized outside College Station.

along the Strand, 25th Street, and the seawall to join in the festivities and watch the first public Mardi Gras parade held in Galveston since 1941. Mardi Gras caught many students by surprise; they were not quite sure what was going on. Organizers of the big Momus night parade invited some of the students to participate: they dressed up like pirates and learned how to toss beads to anyone who yelled out, "Throw me something, Mister!" The Aggie gathering place during that year's parades was the Emporium, a delicatessen and specialty foods store on the Strand.

Former Galvestonian Paul Burka wrote an article in *Texas Monthly* in March about ways to save $1 billion in state taxes. One of his outrageous tongue-in-cheek proposals was to sell Texas A&M University at Galveston to Holiday Inn. Burka said it was hard for him to justify all the money spent for fewer than six hundred students, "most of whom are learning to pilot ships." Except for the small size of the student body, he had most of his facts mixed up. TAMUG administrators tried to correct his notion that the university mostly trained pilots. They invited Burka to tour the campus and take a free summer cruise on *Texas Clipper* so that he could see firsthand what cadets actually do. He declined the invitation.

In its editorial response, the *Galveston Daily News* showed that Burka had his financial facts wrong and warned "Hands off TAMUG!" The *News* noted that TAMUG might be small, but it packed a big educational punch. The smallest of the thirty-five state universities, it was number nineteen in dollars raised for funded research. And far from being only a pilot-training school, it offered nationally ranked science and engineering programs. *Texas Monthly* never corrected its article. In fact, the piece influenced State Representative Paul Colbert of Houston to call for a legislative effort to remove funding for TAMUG. In March Colbert's House Appropriations Committee recommended shutting down both TAMUG and UT's Permian Basin campus. Representatives Lloyd Criss and James Hury persuaded the committee to reconsider its vote and then to table the item indefinitely. They made saving TAMUG their top legislative priority, reported the *News*: "We don't intend to lose."

State Senator Chet Brooks of Pasadena said Colbert's motion was "a cutesy, cavalier move that I'm inclined to believe was done purely as a bargaining chip. It was a completely whimsical and irresponsible act." Colbert himself admitted in the *News* that he had only been "trying to make a point." Funds were restored, but political damage had been done. Rumblings in the legislature led to the creation of another committee to identify ways to save money in higher education. To say the least, it was a dangerous period for TAMUG.

In April the TAMUG Sail Club won the Kennedy Cup at the U.S. Naval Academy in a forty-four-foot Luder yawl, beating the Naval Academy, the University of Maryland, the State University of New York, and other East and West Coast colleges. The eight-man TAMUG team finished with eighteen points, nine points ahead of the second-place team from the University of California at Santa Barbara. TAMUG also won the

In Annapolis, Maryland, during the third weekend of April, 1985, the TAMUG Sail Club wins the national intercollegiate offshore racing championship—the John F. Kennedy Memorial Cup Regatta. The team also went home with the Judge's Trophy for seamanship and maintenance. Source: *Voyager*, 1985.

Judge's Trophy for seamanship and yacht maintenance. This was impressive news for a small university without athletic scholarships of any kind. All members of the team were walk-on students who simply loved sailing and happened to prove that they were great at it. Upon their return they got a hero's welcome from their fellow students, with a campuswide party at the tall ship *Elissa*.

In the summer, TAMUG sponsored its first Sea Camp, attracting about 450 children aged ten to twelve who wanted to learn about marine life along the margin of Galveston Bay. An Advanced Sea Camp for those aged fourteen to sixteen offered fewer recreational activities but longer and more rigorous hours in the field and in laboratories. Students happily slogged around in mud, dragged the marsh for specimens, and dissected what they caught.

In October the campus library, still housed in the engineering building, displayed the one-man nautical art show of Harry Ahysen, professor of art at Sam Houston State University. Ahysen, the state artist of Texas for 1980–81, donated two oil paintings to TAMUG: a seascape of ocean waves and a depiction of *Texas Clipper*.

Construction on the new library building finally began in December. Also in the fall of 1985, the *Gourman Report* ranked TAMUG at eighteen out of the then sixty-four public and private universities in Texas. For years the respected *Gourman Report* had ranked the undergraduate

First Aggie Graduation Held outside College Station

The graduating class of May, 1985, became the first ever to attend an Aggie commencement ceremony in Galveston. On May 4, when they heard their names called, they walked across the stage of the auditorium in the classroom laboratory building on the Mitchell campus on Pelican Island to receive their diplomas. Previous classes had attended what had been called a convocation ceremony in Galveston on Friday, when names of graduates were called out, cadets were commissioned, new corps of cadets officers were sworn in, and awards were announced. Then on Saturday morning students would receive their degrees in the G. Rollie White Auditorium at College Station. From now on, all the ceremonies would take place in Galveston.

The first commencement speaker in Galveston, fittingly, was John C. Calhoun, emeritus deputy chancellor for engineering of the Texas A&M University System. Calhoun had been the intellectual architect behind the growth of TAMUG. He had come up with the idea of expanding the role of Galveston's undergraduate program to include science as well as merchant marine curricula. Calhoun noted how much the campus had grown, both physically and intellectually, over the past fourteen years. The overflow crowd had to watch the ceremony on closed-circuit television from the Northen Student Center. It was obvious that the ceremony needed a larger space, which it would have by the following May.

Construction of the Jack K. Williams Library began in December of 1985. The future entrance to the library is in the indented center of the front façade.

marine biology program as third best in the nation, after Michigan and California–Santa Barbara. And the marine engineering program ranked fourth behind New York Maritime, the U.S. Naval Academy, and the U.S. Coast Guard Academy.

January was a month of accidents, one trivial but the other catastrophic. A bulldozer slid into a ditch and split open a ten-inch water main. The campus was without water for about six hours while a new section of pipe arrived from Houston and was installed. The inconvenience caused by this mishap was as nothing compared to the emotional turmoil on campus over the January 28 explosion of the space shuttle *Challenger*. The proximity of Clear Lake City meant that a number of people at TAMUG had direct or indirect contact with those working on the shuttle program at NASA's Johnson Space Center.

A student-led movement was under way to convince Berkeley Breathed, creator of the popular comic strip "Bloom County" to let his character Opus the penguin be used as the mascot of TAMUG. Breathed responded that copyright restrictions "prohibit such a grand status as mascot for our large-tushed friend." But Breathed added that he was "quite honored that you felt Opus the most appropriate candidate." Students were split over whether their favorite comic strip was "Calvin and Hobbes," which debuted that year, or "Bloom County."

In February, present and former TAMUG students jumped right into the spirit of Galveston's second annual Mardi Gras by creating their own krewe, the Krewe of Thalasar. Members decorated and rode in a float in the Aquarius truck parade, held on Saturday two weeks before Fat Tuesday. (Thalasar also hosted an annual ball, participated in the Adopt-a-Beach cleanup program, and invited people to their Fourth of July barbecue.) The following Saturday night, maritime academy cadets were invited to march in the big Momus parade. But they had some disagreement with College Station cadets over placement in the line waiting for the parade to start: maritime cadets were more than a little miffed at being stuck directly behind the horses. On their own initiative, they blended into the crowd and reentered the line in front of the horses. Now the College Station cadets were upset. A parade official, a local Aggie, solved the problem by separating the two corps groups; he reassigned the maritime cadets, as befitted their status as Galveston's own corps, to the head of the parade.

The Sail Club won the seamanship Judge's Trophy for the second year in a row but finished fourth in the Kennedy Cup regatta. The Texas A&M System Board of Regents had approved a new academic program, Computer Science for Marine Studies, but political opposition from the outside squelched the proposed program before it could get off the drawing boards. The outlook was so uninviting that the next new TAMUG program would not be approved for another eleven years.

1986

In 1986, TAMUG survived the most serious crisis in its history: threatened legislative closure. *Texas Clipper* broke through the so-called Iron Curtain when she became the first American passenger ship or training vessel in ten years to visit Russia. And the campus turned over a new page with the opening of its library building.

State politics soon grew even bleaker. The previous year, as described, State Representative Colbert had proposed shutting down TAMUG and other low-enrollment colleges. Now the Governor's Select Committee on Higher Education, under chairman Larry Temple, looked at closing TAMUG, the University of Texas at Permian Basin, Sul Ross State University at Alpine, and East Texas State University at Commerce. The committee also considered merging institutions like Texas Southern University with the University of Houston at University Park; and Texas Women's Houston Center with the University of Texas Health Science Center. And it considered converting several colleges to branch study centers. Unfortunately, just as TAMUG most needed their support, some of the more influential administrators at College Station were at best lukewarm.

Things looked miserable enough for maritime cadets to be told at a routine Thursday formation on the dock that if the school closed, they might have to finish their academic program at California Maritime Academy. Many faculty members believed they should look for work elsewhere. But the school was not going to give up without a fight. Billboards announced the local resolve to fight the threatened closure. Supporters of TAMUG took out a full-page advertisement in the *Galveston Daily News* saying "SUPPORT TAMUG." The ad noted that TAMUG was the only marine-oriented university in Texas, running the only maritime academy on the Gulf Coast, and that the *Gourman Report* ranked its marine biology and marine engineering programs nationally. The *News* published an editorial titled "Let's Save TAMUG," urging concerned citizens to send letters of support to the select committee. In four days, two hundred letters were collected.

Public sentiment began to swing in TAMUG's favor. In July Governor Mark White said it would be a "tragic mistake" to close any of the five schools, which he called "some of Texas' finest institutions," according to the *Daily News*. State Representatives Lloyd Criss and James Hury, State Senator Chet Brooks, and Galveston Mayor Jan Coggeshall were among those who went to Austin to testify on TAMUG's behalf. Brooks, who orchestrated the defense, had just returned from spending a week aboard *Texas Clipper*. Onboard the ship, he and TAMUG President Clayton had discussed strategy and made a video about the actual hands-on training of maritime cadets. Students and former students got on chartered buses and carpooled to Austin. They talked to anyone who would listen about how important TAMUG was to them.

Senator Brooks showed his *Texas Clipper* video to the committee; they were mightily impressed. One of the more prominent of the select committee members, Norman Hackerman (former president of Rice University), remarked out loud about his personal knowledge of the high academic quality of TAMUG. The last to testify, Texas A&M University System Chancellor Perry L. Adkisson—influenced by the massively positive testimony he had heard—said that, if given the support it deserved,

TAMUG could become as prominent as California's Scripps Institute of Oceanography.

The testimony in defense of TAMUG had been overwhelming. On July 11, the Select Committee on Higher Education voted to recommend not only against closing but also in favor of expanding TAMUG. In an extraordinary move, the committee charged TAMUG to become "a first-class research component of the Texas A&M University System" by investigating "all aspects of ocean and estuary research." The select committee also recommended that TAMUG become an oceanographic research institute serving both Texas A&M and the University of Texas, which led to the creation by TAMUG of the Texas Institute of Oceanography.

Babe Schwartz, who had helped sponsor the legislation to found TAMUG, made it clear what he thought of the aborted proposal to close the school. He gestured to the state capitol grounds: "See those statues? They don't have any statues out there for people who abolish state educational institutions. If they did, every dog in Austin would find that one statue when his bladder got full." The *Galveston Daily News* carried his remarks, much to the delight of the school's supporters.

As this crisis ran its course, a cheating scandal rocked TAMUG. Administrators had discovered that some students had purchased answers to a physics and a celestial navigation test for twenty-five dollars. There was a shakeup within the maritime corps of cadets, resulting in expulsions and the appointment of a new student corps commander.

The commencement ceremony moved to the Grand 1894 Opera House in 1986 for the first of many occasions. The opera house would

THANK YOU GALVESTON

On Friday, July 11, the Select Committee on Higher Education announced their recommendation that Texas A&M University at Galveston not be closed.

Your interest in and support of the University played an important role in this decision. Your continued friendship is greatly appreciated.

On July 11, 1986, TAMUG survived the biggest scare in its history—the threat of legislative closure. The school took out this newspaper advertisement on Sunday, July 13, to express appreciation for members of the Galveston community, many of whom traveled to Austin by chartered bus or carpool to demonstrate their support.

become for Galveston students what the coliseum was for College Station students—the stage for receiving your diploma. The coliseum might be larger, but the opera house was definitely a more beautiful venue. Chase Untermeyer, assistant secretary of the Navy for manpower and reserve affairs, delivered the main address. Bill Hearn, vice president of student services, won the first ever William Paul Ricker Distinguished Faculty/Staff Achievement Award. Since joining TAMUG in 1974, Hearn had been the senior student life officer. He helped develop most of the student services on campus, including counseling, career placement, financial aid, and residential life. The joke that his real title is "administrator in charge of most things" was not far from the truth. At one time or another he headed up the maritime cadet corps, ship operations, new student recruiting, enrollment services, food services, housing operations, and the campus bookstore.

Texas Clipper meanwhile became the first American passenger ship or training vessel to visit a Soviet port in over a decade when it stopped that summer at Leningrad, Russia. Things got off to an uneasy start. To get to the harbor, the *Clipper* had to sail past a Soviet naval base off the port side. As soon as everyone onboard was instructed not to take photos, cadets ran to their rooms for cameras: it seemed as if everyone was taking photos surreptitiously. Cadet Sam Stephenson (later a master of the *Clipper*) said he was called a traitor for raising the Soviet flag on the *Clipper*, as prescribed by international protocol. Off the starboard side seamen on a Soviet ship trained binoculars on the American ship. Things were tense. The Soviet bow tug deliberately took mooring lines across *Clipper's* sharp bow, thus snapping four lines while docking. After the captain of the *Clipper* said, "If one more snaps, we're leaving!" the problem ended.

Guards were stationed on the dock the whole length of ship, from bow to stern. After passing through a metal detector at a checkpoint at the gangplank, those on *Texas Clipper* were relatively free to wander in the city. Many traveled to the world famous Hermitage art museum. However, curfew was strictly enforced: a few cadets were picked up by KGB officials two or three minutes after curfew had expired, escorted back to the ship under guard, and fined forty rubles (a small amount for Americans but quite a hefty sum for Soviet citizens). Throughout their stay, the contrast between Soviet restrictions and American freedom was everywhere apparent.

On August 25, a few weeks after *Clipper* returned to Galveston, the Texas Maritime Academy's generous friend Mary Moody Northen died at age ninety-four. She had a deep interest in education in general and Aggies in particular, remembered TAMUG President Clayton. She liked students, and they liked her. She showed her appreciation in many ways, including her monetary support. In the lobby of the Northen Student Center, named in her honor, her portrait is on permanent display.

At the start of the fall semester, almost the entire student body found themselves no longer legally able to buy a beer. On September 1,

the Texas Legislature, bowing to pressure from the federal government
(which threatened to withhold highway funds), raised the minimum legal drinking age from nineteen to twenty-one; it was the second time in
five years that the age had been raised. According to one student, though,
it made no difference at all: "Almost all students had fake doctored IDs.
Cadets found that the Merchant Marine identification, made out of paper,
was especially easy to fix." Because the age restriction was viewed in Texas
as federal blackmail, it was not at first widely enforced. "At the Old Galveston Club, Santos didn't card us. And nightclubs didn't check IDs."

But because the university could no longer serve alcohol at off-
campus get-togethers, student attendance at school-sponsored parties
dropped precipitously and would not rebound for another three or four
years. For instance, during the Sail Club's annual *Elissa* fund-raising
party, then the largest party for TAMUG, just about everyone (even faculty) subverted the alcohol-free restriction by making frequent trips to
hidden bottles in parked cars. The effort hardly seemed worth it. After
three years of declining attendance, the party died a natural death.

Students wondered whether TAMUG would ever obtain funding to
do some landscaping near the dorms. A *Nautilus* editorial admitted blame
for some of the problem: "Let's face it fellow students, by the time Sunday rolls around the grounds around C-Dorm and sometimes inside
A & B Dorms looks like a trashcan threw up on the lawn (or in the
lobby)."

Do-it-Yourself Library Move Turning a New Page

Thursday, October 23, 1986, was a defining day in the history of
TAMUG. After having survived a depressing spring of threatened leg-
islative closure, the campus community clubbed together to show how the
Aggie spirit of cooperation worked. The new library was finished at last.
Professional estimates had set the time required for installing the collec-
tion at five days, with a moving fee of fifteen thousand dollars.

Although TAMUG did not have much money, it did have plenty of eager volunteers. Students, faculty, staff, and others moved forty-five thousand books from the temporary library area in the engineering building to
the permanent library building; it took just one eight-to-five day, a rainy
day at that. To prepare for the move, the library staff had labeled shelf areas in both the old and new libraries and had labeled a thousand cardboard boxes that were used to transport the books and journals on rented
hand trucks. Following the move, the campus threw itself a party at the
Northen Student Center—barbecue, a live band, dancing, and thirty raffle
prizes including a bicycle, a TV set, and restaurant meals, all donated by
local businesses.

After twenty-four years of making do with cramped substandard quarters, the library seemed vast: it had twenty-seven thousand square feet of
space, with seating for about two hundred people. It also had eighty study
carrels and four study rooms. The motto silk-screened on volunteers'
T-shirts conveyed the rampant spirit of optimism: "We're turning over a
new page."

A survey released by the American Association of State Colleges and Universities singled out TAMUG as the fourth least expensive public college in the nation. Its 1985 cost of $563 a semester for tuition and fees was half the national average.

On November 1, Mitchell campus dedicated two of its buildings to the memory of staunch supporters. One of the first two buildings constructed on the campus in 1971, the old admin building (with the initial classrooms and laboratories) became Emmett O. Kirkham Hall. It honored the man who had been director of industrial relations for Todd Shipyards and who in 1958 had chaired the first chamber of commerce committee that led to the creation of the Texas Maritime Academy. The brand new library became the Jack K. Williams Library, in honor of the TAMU president who helped shape the Galveston institution in the 1970s during its period of greatest growth, from academy to college to university.

On December 2, at 4:18 P.M., all eyes on the campus faced north across the bay to Texas City, where a loud boom was followed by a mushroom cloud that blocked out the sun in Galveston. Butadiene, a highly unstable compound used to manufacture synthetic rubber and plastic, exploded during a loading process. The fire was extinguished three hours later; one person was killed.

1987

In 1987, the population of the world topped 5 billion. The United States and the Soviets banned short- and medium-range nuclear weapons in Europe. The soundtrack for *Dirty Dancing* became a bestseller. The campus experienced its first executive change since 1971. Springfest was invented. Graduating seniors were exempted from final exams for the last time.

William Clayton stepped down as president on January 1. During his sixteen-year term as chief executive officer, Clayton had overseen the period of greatest physical growth of the campus, from two to eleven buildings; during the same period, enrollment had increased by about 500 percent. Chancellor Perry Adkisson said Clayton "pioneered the Galveston program with missionary zeal and achieved things few others could have." The 1987 *Voyager*, the undergraduate yearbook, was dedicated to Clayton.

In a front-page *Galveston Daily News* story, Chancellor Adkisson squelched rumors that TAMUG would phase out its undergraduate program in favor of a research institute. He said Texas A&M was "not going to throw in the towel" but would maintain undergraduate programs and develop a first-class research institute at TAMUG. Sammy Ray, now dean of the Moody College of Marine Technology, was named interim president after Clayton's resignation. Ray said his first priority was to improve living conditions in the dormitories.

Adkisson announced in February that William J. Merrell, assistant director of the National Science Foundation in Washington, D.C., would be named the next president of TAMUG. Merrell was on a leave of absence from A&M when Adkisson, who was on the National Science Board, offered him the job. It was viewed as an internal promotion with Texas A&M University. Merrell had received his doctorate in oceanography from TAMU.

Adkisson also announced the formation of a special task force to "evaluate the role, scope, mission, curricula and intercampus agreements" of TAMUG. In response to questions about whether some programs might be phased out, he said, "Let's talk about phasing in, not phasing out." Merrell, former assistant director for geosciences for the National Science Foundation, assumed the presidency in mid-July. He came with the full support of administrators at College Station, from whom support had been at best uneven since the death of Jack Williams in 1979.

Meanwhile members of the TAMUG Student Advisory Committee decided to tackle a problem "that has been haunting us for years." Searching through their files from 1979, they uncovered about thirty "complaints about the manner in which we are being fed." With the cooperation of the administration, they set up a menu board to advise the food services director about meal choices. The new board would come up with a plan to include a wider variety of entrees. SAC also increased student input on the food services facilities board.

In April, TAMUG held its first Springfest, billed as "a random collection of frivolous events and activities scheduled throughout the week." If you were not careful, you might find yourself in a dunking booth or on the receiving end of a pie in the face. In the spring semester, TAMUG students also founded a drama club, Melanie Cravey Lesko and I serving as advisors. The club's first production was a one-act play called *The Monster*. Tickets were free for students, two dollars for others. The play

In 1987 William "Bill" Merrell was named the second president of TAMUG. He would focus his administration's efforts on hiring faculty members with international reputations, merging the Galveston campus with the College of Geosciences on main campus, and increasing enrollment.

William Clayton: First President

William H. Clayton, born in Dallas, served as a pilot in the Royal Canadian Air Force and the United States Army Air Forces. He earned a B.S. degree from Bucknell University in 1949 and a Ph.D. from Texas A&M University in 1956. Clayton joined the Department of Oceanography and Meteorology at Texas A&M College in 1956; he was named dean of what was then known as the College of Marine Sciences and Maritime Resources in 1971, the year that the Mitchell campus opened on Pelican Island.

He advanced to the rank of provost in 1974 and then president in 1979 of a school by then renamed Texas A&M University at Galveston. He oversaw the beginning of the undergraduate programs in areas other than marine transportation and marine engineering. During his administration, the campus offered its first science degrees and admitted its first female and African-American students.

Clayton stepped down as president of Texas A&M University at Galveston on January 1, 1987; he continued to serve as superintendent of the Texas Maritime Academy until his retirement in August. That same year, he was named president emeritus, in recognition of his long, productive career at the helm of the Galveston campus during its formative years. After he left TAMUG, Clayton served five consecutive terms on the Galveston City Council from 1993 to 2002, when he decided not to seek reelection. He was appointed by then Texas governor George W. Bush in 1998 and then reappointed in 2000 to the Coastal Coordination Council.

was directed by Galvestonian John Moynihan of the Strand Street Theatre. In the fall, students put on his original play *The Mighty Methuselah*.
This first year established the routine of one dramatic production each
semester.

The summer cruise of *Texas Clipper*, delayed by a faulty valve, scheduled visits to ports in the Caribbean and South America. Texas cadets
made room for about eighty cadets from Massachusetts Maritime Academy whose ship *Patriot State* had suffered a major boiler breakdown on
May 1. *Clipper* finally sailed on Saturday, June 7, about a week late. With
a strong favoring current behind her, the old ship hit a record speed of
twenty knots (much faster than her normal maximum cruising speed of
twelve knots) and actually reached the first port on time. About the same
time as *Clipper* departed, another TAMUG ship, the Research Vessel *Gyre*,
was returning to the campus. About thirty miles southeast of Freeport,
the *Gyre* crew rescued a thirty-two-year-old shrimper nineteen hours after he had fallen overboard. The man, who had been spotted by a couple
of sharks, said he would have died had it not been for the sharp-eyed Aggie crew. The Texas Senate passed a resolution honoring Captain Patrick
Modic and his nine crew members for their professionalism and quick
action.

In the summer and for several summers afterward, TAMUG hosted
Youth Opportunities Unlimited (YOU), an eight-week educational experience for underprivileged students. TAMUG geology professor Ernie
Estes put the program together with funding from state, federal, and
private sources. The fourteen- and fifteen-year-old participants earned
money in part-time on-campus jobs and earned high school credit to help
them graduate and find jobs. About a dozen college campuses around
the state hosted similar programs. That same summer the Pelican Island
causeway, connecting 51st Street with Seawolf Parkway, was renamed the
Herbert E. Schmidt Causeway, after a man who survived the 1900 Storm
(it hit just two months before he was born), graduated from Texas A&M
College in 1922, worked for the U.S. Army Corps of Engineers, and
served on the Navigation District Board. Schmidt died in 1991.

In the fall semester, undergraduate enrollment recorded a modest
gain. It was at last moving in the right direction. This gain was especially
welcome after the stagnation and decline of the past eight years. Part
of the reason for the turnaround was the grass-roots effort of volunteer
recruiters. Faculty, staff, and students took TAMUG brochures to high
schools around the state and manned booths at college fairs. It was clear
that if TAMUG were to fulfill its promise under the watchful eye of the
state legislature, it was going to have to grow. People were understandably nervous about how the institution's small size had made it vulner-
able the year before.

In November, the Williams library held a reception to acknowledge
its opening-day collection of sculpture and paintings by Texas artists.
The premier piece, installed in the foyer, was a nine- by thirty-foot pol-

ished aluminum artwork by Charles A. Pebworth, professor of art at Sam Houston State University; its reflective surface was designed to give the impression of rippling like water as patrons entered the library. Within the overall abstract design of the curved panels were recognizable motifs of sea-related science and technology. Harry Ahysen, Howard Bond, Peggy Bryan, Lise Darst, Stella Dobbins, Susan Eckel, Pam Heidt, Alfred Lee, and Lucinda Johnson had created the other works in watercolor, oils, and monotype. The works remain part of the library's permanent art collection.

Final exam week in December marked the last time that all graduating seniors were exempted from having to take final exams. Under Texas A&M University rules, seniors would leave ongoing class meetings a week early so that they could receive their diplomas on the Saturday *during* exam week. Clever students worked the system to their advantage: they would put off taking courses with killer final exams until the semester they graduated. Then they played their get-out-of-finals-free card and walked across the stage while their less fortunate classmates were still cramming for that exam. The rationale for this lost academic week probably stemmed from the days when every Aggie was a member of the corps of cadets. At that time, all graduating seniors received not only diplomas but also commissions on the day of graduation. Getting commissioned a week early gave them a leg up: it made them eligible for earlier promotions than their counterparts at other military academies who had a later date of rank. Or so the story goes. At any rate, it all would change after December of 1987.

On Saturday, April 9, TAMUG held its first fun run, billed as the "Aggie 5K Pelican Trot." The fund-raiser began and ended in front of *Texas Clipper*. Also in April the TAMUG campus hosted sixteen hundred participants in a marine education symposium, sponsored by the Texas Sea Grant College program and TAMUG. Costume parties were the in thing that year. Students dressed up—or down—for the pimp-and-whore party (later discontinued due to lack of political correctness) and the Halloween pagan ritual party. The latter, started in 1987, was held off campus and featured movies, a haunted house, games, and refreshments.

During final examinations week, the campus cafeteria began the tradition of serving "midnight breakfast," offering a rich and varied selection including custom omelets, waffles, and pancakes. Many said their favorite was the homemade breakfast taco, prepared by printshop manager Willie Gomez. And one of the faculty members would, by request, perform a sung rendition of the nursery rhyme "I'm a Little Teapot," complete with arm gestures. Students trooped over to the cafeteria in the middle of the night to take a fortifying break from their last-minute cramming. The new breakfast tradition was small compensation for graduating seniors who had lost their old skip-week tradition. The rules, changed by College Station, applied to the Galveston campus as

1988

In 1988, the *Texas Clipper* sailed with a woman captain for the first time. The campus narrowly avoided being downwind of a fish-processing plant. And an undergraduate, apparently the victim of an off-campus abduction, disappeared.

well: from this time forward, graduating seniors had to attend the last week of class meetings and suffer through finals with everyone else. No more special last-semester privileges.

Ann Sanborn, thirty-four, class of 1979, captained the summer cruise of *Texas Clipper*. She was the first woman TMA graduate and one of the first women nationwide to receive a master's license. News releases boasted that she was now the first woman to serve as master of a deep-sea merchant vessel sailing under a United States flag. Sanborn had previously held positions with Exxon, the University of Washington, and Sabine Towing and Transfer; she also taught at TAMUG and had sailed on *Texas Clipper* as instructor. The first port for the *Clipper* was Baltimore, Maryland, near Sparrows Point, where the ship had been built and launched as USS *Queens* at the Bethlehem Steel Company shipyard on September 12, 1944. On the way to Reykjavik, Iceland, the *Clipper* deliberately detoured to cross the Arctic Circle so that students could be initiated as blue noses. Four years earlier, an attempt to cross the circle had been aborted because of hazardous icebergs in the area. The cold-

In the summer of 1988, Ann Sanborn (TAMUG class of 1979) became the first woman to sail as master of a deep-sea merchant vessel sailing under a United States flag. She captained *Texas Clipper*, the ship she learned on as a cadet.

blooded ceremony demanded that initiates walk like a penguin, sit on a block of ice, wear a piece of ice, dunk their heads in ice water, and have their nose painted—blue, of course.

It was now happily clear that the enrollment increase had signaled the start of a dramatic turnaround. Acceptances of freshman were going up again, about 80 percent in the fall, partly due to a well-funded recruiting effort locally and support from College Station. As administrators breathed a sigh of relief, they smelled something else in the air that threatened to stifle enrollment growth. An international company proposed setting up a fish-processing plant in the former facility of Todd Shipyards, just east of the Mitchell campus on Pelican Island. The facility expected to process forty thousand tons of menhaden a year. Agents, seeking a state permit for the proposed plant to operate, said it would have "practically no smell." Former senator Babe Schwartz countered that "roses have 'practically no smell' if you are far away from them." Unfortunately, the campus was nearby and downwind.

A public meeting was held in the jury assembly room of the Galveston County Courthouse to examine the merits of the proposed plant. Schwartz had come prepared: "Before the meeting I hid some of the fishmeal between a rail and a chair. People couldn't see it, but they sure could smell it. What was it that smelled so bad, they asked." He pointed to the bag and urged the decision makers to trust not promises but their own senses. After that, said Schwartz, "nobody there would have voted for the fish plant."

A panel of three experts recommended opposing the construction of the plant because of "the potential for significant adverse environmental and economic impact" on TAMU and tourism in Galveston. After a spirited political battle, the "pogy-plant" withdrew its construction proposal and relocated in Brazoria County. It eventually shut down soon after its odor forced the cancelation of an Angleton high school football game— *more than ten miles* downwind.

A scare created by Hurricane Gilbert, initially a category 5 storm, had a greater impact on traffic than weather. By September 16, more than half of Galveston's residents had left the island because of the size of the storm and an official evacuation recommendation (by state law, communities cannot "order" evacuation). When Gilbert did not strike Galveston, angry evacuees complained loud and long. Recalling the false-alarm evacuation for Hurricane Allen in 1981, many vowed they would no longer pay any attention to official calls for evacuation. Campus students, who had been caught up in the traffic jam, found the alert a diversion from classes. But TAMUG officials, who had seen what Hurricane Alicia had done just five years earlier, continued to take evacuation calls very seriously. Soon afterward, the Student Advisory Committee came up with an unsuccessful campaign to convince the administration to authorize a canine mascot for the campus. The dog would have been named Gilbert, after the hurricane.

The fall semester saw many positive changes. Undergraduate enroll-ment was up 35 percent to 742 full-time students—the largest percent-age increase that year for any Texas university. The campus also experi-enced growth of another sort. More than one thousand shrubs, plants, and trees were placed throughout the grounds, which now featured a new football and soccer field (the old intramural field had been plowed under to make room for the Williams library). The MASE department collapsed its three options into one combined program to improve its likelihood of continued national accreditation. TAMUG research fund-ing had increased an astounding 211 percent over the previous year. And the overall budget for the campus exceeded $10 million for the first time. These were not bad statistics for a university that had been threat-ened with closure a mere two years before. Things were also looking up in the relationship between TAMUG and main campus. William H. Mob-ley, named the new president of Texas A&M University, would estab-lish a record of paying close, helpful attention to issues that concerned Galveston.

In October the student body reeled with the shock of an apparent criminal abduction in Galveston. Suzanne René Richerson, twenty-two, a senior at TAMUG, disappeared from Casa Del Mar Hotel where she worked. She was last seen by security guards an hour before her night shift was to end. A half hour later, Richerson was missing with no sign of a struggle. Her purse, school books, and car were left behind; one of her shoes was found in the parking lot. Early the next morning students distributed about forty thousand flyers (donated by printers in Galveston and in Austin) to local merchants and to motorists. Hundreds gathered at a candlelight vigil on campus. A billboard and more than two dozen television spots were donated to publicize the search for Richerson. It was a sobering experience for the campus: the most common response was disbelief that it could happen here. A year after her disappearance, TAMUG students planted a live oak sapling in front of the northwest cor-ner of the Northen Student Center in her honor; as this book was be-ing published, the tree was more than twenty feet tall with a luxuriant canopy. Despite extraordinary investigative effort and nationwide pub-licity—the incident was even featured on the national network televi-sion show *Unsolved Mysteries*—the case remains unsolved.

1989

In 1989 the Berlin Wall fell. Hundreds of rioting students were killed in Beijing's Tiananmen Square. *Texas Clipper* took its silver anniversary train-ing cruise and *US News & World Report* recognized TAMUG's national aca-demic reputation.

The TAMUG shuttle extended its schedule to seven days a week. It was designed to help dorm-bound students without cars take advantage of what Galveston had to offer. From about 5:00 P.M. until 11:00 P.M. each evening, students could board the white van beside the Student Center. On weekends its last run was at about 2:30 A.M.

A tongue-in-cheek letter to the campus newspaper *Nautilus* by a student who signed himself "Bewildered" asked whether it was okay to swim "in the pond in front of the library." The editors responded in kind: they said it was not a swimming pool but a "reflecting pool." An effort to

capture the feeling of wetlands on campus, the pond never garnered appreciation or support. Too small to establish its own healthy ecosystem,
it was usually clogged with green scum. After the pond was filled in by
popular demand, the area featured a raised flower bed planted with a variety of rose bushes. Students would discover much to their economical
delight that the rose garden made for easy pickings when they did not
have enough money to buy a corsage for a date.

In February TAMUG held its first job fair on campus with representatives from a dozen organizations—including UTMB, Sealift Shipping,
and Texas Parks and Wildlife—interviewing students in the student center. On the lighter side, students organized the Gong Show, an amateur
talent show, with the emphasis on the quirky. Lip synchers, magicians,
stand-up comics, and musicians competed for the top honors. It was part
of that year's Springfest week.

In March the TAMUG surf club invited sixteen colleges to participate
in its first intercollegiate surfing and bodyboarding tournament, held off
Galveston's seawall during spring break week. TAMUG came in first, followed by TAMU–College Station and the University of Houston–Clear
Lake. Other university-sponsored sports that semester included a dive
club, an outdoor sports club, and the Sail Club. Since just about every
club had its own specially designed T-shirt, the surf club hit on the idea
of holding an informal T-shirt competition to help the clubs raise money.
The winner was the club that sold the most shirts. That same month
TAMUG was authorized to use facilities of the National Marine Fisheries Service at Fort Crockett and East Lagoon, including the turtle
hatchery and the seawater laboratory. The turtle hatchery, internationally renowned for its tireless attempts to raise endangered Kemp's ridley
turtles, released them into the ocean as a means of helping restore the
depleted populations. This was called the headstart program.

In April, an impressive tradition of fifteen years' service by the Student Advisory Committee (SAC) came to an end. As its name implied,
SAC had advised the administration about what students were thinking. The Student Senate, which took its place, was an elected represen-
tational body with stronger powers, including that of passing resolutions. The senate at TAMUG came into being when its constitution, a year
in the writing and revising, was approved by the campus administration.
It was a popular move: the referendum to establish a senate passed over-
whelmingly, with 91 percent of students in favor. And the transition was
smooth.

Walter Littlejohn III, a MARA sophomore and chair of the now de-
funct Student Advisory Committee, had been the driving force behind
the drafting of the constitution. He was elected the Student Senate's first
president—a position that carried with it the functions of a student body
president. In fact, the senate president would commonly be referred to
as student body president in official correspondence. It is a tribute to the
open racial atmosphere on a predominantly white campus that the first

As part of Springfest, TAMUG students in the campus swimming pool adjust their SCUBA gear as they await the start of the underwater banana-eating contest. The other big swimming-pool event is the bellyflop contest. Both events inevitably draw more spectators than participants.

elected president was an African American student. That year, the new Student Senate passed resolutions about a path for pedestrians and bicyclists along the bridge between Pelican and Galveston islands, extension of mailroom window hours, medical services for students, and a walkway between the C-dorm parking lot and the newly constructed gravel lot to the north.

Also in April James Young, the popular director of student financial aid, died suddenly at age fifty-one. Many members of the TAMUG community attended his memorial service at First Presbyterian Church in Galveston. Young's widow established a scholarship in his name.

In May, TAMUG had a new student association, the Cave Club (later named the Galveston Grotto), for those who liked to spend their weekends underground. The club members would sell hot turkey legs at the Dickens on the Strand festival to raise money for trips throughout Texas and into Mexico. The May commencement speaker William Evans, undersecretary of commerce for oceans and atmosphere and the administrator of the National Oceanic and Atmospheric Administration, accepted the position of dean of the Texas Maritime College, TAMUG.

Texas Clipper celebrated its twenty-fifth year as a training ship for the maritime academy. The silver anniversary cruise visited European ports. When it returned to campus, the ship celebrated its forty-fifth birthday with a reception, birthday cake, guided tours, and videos from past cruises. A number of former preps, cadets, crew, and even medical personnel turned up to show their affection for a fine old ship that had supplied irreplaceable memories. Mary Gardiner, novelist and TAMUG En-

glish teacher, celebrated a quarter century of memories in the sixteen-
page booklet *The Twenty-Fifth Voyage of the* Texas Clipper: *A Proud Lady
Earns Her Silver Hair.*

College students always complain about food in campus cafeterias,
and TAMUG was no exception. But a criminal case proved that TAMUG
students had indeed had something serious to complain about. In August James Newlin, who had been director of food services from 1978 to
1988, pleaded "no contest" to the felony charge of stealing about sixty-
six thousand dollars from the university. The district attorney's office
charged that he had set up a bogus company called B&J Wholesale to
which he paid money, ostensibly for food. Investigation discovered that
the "company" consisted of nothing more than a post office box and a
checking account in his name. There was no evidence that the dummy
company had ever delivered any food. He was found guilty of the charge,
and it turned out that Newlin was not even his real name; he had been
using an alias all those years. When students had complained that their
meals should have been better, he had pleaded "budget limitations."
Whether the cause was inadequate budget or theft, former students of
that era vividly recall being served hamburgers—called "Moody bur-
gers"—that had been kept swimming in hot water the night before. It
was that or nothing. A standard joke on campus was that the easiest way
to lose weight was to eat in the cafeteria.

TAMUG doubled its research funding to $769,663 and doubled the
number of students in its freshmen class. And the Texas A&M Board of
Regents approved $3.5 million for the design and construction of a gym-
nasium on the TAMUG campus. Students had been campaigning for a
gym from the day the Mitchell campus opened. Now it looked as though
their wish would finally come true. In a related move, the regents also
gave the campus $700,000 to continue landscaping.

The decade ended with TAMUG getting the academic recognition
it had long deserved. In September Texas A&M University at Galveston first appeared in the *US News & World Report* top-ten rankings for
small colleges in the West. TAMUG was ranked in the category for liberal arts colleges, said the magazine, because there was no category for
special-purpose colleges. The other four Texas colleges and universities
placed in top-ten rankings in their categories—Rice, Trinity, Southwestern, and Texas Lutheran—were private institutions. TAMUG was the
only Texas public university. The rankings weighed such criteria as quality of faculty, academic reputation, selectivity of student body, and financial resources.

As the university's reputation grew, so did its enrollment. For the
second consecutive year TAMUG experienced the largest percentage increase in undergraduates in the state. Because the student population
could not fit into campus dormitories, the administration came up with
the innovative solution of arranging for temporary dorms in hotels and
motels in the city. The students made welcome tenants. In that first year,

only one complaint was registered about excessive noise: but it was a student who had lodged the complaint about a retired neighbor. It seems that at night the older gentleman would turn off his hearing aid and turn up the volume on the TV so high that the student found it difficult to study.

The year had been plagued by lousy weather. In February an ice storm kept crowds low for Mardi Gras. Then in the summer Galveston was hit by three named tropical storms—a record. Tropical Storm Allison came ashore on June 26 at Bay City. Galveston experienced winds of fifty-six miles per hour and suffered only minor street flooding. But more than a hundred passengers were inconvenienced when strong tides drove a Bolivar ferry aground on a sandbar for one and a half hours until it was freed by a tugboat. On August 1 Hurricane Chantal made landfall at nearby High Island; Galveston experienced winds of fifty-two miles per hour and more street flooding and beach erosion. Then on October 15, the latest date ever recorded for a hurricane landfall in Galveston, Hurricane Jerry showed up with heavy rains. In some offices and classrooms on the Mitchell campus people had not yet taken down the masking tape on windows from the previous storm. The last storm flooded the ground floor of the dorms, but students viewed it as an opportunity for fun. At night, they splashed outside in the mud and went skim-surfing in the parking lots.

The Galveston Bay Information Center, funded by the Galveston Bay National Estuary Program, was established in the Williams library. Re-

Members of the Krewe of Thalasar throw beads and doubloons to the crowd and ride their float down Seawall Boulevard in the Aquarius truck parade, two Saturdays prior to Fat Tuesday. The krewe, created by former and current students of TAMUG, decorated an old lifeboat on a flatbed trailer as a pirate ship. Source: *Voyager,* 1985.

ceiving the contract to establish the center had been a real coup; several
area libraries had competed for the project. The center began creating
a computerized bibliography of research on the bay. It put the campus
library on researchers' maps throughout the world. In November the
Texas Engineering Experiment Station, a research entity supporting the
public, business, and industry, named TAMUG the seventh state university to participate actively in its programs.

Students had a dramatic rat sighting that year. A male resident of
C-dorm awoke one night to find a rat on the pillow next to him. He let
out a scream that awakened just about everyone. After an informal conference, C-dorm declared all-out war on the rat. Traps were set throughout the dorm. The most elaborate was manufactured by the pillow
screamer himself: he placed a hunk of cheese underneath a box, one edge
of which was held up by a stick. He held the other end of a pull-string
tied to the stick and waited with a loaded spear gun. One of the traps
must have worked, for the rat disappeared and nighttime was once again
peaceful and calm.

Gregory Slotta of the U.S. Department of State inspired a lighthearted
moment when he addressed the TAMUG campus in November about the
foreign policy of the first Bush administration. The auditorium was filled
to capacity by an appreciative audience. However, the greatest applause
came not from anything Slotta said about politics but from his reply to
a question about whether he had appeared as an extra next to the guitar
player on the stairs in the 1978 college cult-classic movie *National Lam-
poon's Animal House*. When he admitted that he had, undergraduates in
the audience whooped in appreciation. Anyone could work for a U.S.
president, they reasoned, but only a select few could appear in a movie
with John Belushi.

After students had left on Christmas break, the year ended with a big
freeze. Sleet and snow began falling on Galveston on December 22; the
next day the mercury plummeted to 14 degrees F. Below-freezing temperatures for fifty-six consecutive hours kept the snow on the ground,
giving Galveston a frozen-slush white Christmas. But most TAMUG students missed it.

The decade of the eighties was a rough coming of age for TAMUG.
Things looked ominously dark at the start: Hurricane Alicia slammed the
campus with damaging results. Then an offhand remark on its uneco-
nomic size in a *Texas Monthly* article led to a truly worrisome legislative
effort to close the school. But the sun slowly emerged through the clouds.
TAMUG successfully fought off the legislative attack, opened its first real
library, and experienced its second big enrollment surge. Almost miraculously, things came together: after twenty-seven years TAMUG was
suddenly a success. The high quality of its students and faculty members
and the quality and quantity of faculty research finally got the attention
they deserved. The decade closed with a rave review in the *US News &
World Report* college rankings. A new day had dawned.

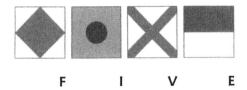

National Reputation, 1990–1999
Merger and De-merger

THE 1990s were seen by some as America's second Gilded Age. Making money in the stock market was a given; every week the Dow Jones seemed to set a new high. Dotcoms and technology companies could do no wrong. Everyone surfed the Internet. The so-called grunge look was definitely the fashion, or antifashion. Science unlocked the secrets of the genome, and cloning was in the news. Even more in the news were celebrities, gossip, scandal—the American public taste for these things seemed insatiable. The presidency was rocked as we learned more than we wanted to about nonpresidential affairs of Bill Clinton.

In the 1990s, Nelson Mandela was released from prison in South Africa. Lech Walesa was elected president of Poland. The first Iraq war started. The Soviet Union split up into fifteen countries. A riot broke out in Los Angeles over finding the police not guilty in the Rodney King trial. On TV, *Cheers* ended and *The X-Files, Seinfeld,* and *The Sopranos* debuted. In Hollywood, *Toy Story* became the first feature movie with all-computer animation and *Titanic* became the top-grossing movie ever. IMAX 3-D films were introduced to America. The governmental siege of the Branch Davidian compound in Waco, Texas, ended in a fatal fire. Bomb blasts rocked Oklahoma City, the World Trade Center, and the Atlanta Olympics. After seventeen years, the Unabomber was captured. Great Britain handed over Hong Kong to China and U.S. control of the Panama Canal ended. DVD players were introduced. Tiger Woods became the youngest person and the first African American to win the Masters golf tournament. The first Harry Potter book was published.

At the start of the decade, TAMUG was in the midst of its second and larger growth spurt, the first having come in the 1970s. Following a temporary merger with another college at main campus, enrollment would dip for four years, then recover. TAMUG would also replace its training ship, build a physical education facility, and then end the decade with a high ranking from the prestigious Princeton Review in *Time* magazine.

In January of 1990 Sammy Ray, aged sixty-nine, officially retired from teaching. He would continue to work with TAMUG sea camps and continuing education programs and would still devote time to his ongoing passion—oyster research. About three hundred people attended a reception sponsored by TAMUG at the San Luis Hotel Ballroom honoring Ray for thirty-one years of service. He was feted as one of the most beloved teachers in the school's history, a man who had influenced generations of undergraduate and graduate students in marine biology.

George Mitchell, who had donated the Pelican Island campus, gave the May commencement address. Afterward he was presented with a plaque rededicating the campus to his parents, Mike and Katrina Mitchell; the original 1968 dedication had been to his father only, but as George said, "It's the name of the whole family." Chris Perrocco succeeded Walter Littlejohn as student body president.

In the summer *Texas Clipper* visited European ports. Stavanger, Norway, a sister city of Galveston-Houston, held a special reception for students, faculty, and crew on the ship. Meanwhile, faculty member Captain Cindy Smith and eight cadets left Galveston for a trip on *Druzhba*, a 360-foot, three-masted square-rigged sailing ship operated by the Odessa Maritime Academy in the Soviet Union. All in all forty-two Americans (from the Maine, Massachusetts, California, Texas, and Kings Point mar-

1990

In 1990, Galveston's Sea-Arama Marineworld closed its doors as a public amusement park. In the fall, TAMUG enrollment broke the one thousand mark for the first time. The 26 percent increase from the previous fall and 70 percent increase in the previous two years made it the fastest growing college in Texas for those years.

At commencement in May, 1990, TAMUG President William Merrell (left) presents George Mitchell with a plaque indicating that the Mitchell campus is dedicated to the memory of his parents, Mike and Katrina Mitchell. The plaque recalls the campus groundbreaking ceremony held on Pelican Island on October 18, 1968.

itime academies) joined the ship as part of the total of 160 people aboard. Texas Maritime was the only American academy that contributed an instructor.

Texans had boned up on their Russian. They had also practiced handling square-rigged sailing ships by working on the *Elissa,* a century older than the Soviet ship, at the Texas Seaport Museum. *Druzhba* ended its voyage in Baltimore in August. According to newspaper reports, Smith and one cadet were the only women aboard the ship. Elsewhere, Captain Ellen Warner (TMA, 1978) became the first woman graduate of TAMUG to become master of a tanker, *SS Knight,* chartered by British Petroleum from American Heavy Lift Shipping of Houston.

That same summer, back in the Gulf of Mexico, an oil spill made headlines. On June 8, an onboard explosion caused a fire in the pump room of the *Mega Borg,* spilling 5.1 million gallons of oil sixty miles southeast of Galveston. The Norwegian tanker leaked oil and burned for four days. The spill affected TAMUG in several ways. Those who had trained in the TAMUG oil-spill control school had their hands full. The Research Vessel *Gyre* analyzed water samples at various depths to gauge contamination levels. And TAMUG professor Bernd Würsig published a study about the effects of the spill on the behavior of bottlenose dolphins.

In June the TAMUG Rowing Club hosted its first regatta. The University of Texas dominated the competition, but members of the relatively untried TAMUG crew, which had competed only once before, were satisfied with their second-place finish.

The fall semester began with a bang. For the third consecutive year, TAMUG led all other state colleges and universities in growth, with a gain of 14.9 percent. The campus hosted a couple of significant showcases. In August the Williams library held a reception to recognize the achievements of the TAMUG faculty. The library displayed publications by faculty and descriptions of their research projects. Alan Shepard, the first American in space, was the guest of honor. In 1961 he had flown aboard the Freedom 7 spacecraft 116 miles up into space, and ten years later he set foot on the surface of the moon. Then in September, TAMUG held an Engineering Exposition to highlight its two undergraduate programs in the field: marine engineering (shipboard power plants and seagoing careers) and maritime systems engineering (offshore and coastal structures).

The city was doing well too. The September issue of *Money* magazine rated Galveston the best place in Texas to live: Galveston was rated thirty-second in the nation.

Texas A&M University System Chancellor Perry Adkisson announced in October that Texas A&M University at Galveston would start planning to merge with the College of Geosciences. The merger was intended to strengthen ties between the College Station and Galveston campuses, expand graduate programs at Galveston, eliminate duplication, and allow for exchange of faculty. To many, however, the merger looked like a step backward. When the Mitchell campus had opened in 1971, the school had been headed by a dean and was one of the colleges of Texas A&M University. Now, twenty years later, the plan was to reduce it once more to a college, headed by a dean, except that now the chief executive officer on the TAMUG campus would be subordinate to that dean, who resided in College Station.

In November TAMUG accepted an oil portrait of retired Rear Admiral Sherman Wetmore, chair of the 1959 Galveston Chamber of Commerce committee that had worked to create the Texas Maritime Academy. He had also served as chair of the academy's first Board of Visitors in 1962.

That same month a group calling itself TOCSICK (a deliberate play on the word *toxic*), made up of TAMUG students and other concerned citizens, stood on the Galveston Seawall across from the San Luis Hotel with a thirty-foot-long handpainted sign reading "Mitsubishi: Don't Dump in Our Bay." They also carried a sign written in Japanese, which translated as "Don't Ruin Our Water." They were protesting the plans of Mitsubishi Metal Corporation to build its Texas Copper Corporation smelter in Texas City. The president of Texas Copper was attending a banquet at the San Luis. Eventually environmentalists prevailed; the corporation withdrew its plans for the smelter.

The spring semester was full of activity. In March, the Institute of Marine Life Studies was created by the Texas A&M System to enhance research at TAMUG. The institute was started as a joint effort of TAMUG,

1991

In 1991 William Merrell ended his term as the last president of TAMUG. As communist rule was ending in the Soviet Union, a famous Soviet environmentalist gave the May commencement address, and a Soviet ship kept company with *Texas Clipper*.

Ashanti Suné Johnson (left) is among the many volunteers for the annual Beach Cleanup Day, 1990. She would serve two terms as TAMUG student body president, 1991–93. Students, faculty, and staff from the campus joined others from around the state to collect trash from the West End of Galveston Island. Source: *Voyager*, 1990.

TAMU, and what was then called Corpus Christi State University, to help
deal with environmental issues along the Texas coast. The Pelican Island
campus planned to spend half a million dollars on landscaping. Before
the start of final exams, faculty and staff put on aprons in the cafeteria to
cook and serve a banquet breakfast to students.

Because it was increasingly clear that the training ship was showing
her years, the university was looking for a replacement. Students were
well aware that the ship had seen better days. The *Nautilus* carried a humorous top-ten list of reasons "Why the University Still Has *Texas Clipper*." Among the reasons: students didn't *really* need to get to port on
time; holes in the rusted hull made for easy room ventilation; the engine room had convenient saltwater showers; Texas needed somewhere
to burn old tar from its highways; and the university did not want homeless cockroaches to move from the ship to campus dorms. And the number one reason: "If you can sail the *Clipper,* you can sail anything."

Alexey V. Yablokov, deputy chairman of the ecology committee of
the Soviet Union Supreme Soviet, addressed graduates at the May commencement. As Boris Yeltsin's counselor for ecology, he had tried to
wean the Soviet government from environmental irresponsibility such as
nuclear dumping. At the end of his remarks he pounded on the lectern
and repeated several times, "Remember, there is no such thing as a free
lunch." Students knew that Yablokov was speaking from experience: he
had risked his freedom and even his life in a secretive country by trying
to uncover the truth about ecological issues and by working to reform
Soviet politics. What students did not know was that he had warned the
school to arrange for an alternative speaker just in case Yeltsin's coup was
reversed, and the Soviet Union arrested Yablokov as a dissident. Luckily
for TAMUG students and the rest of the world, Yablokov's side won.

Texas Clipper carried a record number of women on its summer training cruise board in 1991: 62 of the 189 cadets were women. The percentage of women in the maritime corps of cadets had doubled over the last
two years, from 15 to 30 percent. Texas Maritime Academy continued
to hold the distinction of enrolling more women cadets than any other
American maritime academy. Back on campus Ashanti Suné Johnson, an
African American woman, became the third student body president.

In June TAMUG students entered the eleven-foot *Sublime,* named for
its bright green paint job, in the national two-person human-powered
submarine race, held in Florida. The team of MASE, MARB, and MARE
undergraduates designed and built the sub, based on a wooden proto-
type, all by themselves with a little advice from their professors. They did
not win the race, but they put on a respectable show, placing fourteenth
out of thirty-six, and learned a great deal about effective underwater design. It was their first minisub. Four years later they would put all they
had learned into a revised model.

In August *Anichkov* docked at the campus for a week-long visit. The
Soviet ship was the training vessel for 137 cadets of the Odessa Higher

In 1991, engineering undergraduates designed and
built the two-person human-
powered submersible *Sub-*
lime, its manatee-shaped hull
painted lime green. Following a race in Florida the sub
went on display in the library
foyer.

Engineering Marine School in the Ukraine. Her visit to Galveston was
part of a continuing relationship between the American and Soviet
schools. Earlier that summer *Anichkov* and *Texas Clipper* had exchanged
a number of cadets: one Texas cadet became the first woman ever to fire
up the engine of a Soviet ship. The two ships sailed in tandem from port
to port. At Panama, *Clipper* had to restock its collection of toilet paper and
condoms—two hot commodities in the Soviet Union. It was suspected
that enterprising Soviet cadets had stockpiled the stuff to sell back home.

The night before the cruise ended, with the lights from Galveston visible on the horizon, cadets from both schools formed an international
pickup band that played for a dance on the deck the *Clipper.* The event
launched more than one romance—the all-male cadets of *Anichkov* were
much taken with the women of the Texas Maritime Academy. As the
Cold War was receding into memory, said the captain of *Anichkov,* he
and his students felt the warmth of the welcome they had received: "We
are hot from the hospitality and kindness here."

The visit also gave them an opportunity to visit an ill countryman.
When they discovered that a fifteen-year-old Ukrainian boy was under-
going treatment in Galveston's Shriners Burns Institute, a few of the
Odessa cadets and their captain paid the boy a visit. And they engaged in
some Western capitalism. While in Galveston, the captain bought several used cars to sell for a profit upon his return to Soviet Georgia: their
merchant marine school had to pay all its own expenses by such oppor-
tunistic trade.

That fall semester, Carl Sanders (TMA, 1974) became the first former
student appointed to the Board of Visitors. And William Merrell resigned as president of TAMUG. It marked the last time a chief executive
of TAMUG would hold the title of president, first conferred in 1979. A

William Merrell, the Last President

William Merrell was born in Grand Island, Nebraska. He earned his bachelor's degree at Sam Houston State University, completed a master of arts degree in physics and mathematics, and earned his Ph.D. in oceanography from Texas A&M University in 1971. In 1985 President Ronald Reagan named him assistant director for the National Science Foundation in Washington, D.C. Merrell also had an appointment as professor of oceanography at Texas A&M University, where he was a former associate dean of geosciences. He testified before the U.S. Congress on the need to focus scientific programs on the study of the earth as an integrated system. He received the 1990 Geosciences and Earth Resources Achievement Medal for exceptional contributions to exploration, development, and conservation.

From 1987 to 1991 he presided over Texas A&M University at Galveston. During that time undergraduate enrollment experienced its highest percentage rate of growth ever. When asked which were the greatest achievements of his administration, he named three: "getting the enrollment back up, improving the relationship between Galveston and College Station, and putting faculty in charge of TAMUG." Consonant with his successes, a local newspaper gave him a more elevated title than president. The *Strand Sentinel* ran a story entitled "William Merrell: The King of Texas A&M Galveston."

He stepped down as TAMUG president in 1991 to accept a newly created post as vice president for research policy at TAMU. He would thus become one of four senior vice presidents at TAMU, and the only one in residence at Galveston. In 1993 he was appointed vice chancellor for strategic programs with the Texas A&M University System. In the fall of 2001, he turned his administrative experience into an amateur drama spoofing academic politics: Galveston's Strand Theatre produced his play *The Boating Party* as a fund-raiser. Splitting his time between Washington, D.C., and Galveston, Merrell took an active role in national affairs as president and senior fellow of the H. John Heinz Center for science, economics, and the environment.

national search was on for a campus dean, the new title for the next chief executive officer.

TAMUG received more kudos that semester. Locally, the school was named business of the month by the Galveston Chamber of Commerce. Nationally, the school appeared once again in *US News & World Report,* this time advancing to the number three spot in the category of small colleges in the West. Strangely, the magazine had not even considered TAMUG in 1990 because an administrative official at College Station had told *US News* that TAMUG was entirely a dependent part of TAMU and therefore not eligible for the rankings. Since then the administrative official had been removed, and TAMU had correctly informed the magazine that TAMUG, with an independent budget and administration, ought to be considered. TAMUG thereafter continued to be ranked. When asked why a university offering only bachelor of science degrees was classified as a liberal arts college, a spokesman for *US News* said "it wasn't big enough" for any other category. In addition, the federal government classifies biology as one of the liberal arts; since marine biology had by far the largest enrollment on campus, TAMUG was considered a liberal arts college.

The magazine also named the school a "best buy." That year, annual tuition and fees plus room and board for TAMUG students were about $4,000 for Texas residents; about $7,100 for out-of-state students; and about $4,600 (including the summer cruise) for maritime cadets. Low cost plus high quality helped attract more freshmen. Rapid enrollment growth meant that demand had outstripped the supply for on-campus housing. More and more students had to find a place to stay in the local community.

In October TAMUG began its first intercollegiate lacrosse team, playing under the name Bay Area team. It joined the Southwest Lacrosse Association with teams from Louisiana State, Rice, Sam Houston, and

Carrie Gretzckie (left) and Jed Silverman add a decidedly TAMUG twist to their costumes for Dickens on the Strand, held on the first weekend of December. Anyone wearing Victorian garb gains free entrance to the festival, an annual Galveston tradition since 1974. Source: *Voyager,* 1991.

Stephen F. Austin universities, TAMU, the University of Houston, and the University of Texas. And in November the campus opened its first office devoted entirely to job placement of students.

1992

In 1992 the Internet began with 1 million linked computers. TAMUG merged with another academic college on the main campus. The first fall graduation ceremony was held.

In January TAMUG established its own Elderhostel, part of a worldwide program offering continuing education for senior citizens. Week-long Elderhostel classes focused on the history, culture, and biology of the Texas

The Uneasy Merger with Geosciences

Starting in January of 1992, TAMUG was diverted down a bizarre administrative detour. TAMUG was officially merged with the College of Geosciences at the College Station campus of TAMU—the hybrid College of Geosciences and Maritime Studies was the result. The chief academic officer of the Galveston operations was downgraded from the rank of president to the rank of campus dean. In effect, TAMUG was demoted from the ranks of one of the eight universities (like Prairie View A&M, Tarleton State, and Texas A&I) in the Texas A&M University System. Instead it was relegated to being merely a part of one of many academic colleges at TAMU, like the College of Liberal Arts or the College of Engineering. The result was loss of autonomy: before the merger the TAMUG president had been high up in the academic hierarchy; after the merger the TAMUG campus dean was not even allowed to sit in on key meetings with the president of Texas A&M University. This meant that the campus dean often had no voice in issues that affected Galveston; sometimes he was not even told about decisions until long after they were made.

The justification for the merger was political: TAMUG would be protected by TAMU–College Station, presumably against any possible threats of closure as in 1985–86. And there were plans, which never came to fruition, that TAMUG could gain power through a reorganized Texas Institute of Oceanography. But in practice the merger meant that TAMUG had an absentee landlord, 150 miles to the north. Galveston administrators put a positive spin on the merger: it was a "good thing," they said. A student cartoon in the *Nautilus*, however, portrayed the underlying anxieties. A harmless little TAMUG butterflyfish about to become dinner for a huge TAMU shark in a cartoon titled "The Merger."

From the College Station perspective, the College of Geosciences needed its small enrollment bolstered. When TAMUG undergraduates were added in, the new combined college had a healthy overall enrollment. At least at the start, it looked as if the merger might solve two problems. Instead, it created some thorny new problems.

Some compared the merger to the corporate decision to abandon the original formula of Coca-Cola in favor of New Coke. Classic Coke would reclaim the original formula, and TAMUG would eventually split off from the College of Geosciences, which got its original name back. In spring of 2001 the last administrative remnant of the merger disappeared as Galveston's Department of Marine Sciences was divorced from College Station's Department of Oceanography. The Board of Regents officially recognized the existence of "separate and autonomous administrations on the two campuses," thus ending a peculiar era of split administrations so confused and confusing that Galveston-based faculty members in the Department of Marine Sciences were ineligible to vote in Galveston faculty elections.

coast. Participants learned about birdwatching, hatcheries, sailing, seining, and singing chanteys. It soon became a common to see a group of white-haired men and women with nametags attending classes on campus. The Center for Marine Training and Safety, another continuing education program, expanded at the Offatts Bayou campus (which TAMUG had been using since 1988). All told, continuing education was estimated to have an economic impact of about $2 million on Galveston.

Beginning in January TAMUG gained a new chief executive, the sixth in its history. David Schmidly, former head of Texas A&M University's Department of Wildlife and Fisheries Sciences, was named campus dean. The title, a new one for the Galveston campus, reflected Galveston's merger into the College of Geosciences and Maritime Resources. As a campus dean, Schmidly reported to the dean of that college, Robert Duce, who reported to the provost, who reported to the president of Texas A&M at College Station. The Galveston campus was submerged under two additional bureaucratic layers.

Academically, TAMUG's reputation had never been better. Enrollment had more than doubled and research funding for faculty had soared 500 percent in five years. The campus enjoyed an academic mystique and a burgeoning nationwide reputation. Students prided themselves on how hard their classes were. And they had good reason to boast that college experience was different for them than for other undergraduates in Texas. Statistics showed that the average TAMUG student enrolled in twice as many science and technical laboratory courses as did students in other Texas colleges.

In the spring semester TAMUG decided to hold a separate awards ceremony to honor graduating seniors and others for outstanding service, scholarship, and leadership. This marked the first time that awards

In its April 23, 1992, issue, the student newspaper *Nautilus* published this dramatic image of one way to look at the merger of TAMUG with the College of Geosciences on the main campus. The anonymous undergraduate artist clearly believed that the results of merger would not favor the little butterfly-fish labeled TAMUG.

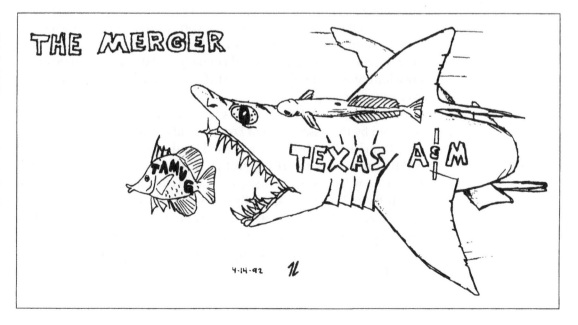

were given other than at a May graduation ceremony. Back in 1966 awards had accompanied cadet licensing and commissioning; in 1975 awards were expanded to include students other than cadets. Over the years the growth in numbers of graduates and of awards had prolonged the commencement uncomfortably. The 1992 split allowed awards to take center stage in their own right and meant each ceremony could be completed within a reasonable time.

Hopes for a gym on campus were dashed in May. The Texas Higher Education Coordinating Board, anxious about escalating future costs to the state in utilities and maintenance for another building, withdrew permission for TAMUG to build a gymnasium. It was heartbreaking news. In attempting to justify their reneging, the coordinating board said: "The institution has gotten by since the campus was built in the early 70's without a gymnasium and is doing an excellent job so no gym is needed." TAMUG student body president Ashanti Suné Johnson objected. She noted that the Student Senate was trying to arrange for the use of physical education facilities at Galveston College, UTMB, and College of the Mainland; it was inconvenient, to say the least. Intramural basketball, a popular sport among students, had to fit its abbreviated season into the already overfilled schedule at the Galveston Boys Club. During inclement weather, the only place on campus to get up a game of basketball was still inside one of the cargo holds of *Texas Clipper*. In a letter of appreciation to two TAMUG supporters, State Representatives James Hury and Mike Martin, Johnson wrote: "Needless to say, our students are devastated by the Board's decision." The battle had been lost, but the war was not yet over. Fierce lobbying continued.

Meanwhile, Texas Comptroller John Sharp was in Galveston to comment on the success of the brand new Texas State Lottery. Actual revenue from ticket sales far outstripped earlier estimates. First-day sales of $24 million were 40 percent higher than expected, and first-week sales of $102.4 million broke the previous record set by Florida. Local educational institutions, including TAMUG, hoped that lottery revenue would offset recent state deficits that had cut budgets. Students joked that buying a lottery ticket might be the best chance the Mitchell campus would ever have to get a gym.

In May two TAMUG professors walked away with the highest honors given by the Association of Former Students of TAMU–College Station. Douglas Klein became the second faculty member in the history of TAMUG to receive the Distinguished Achievement Award for research (Sammy Ray had been the first). The award cited his work in theoretical chemistry and physics, especially concerning the 60-atom carbon molecule called Buckminsterfullerene. I was honored to be named the first TAMUG recipient of the Distinguished Achievement Award for teaching, acknowledging my role in writing and literature instruction at the school since 1973.

On August 26, five days before the start of the fall semester, TAMUG evacuated its campus as a cautionary measure because of the monstrously strong Hurricane Andrew, the most likely landfall of which was projected to be western Louisiana. The storm had been highly destructive in Florida, and a minor direction change could put Galveston in harm's way. Students unable to return home were bussed to the College Station campus, where they found temporary and often crowded lodging in dormitories. The powerful storm went ashore in Louisiana, as predicted. It produced no damage in Galveston beyond the evacuation causing some confusion during the normally busy time of preregistration.

TAMUG announced in October that the aging 475-foot-long *Texas Clipper* would soon be replaced by the 393-foot *Chauvenet*, used during the Persian Gulf War. Launched in 1970, *USNS Chauvenet* was the first Navy vessel designed specifically for coastal hydrographic surveys. She had been named after mathematician William Chauvenet, who had helped found the U.S. Naval Academy at Annapolis in 1845. On May 24, 1967, her keel was laid by Upper Clyde Shipbuilding Corporation of Glasgow, Scotland. She was launched on May 13, 1968, and delivered to the US Navy on November 13, 1970. In her naval career *Chauvenet* earned the Navy Battle E Ribbon, National Defense Service Medal, Southwest Asia Service Medal, and Kuwait Liberation Medal (Kuwait).

The ship was scheduled to undergo about $11 million in renovations to become suitable as a university training vessel. It was hoped that the replacement ship would be ready in 1994. There was already a connection between the new ship and the school: Patrick Michael De Charles, a former student of Texas Maritime Academy (class of 1976), had sailed on board *Chauvenet* as second mate.

In November, the school was encouraged by news that its gym had been put back on the drawing board. After persistent local lobbying, the Texas Higher Education Coordinating Board approved the design and construction of a new $3.6 million physical education building. What had convinced them to change their minds was a promise by TAMUG to pick up all utility and maintenance costs incurred by the gym for the first few years. The news was greeted with much rejoicing. Now TAMUG students could look forward to intramural sports on campus during all kinds of weather; now they could play a pickup game of volleyball after dark; now they, just like students on every other campus in the Texas A&M System, could take physical education classes. The coordinating board also approved the purchase of the Offatts Bayou campus, which TAMUG had been renting; it was used primarily for continuing education in the maritime industry.

That fall the campus experienced a resurgence of interest in Aggie traditions. Yell practices, held in Galveston on Thursday nights before Aggie football home games, ended with throwing yell leaders in the swimming pool. The next day, TAMUG students would drive to the Fri-

"Hump it, Ags!" Students show their Aggie spirit at organizations night, held at Galveston's 1880 Garten Verein pavilion on September 2, 1992. Left to right: Mike Eyman, Ted Engelhardt, Heather Madsen, Diane Jackson, Bonnie Hardie, and Kathy Dudley. Source: *Voyager,* 1993.

day night yell practices at College Station. TAMUG even assembled its own smaller version of the Aggie bonfire out on Bolivar beach. There had been previous Galveston bonfires before some Aggie-Longhorn football matchups, but this was the rebirth of an organized annual effort in Galveston. The stack was a ferry ride away at the beach on Bolivar Peninsula: on the ride over, yell leaders stirred the crowd with some prebonfire yells. Atop the structure of pallets, scrap wood, and telephone poles was an effigy of Bevo, the University of Texas mascot. If anyone challenged their being "real" Aggies, TAMUG students could truthfully say they attended twice as many yell practices and twice as many bonfires as College Station Aggies.

Two victories made news on campus. Arkansas Governor Bill Clinton became the forty-second president of the United States. TAMUG students had picked the winner in a campuswide straw poll: they had chosen Clinton (36 percent) over Bush (19 percent) and Perot (17 percent); undecided came in second with 28 percent. But more students were interested in local sailing than in national politics. The sailing team won a regional competition in New Orleans that qualified them to compete in the sloop-racing nationals in Hawaii. Continental Airlines cut airfare prices by more than 60 percent, making it affordable for team members to fly to the competition.

C-dorm had badly needed repairs for a long time. Although it was welcome, the construction work caused inconveniences. When repairs began in November and continued into December, students dubbed C-dorm a "building under siege!" Every day from 8:00 to 5:00 the staccato of jackhammers and the constant whoosh of sandblasting reverberated in the residence hall, making it difficult to concentrate. Reading and studying were next to impossible. Construction dust filled the air and made its way into the rooms, where it coated surfaces and got into clothing. It was a gritty, earsplitting mess. The noise at least stopped on dead day, the day before the start of final exams, and did not resume until finals were finished. By that time students had left campus. When they returned at the start of the next semester, C-dorm had been refurbished and was blessedly quiet.

More than 75 percent of TAMUG undergraduates were majoring in science or engineering; that contrasted dramatically with 34 percent at the next closest state institution. Moreover, the campus was bucking a nationwide trend: while enrollment was declining everywhere else, it had been increasing at TAMUG for the past seven years in a row. An expanded TAMUG also made the City of Galveston happy. A study conducted by researchers at the University of Houston–Clear Lake calculated that TAMUG generated an economic impact of more than $26.5 million annually. The figure included the business conducted by the campus, the personal income of employees, and the value of businesses that exist because of the school and its students.

In March the contract was awarded for construction of the new physical education facility. The TAMUG community was cautioned to refer to it by that three-word phrase "physical education facility"—it was definitely not to be called a gymnasium. The state, said university officials, builds educational facilities only, not gyms. Galveston opened a great new tourist attraction that month when the ten-story rainforest pyramid opened. The first of three pyramids to be built in Moody Gardens, the rainforest is a climate-controlled greenhouse featuring tropical vegetation and some wildlife, including birds, fish, and butterflies.

1993

In 1993, TAMUG purchased the Offatts Bayou campus and added land to the Mitchell campus. *Texas Clipper* was honored in a big farewell tribute. Ground was broken for construction of the physical education facility.

First December Graduation Ceremony

In December of 1992, TAMUG held its first fall graduation in the Grand 1894 Opera House. Enrollment growth had made this additional annual ceremony desirable and necessary: the opera house was running out of space to fit an entire academic year of graduates into one ceremony. This December ceremony came seven years after the first commencement ceremony outside College Station had been held in Galveston in 1985. Dr. Alvaro Romo de la Rosa, director of the international program at the Universidad Autonoma de Guadalajara, was the first December commencement speaker.

Groundbreaking for the physical education facility was in July of 1993. Holding ceremonial shovels are (left to right) Peter Perrault of the TAMUG Board of Visitors; David Schmidly, TAMUG campus dean; Bob Duce, dean of Geosciences and Maritime Studies; Galveston State Representative Patty Gray; Galveston State Senator Mike Martin; and Billy Clayton of the TAMUS Board of Regents; the three on the far right are unknown.

In April *Akademik Mstislav Keldysh,* a research vessel run by the Russian Academy of Sciences, docked next to *Texas Clipper.* The Russian ship, which had helped explore the sunken *Titanic,* carried manned submersibles capable of diving four miles under the ocean's surface. The submersibles shot documentary film that was made into a ninety-minute IMAX movie. *Keldysh* was open for tours as part of Earth Day activities, which also included the five-kilometer Pelican Trot fun run, exhibitors' displays, games, and live music.

Meanwhile, TAMUG had finally closed the $1.3 million deal to buy 10.2 acres off Teichman Road on Galveston Island. The Moody State School for children with cerebral palsy had once occupied the site. TAMUG planned to put a barge at the dock to train mariners in barge loading, inspection, and survival techniques. The new campus—variously referred to as the Offatts Bayou, Teichman Road, or Waterfront campus—would also offer courses in oil-spill containment. On Thursday afternoon almost every week, members of the oil-spill control training

Galveston Aggies Ain't Fit to Kiss Pigs

In May TAMUG organized Aggie Fair Day to raise money for the United Way with activities like pie tossing, dunking, and cookie judging. The highlight was the pig-kissing booth. However, it turned out that Elliott, a hundred-pound pot-bellied pig, cared more for swilling down cranberry juice and munching on currants than for kissing humans. One woman student, unable to convince the pig to face her for a kiss, joked, "I've never felt so rejected."

program intentionally dumped cottonseed hulls into Galveston Bay. The hulls acted a lot like crude oil, and students had to use all their book learning to clean up the simulated spill.

In the first week of June TAMUG held a farewell tribute to the original *Texas Clipper*. The shindig began on Friday night with a buffet and live music at the Texas Seaport Museum, where a fund-raising auction was held. Then it moved to the Pelican Island campus on Saturday for fun, games, and lectures by various faculty members. Tours visited the Offatts Bayou and Fort Crockett campuses. That night the Texas Southern University Jazz Ensemble rounded things off with music at a reception held at Pier 21. The ship then departed on what was billed as her final summer cruise, her twenty-ninth annual trek as a university training ship, to Las Palmas in the Canary Islands; Cork, Ireland; Gdynia, Poland; St John's, Newfoundland; and Baltimore, where the ship had been built forty-nine years before. A leaking fuel line delayed departure from Galveston by a few days. A newspaper in the Canary Islands ran this romantic account (translated into English) of the lives of the cadets: "The style of these young people is unmistakably that of the Americans of television movies, where the beautiful sex is the one that commands onboard. . . . The docking maneuvers yesterday were spectacular to see, with youngsters of both sexes working together." Everywhere the ship went, it attracted visitors who wanted to see one of the oldest American merchant marine ships still afloat. Bosun Joseph Gooby, who had joined the Navy just two weeks after the *USS Queens* was launched, built a thirty-inch scale model of the *Clipper* out of found material like cardboard, thread, wire, and even coins; the model is often on display in the Williams library.

Campus acreage was growing. The Kempner Fund donated 156 acres of wetlands on West Galveston Island, near Snake Island Cove. George Mitchell, who had donated the original hundred acres of the Pelican Island campus in 1965, added another 1.5 acres in June of 1993. When the ten-acre waterfront campus at Offatts Bayou and the three-acre Fort Crockett campus were added in, the total came to about 115 acres of campus lands. In addition TAMUG had title to more than three acres of undeveloped wetlands for research and laboratory use. In July, State Representatives Patty Gray and Mike Martin, Campus Dean Schmidly, College Dean Robert Duce, and other dignitaries broke ground at Pelican Island to mark the long-awaited start of construction for the physical education facility. It was the first major construction on campus since the library had been completed in 1987.

Enrollment had increased 4.6 percent over the previous fall to reach a record high of 1,337. There simply was not enough room, said some faculty members, to accommodate that many students. The Department of Marine Biology especially felt the crunch. It had by far the largest enrollment on campus, and its faculty complained of facilities being stretched to breaking point. The phrase "enrollment cap" was bandied about campus—and those in charge began listening. Money and resources were removed from the recruiting effort. The feeling was that the school had grown prestigious enough to attract new students without having to go to the expense and effort of printing new brochures, buying addresses of prospective students, and orchestrating direct-mail campaigns to market itself. The deemphasis on recruiting would work only too well. For the next four years, freshman classes would be small, and overall enrollment would shrink by almost 17 percent to dangerously low levels.

In September, at College Station, William Mobley was promoted to chancellor of the Texas A&M System, and E. Dean Gage took over as interim president of TAMU. Changes were also in the works for the Galveston administration. The Galveston campus dean got a title boost to chief executive officer and campus dean. There had been a problem with the way most people interpreted the older title: a campus dean sounds like a junior assistant, not the leader of a university. In practical terms, doors did not open for a campus dean. In order to be effective at raising funds and addressing the legislature—both essential tasks for the person in charge of TAMUG—a more prestigious label was needed. Before 1991 the jobholder had been named president, an obviously important title. But that title was no longer obtainable because a president in Galveston would have had a higher rank than his boss, a college dean in College Station. So the addition of *chief executive officer* represented a compromise. A&M President Gage said the CEO title clearly conveyed "the key leadership role" of the Galveston office holder. However, further experi-

The Rowing Club works on building a two-man rowing shell in 1993. Left to right: club president Annette Ramirez, Don Irwin, and Paul Busse. Source: *Voyager,* 1994.

ence would prove that outside the boundaries of the campus, even this new title conveyed little force.

In the fall Paul Hille, who would later work for TAMUG as the associate director for student relations, succeeded Ashanti Suné Johnson as student body president, and the campus rejuvenated the Rowing Club. Club members built the *Double,* their first two-person shell, with their own hands at the Offatts Bayou campus. The club would grow and compete in crew meets. Students also dressed up in tie-dyed shirts or peasant blouses and bell-bottom jeans for Hippie day. The cadets' drill team reorganized itself and began to turn heads on both the Galveston and College Station campuses. They made such a favorable impression at the pregame Kyle Field march-in that they would be invited back every year afterward. At 6:00 A.M. several mornings a week, drill team members were hard at work honing their routines in the parking lots.

For years the spring semester had usually started on the third Monday of January. In 1983 that date also became the observed birthday of Martin Luther King Jr. At TAMUG, faculty and students observed the day by holding impromptu oral readings of King's writings and listening to remarks by speakers such as Galveston County's first African-American commissioner, Wayne Johnson. By 1986, the day had become a federal holiday. Eight years later the Aggie class schedule, set by College Station, finally marked the day as a school holiday. Aggies in both College Station and Galveston celebrated their first Martin Luther King holiday on January 16, 1994. Classes began the next day. The year opened with some high hopes for TAMUG. The school planned to build a $1.3 million oil-spill-response simulator and a $700,000 computerized simulation center for maritime training.

Aggie football was due for a revolution. In 1994, two years after the departure of the University of Arkansas (its last out-of-state member), the eighty-year-old Southwest Conference faded away with barely a whimper. Although the conference had been tarnished by widespread recruiting scandals and NCAA probations, the main causes for its demise were money and uneven competition. The more competitive schools had decided that they could earn more revenue by playing only other big-time football teams. The TAMU System Board of Regents voted to accept an invitation from what was then called the Big Eight Conference, soon to be renamed the Big Twelve Conference with the addition of ex-Southwest Conference members Baylor, Texas A&M, Texas Tech, and the University of Texas.

The TAMUG campus held its first Big Event, a day devoted to volunteer service in the community, on April 10. The highest profile volunteer effort of the event was driving to 18 Mile Road to fill up plastic bags with beach litter. However, this was not the first community-service project for the campus; students, faculty, and staff had been picking up trash for years as part of the Texas Beach Clean-up.

1994

The Houston Rockets inaugurated the brand new gym on Mitchell campus. The campus celebrated the opening with a Sea Aggie Gala. *Texas Clipper* made its second annual farewell cruise. TAMUG held its first summer commencement ceremony. Undergraduate enrollment began a four-year slide.

The next day the physical education facility opened up for student use. Students walking through the building felt like children with a sweet tooth in a candy store. The building had racquetball courts, a hardwood gym with retractable bleachers, an exercise room for aerobics, and a strength-training room with fixed and free weights. That same month, Ray Bowen was named the president of Texas A&M University in College Station. (He replaced E. Dean Gage, who had been interim president for almost a year.) Bowen was to carry on Mobley's legacy of strong support for Galveston programs.

Building a concrete canoe sounds like the punch line to an Aggie joke, but in fact it is a widely respected competition for engineers. TAMUG students had entered the competition twice previously. In 1990 their first effort resulted in a 365-pound canoe, built in a week and sailed before the concrete had had time to cure completely. In 1991 they improved the design, coming up with two canoes that weighed only about 170 – 180 pounds each. That year TAMUG won first place in the category of best presentation. In 1994 the TAMUG chapter of the American Society of Civil Engineers once again entered in the concrete canoe competition, this time held at Corpus Christi.

While being transported, their canoe *Heart of Gold* suffered a crack from a bumpy ride over railroad tracks, but the damage was fortunately above the water line. Another mishap cropped up during the flotation competition, when one team member put his knee through the canoe's

On April 23, 1994, TAMUG seniors Amy Wilke and Stephanie Neuwiller win their sprint heat with Texas Tech and place second overall in the concrete canoe competition at Corpus Christi, Texas.

bottom. Epoxy filler repaired both the hole in the bottom and the crack in the side of the sixteen-foot canoe. On Friday the TAMUG team took second place academically for a five-minute presentation on their creation of the canoe. On Saturday races were held for men, women, and coed two-person teams. *Heart of Gold* performed very well, placing second in both the men's long course and the women's sprint. Although a canoe from main campus split apart during practice, College Station Aggies proved they were good sports by cheering on their Galveston counterparts. Overall, TAMUG finished third, behind the University of Houston and University of Texas–Austin. And the team members graciously used leftover concrete to patch cracks in Mitchell campus sidewalks.

Campus Dean David Schmidly had a national reputation for his study of bats, but it was a play involving a human vampire that made news that spring semester. In April, TAMUG's Drama Club received national publicity when one student actor accidentally stabbed another during the climactic scene of a campus production of the Dracula story. Amazingly, the injured actor Paul Bishop finished the play, minus a few lines: "I was trying to milk it for all it was worth," he said the next day from his hospital bed. Bishop was such a trooper that he offered to go back onstage if only the hospital would release him. But by the time he was released, the remaining two performances of the play had been canceled.

A few months before the official grand opening of the physical education facility, the Houston Rockets inaugurate the gym on April 26, 1994. At the same time they launch their first successful championship series. Hakeem Olajuwon, number 34, shows the stuff that would make him the most valuable player in the NBA. Source: *Voyager,* 1994.

TAMUG-Trained Team Wins NBA Title

On April 26 through 28, 1994, before the start of their playoff opener against Portland, the Houston Rockets spent three days shooting hoops at the new TAMUG gym. What a way to inaugurate the long-awaited facility. Head coach Rudy Tomjonavich, who had previously held training camps at Galveston's Ball High School, said he liked Galveston as a nearby getaway where the team could focus on the game without all the distractions in Houston. Taking his first practice shot, the Rockets' seven-foot-plus center Hakeem Olajuwon said the basket was half an inch too low. After the practice a TAMUG official put his claim to the test. A tape measure proved Olajuwon was exactly right. The basket was raised a half inch before the Rockets' next practice.

Everyone loved the gym. The Rockets liked the site so much that they returned on June 2, just prior to the start of their NBA finals face-off against the New York Knicks. How did they do? They won their first ever NBA championship, taking four out of seven games from the Knicks. Olajuwon was named the league's most valuable player, and Sam Cassel was named rookie of the year. Aggies, of course, believe it was the TAMUG touch that finally turned the trick for the Rockets.

In May the Honorable Jack Brooks, member of the U.S. House of Representatives for the past forty-two years, was the spring commencement speaker. Brooks had been instrumental in acquiring the ship *Chauvenet*. But *Chauvenet* was not quite ready, so the original *Texas Clipper* had to limp through one more trip, inevitably labeled its "Second Annual Final Cruise." Only Aggies, went the joke, could do this twice. On June 7, 1994, under the command of Captain P. Jaime Bourgeois, the fifty-year-old ship embarked on her thirtieth training cruise. On August 4 when she returned, her sailing days would indeed be over for good.

For three days before the *Clipper*'s second annual final departure Galveston celebrated the Sea Aggie Gala, on June 3–5, hosted by honorary chairpersons Associate Dean for Student Services Bill Hearn and his wife Mary. The event was molded around the official opening of the $3.1 million, 28,400-square-foot physical education facility. (Informally, students, staff, and faculty members were already using the gymnasium, racquetball courts, weight room, and aerobics room.)

The gala began Friday evening with commissioning of cadet officers, a barbecue, ceremonial cutting of a maroon-and-white ribbon, dancing to a live country and western band, and a silent auction—all inside the gymnasium, where the floor was covered. Early the next morning the group embarked on an all-day cruise aboard Galveston's gambling ship *Star of Texas*. In addition to organized activities for children and adults, the ship opened its gaming casino while in international waters. Sunday ended the weekend with tours of the Fort Crockett turtle hatchery and brunch at the San Luis Hotel. James F. Moore (class of 1973) and Carl

Sanders (class of 1974), who the previous year had been named Outstanding Former Students, presented a plaque naming Patricia "Tricia"
Ann Clark (class of 1979) the third to be so honored.

In July TAMUG hosted its first corporate invitational fishing tournament as a way to raise funds for research and scholarships. Forty-two
teams of six anglers each competed for landing the largest red snapper,
kingfish, ling, and dorado of the day and finally the largest fish of the
week. The team from Galveston's Liberty Seafood came in first.

In previous years, summer graduates had traveled to College Station
to receive their diplomas. By 1994 TAMUG had grown large enough to
hold its first ever summer commencement ceremony, on August 13. A
fall commencement ceremony had been added in 1992. Now, no matter
which semester you graduated, you could receive your diploma immediately in Galveston. The first summer ceremony in Galveston took place in
the campus auditorium. William Merrell, Texas A&M University System
vice chancellor for strategic programs and former president of TAMUG
from 1987 to 1992, gave the first summer commencement address.

David Houston Jr. succeeded Paul Hille as student body president.
Houston, like his predecessors Ashanti Suné Johnson and Walter Littlejohn, was an African American. For four of the first six years that there
had been a student body president, students had elected African Ameri-

On June 5, 1994, the Sea
Aggie Gala takes to the high
seas aboard the Galveston-
based gambling ship *Star of
Texas*. The event celebrated
the new physical education
facility, which had been officially opened the previous day.

cans. Although predominantly attended by white students, TAMUG was evidently a place where students could be judged, as Martin Luther King had dreamed, not "by the color of their skin but by the content of their character."

When the fall semester began, TAMUG had a brand new—and very noticeable—group of students on campus. TAMUG helped launch the Seaborne Conservation Corps, part of President Clinton's AmeriCorps plan to educate and give job training to at-risk students aged seventeen to twenty. Initially there was some hope that the Seaborne Conservation Corps could find permanent residence aboard the original *Texas Clipper,* thus saving her from the scrap heap. President Clinton swore in about twenty thousand AmeriCorps students in a live satellite feed that was broadcast to the TAMUG campus. The first nine-month class graduated in July of 1995. A second group had already begun in April, and a third was ready to begin the next month. A new sound filled the air. The cadence chants of seaborne cadets, always in uniform, echoed off buildings as they marched or jogged around campus.

As the Seaborne program was growing, the TAMUG undergraduate program began shrinking. Enrollment that fall dropped by 7.5 percent. Some were pleased that the so-called enrollment cap—or passive recruiting—was having its desired effect. But they would not be pleased for long. Fall 1994 marked the beginning of an uncomfortable four-year enrollment slide.

Just before classes began, the campus sponsored the first ever Sea Aggies Learning Traditions or SALT camp, based on the model of the Howdy Camp or Fish Camp at College Station. SALT, said the upperclassmen, was designed to "build Aggie spirit, camaraderie, and student involvement on campus. Oh yeah, we also teach those Aggie traditions." The program worked so successfully in its first year that it became a permanent and increasingly popular part of orientation. With the opening of the gym, TAMUG students, like all other Aggies, now had to take kinesiology (renamed from physical education) courses to graduate. As a whole new world of indoor exercise was made available, one old form of outdoor exercise was removed. To ensure safety and reduce insurance risk, TAMUG dismantled its three-meter diving board; at its deepest end, the pool had only eight feet of water, much too shallow for a board that was almost ten feet high.

For the second year in a row the Houston Rockets decided to make TAMUG home for their preseason camp as they prepared to defend their NBA title. They hoped the good luck would continue. Rockets co-captain Otis Thorpe said the Pelican Island setting helped team members set aside everyday worries and get more focused. In return for the use of the gym, Coach Tomjonavich contributed much to the local community: he chaired a golf tournament, played in it, and ran a Houston Rockets intersquad game—all in Galveston. The result was more than thirty thousand dollars raised for a scholarship program: high school graduates of Galveston County who enrolled at Galveston College or TAMUG received fifteen hundred dollars a year. The intersquad game attracted a standing-room-only crowd in the TAMUG gym and gave many people a chance to see their favorite NBA stars up close.

Although pro basketball was the hot topic of sports conversations on campus, TAMUG had some local success with its own amateur teams. The soccer team played a full season against Houston Community College, Lamar University, Alvin Community College, and the University of St. Thomas. In November the TAMUG crew rowing team won the 1.5-mile Head of Colorado race in Austin. The field included teams from the Austin and Bay Area rowing clubs, University of Texas–Austin, Northwestern Louisiana, Rice, and Southern Methodist University.

Hurricane Opal on October 3 caused some excitement but did little damage. Greater damage was done by a tugboat that crashed into the Pelican Island drawbridge at 6:00 P.M. on October 6. It took out two power poles, blacking out the campus for four hours. Students, unable to watch TV or study during the blackout, spent the warm evening outside their unairconditioned dorm rooms. Because Opal illustrated the need for up-to-the-minute storm warnings, the Student Senate passed a resolution asking for the addition of the weather channel to TAMUG cable services.

The annual local bonfire was bigger than ever. Student committees organized to collect fuel around town. The stack had a distinctly sea-related makeup, mostly old pallets donated by Galveston's port industries. The school administration publicized the effort and helped defray the cost of lugging fuel to the bonfire site on the Bolivar Peninsula. TAMUG's Blazers and Flamers built a stack three times the size of the previous year's. Its nighttime glow could be seen for miles.

John C. Calhoun, one of the founding forefathers of TAMUG programs, gave the commencement address in December. Emeritus deputy chancellor for engineering and distinguished professor of petroleum engineering, Calhoun had begun his career at Texas A&M in 1955. It was his idea to expand Galveston undergraduate curricula by adding marine sciences degrees (marine sciences, marine biology, and maritime systems engineering) to the merchant marine degrees in marine transportation and marine engineering.

TAMUG welcomed Dr. Connie Strode, an English teacher, as the first woman to assume a top administrative position on the campus. She was named associate campus dean for academic and administrative services. In April another TAMUG English teacher, Sara Gragg published a history of Galveston's Jamaica Beach.

Activities in the annual Springfest included smashing a car donated for that purpose by the campus police, playing tug-of-war while balancing on milk crates, and throwing baseballs at a target to dunk faculty members. The Big Event of this year's Springfest activities was reconstructing a city park. TAMUG students helped build elaborate intercon-

1995

Texas Maritime Academy, between ships, had to send its cadets on New York's *Empire State IV*. The Houston Rockets came back to TAMUG and repeated as NBA champions. The campus installation of the anchor from *Texas Clipper I* started a new Sea Aggie tradition. Texas A&M began its confusing practice of redefining the names of weekdays at the semester's end.

During Springfest, members of the Propeller Club give a symbolic shine to the huge propeller embedded in concrete beside the library. The prop glistens in the sun for the first time since it was donated to the campus back in 1984. The Propeller Club promotes the interests of the national and international maritime community. Source: *Voyager,* 1994.

nected wooden play structures at Schreiber Flagship Park, near 83rd Street and Stewart Road. The completed park won the 1995 "Excellence in Design" Achievement Award from the Texas Recreation and Parks Society. "It was a terrific way to give something back to the Galveston Community!" said the yearbook editors.

That spring, the breakfast served to students by faculty and staff before finals moved from morning to night. The time change proved successful in attracting more students: not surprisingly, they said they would much rather stay up late than get up early. The event was renamed Midnight Breakfast, "but in true Aggie tradition," said yearbook editors, "Midnight Breakfast is not held at midnight." It actually started about 10:00 or 11:00 P.M.

William Clayton, president emeritus of TAMUG, delivered the commencement address in May to a record 121 graduates. He told them they were ready to make their mark in the world: "You are much better in terms of success and achievement potential than you think you are." The event strained the thousand-seat capacity of the Grand 1894 Opera House.

Summer found TAMUG in an awkward position, in between training ships. *Texas Clipper II* was not ready; *Texas Clipper I* (having added the Roman numeral "I" to its name when its successor was named with a "II"), no longer operational, was being used as a dormitory for the Seaborne Conservation Corps. Hence arrangements were made for TAMUG cadets to travel to New York to board *Empire State VI* at Fort Schulyer;

the ship took them on a European cruise. There was a déjà vu quality in
this, for in 1963 Texas Maritime Academy cadets had taken their first
ever cruise aboard the New York ship's predecessor, *Empire State IV*. Coincidentally, Naples was on the itinerary for both the 1963 and 1995
cruises. Having no Texas training ship meant that summer school at sea
for newly graduated high school students could not be held that year,
though their predecessors had been sailing aboard *Texas Clipper* for the
past thirty years.

After another successful regular season, this one sparked by the
acquisition of Clyde Drexler, the Houston Rockets were back on the
TAMUG campus that summer to prepare for the playoffs. "This is a great
place to come to," said Coach Tomjonavich. A billboard in town proclaimed: "Go Rockets, Galveston Loves You!" Hundreds of basketball
fans lined up along Seawolf Parkway from the Pelican Island bridge to the
campus entrance, holding up signs with slogans like "Believe it, again."
Guardrails along the bridge were festooned with streamers in the team
colors of red and yellow.

TAMUG received free national publicity as the Rockets were photographed shooting baskets in front of a mural that read "Texas A&M University at Galveston, Island Home of the Houston Rockets." No one can
prove that practicing at TAMUG gave them the edge they needed, but
once again they came up winners, and even more convincingly. They
swept the Orlando Magic to become only the fifth franchise in NBA history to repeat as champs. Two years at TAMUG, two NBA titles.

Jane Young, artist and former TAMUG student, began directing
youngsters in painting murals with marine themes. It was part of a
TAMUG program called Galveston Island Adventure. One of the early

Students get a great deal of
satisfaction out of smashing a
car to work off their frustration over outstanding parking tickets. The campus police department painted the
message on the car, which
they had donated for Springfest 1995, along with supplying the helmet and sledgehammer. Source: *Voyager,*
1994-95.

Having the Houston Rockets on Campus

The presence of the Rockets generated a number of good anecdotes. Before each practice, TAMUG officials would clear the gym to make sure that the Rockets had the facility to themselves. On the last day of practice before the Miami finals, they overlooked a TAMUG professor taking a shower. When he finished, the professor wrapped his towel around him and walked into the locker room. There he found himself surrounded by the entire Rockets team, without their towels. One of the women on the TAMUG staff, when she heard him tell the story, said, "You were in *my* fantasy!"

Another story concerns a prospective student, unaware of what was going on, visiting the campus with her father. When the two of them entered the building, the father opened up the gym door to see what was going on inside. He watched the Rockets in unlabeled sweats practicing. "I just can't believe it," he said. "How can a small school without athletic scholarships get so many good, tall basketball players?"

murals, on a brick wall facing a vacant lot on the corner of Avenue P and 23rd Street, features swimming whales and dolphins. The foray led to the much more ambitious project of painting miles of murals on the Gulf side of the seawall.

That summer the City of Galveston began a beach replenishment project that dumped hundreds of thousands cubic yards of new sand on beaches between 10th and 61st streets, adding about 150 feet of new beach from 1995 through 1997. TAMUG scientists followed the procedure with professional interest; some predicted that the new sand would soon wash away (which it did).

During the fall semester, restoration work began on the footings of the middle section of the Pelican Island bridge. Cars had to wait in line to cross the single open lane on the bridge. And because the span could not be lifted during construction, ships and boats had to take the northern route around Pelican Island. Reports estimated that about a thousand permanent workers and thirteen hundred students crossed the bridge during weekdays, and the span was lifted about three thousand times a year for marine traffic. As the yearbook editors grumbled, "There's only one way on and one way off. The Pelican Island Bridge is always against you!" Some students actually preferred having the bridge under repair— it gave them a surefire excuse for showing up late to class.

The campus also received a major facelift: the parking lot next to the library was enlarged and paved; the small boat basin was renovated; rocks and railroad ties (leftovers from the old train tracks across the Pelican Island bridge) were removed from the campus border; and trees and shrubbery were planted along Seawolf Parkway and at the entrance to the campus. The student center enlarged the bookstore and added office spaces. And for fans of televised Aggie away games and Monday night pro football, the giant screen TV in the campus auditorium was wired for cable.

One poignant change was a memorial to *Texas Clipper I.* The ship's anchor was placed in the center of the quadrangle bordered by the classroom building, library, and student center (in 2002 the anchor would be moved to near the entrance of the library to make way for a clock tower). Set at a forty-five-degree angle, the anchor leaned on its own welded chain links. Affixed to the anchor was a plaque engraved with these words, written by students and administrators: "She served Texas A&M University at Galveston for 32 years, traveling over a quarter of a million miles visiting 49 foreign ports. . . . Having trained thousands of cadets, T/S *TEXAS CLIPPER* will sail in our hearts forever."

Campus Dean Schmidly remembered thinking, when he installed it in the quad, that students were sure to come up with some creative use of the anchor for a new Aggie tradition. He was right: the entire anchor became a good luck talisman, just like the toe on the statue of Lawrence Sullivan "Sully" Ross at main campus. Students rubbed their anchor for good luck, especially during final exams.

That fall Rear Admiral William McMullen was named the new superintendent of the maritime program. He was hardly new to the school. In 1963, while a cadet at New York Maritime aboard the ship *Empire State,* he had assisted the first class of Texas Maritime Academy cadets on their first summer cruise. He joined the faculty of the Texas Maritime Academy in 1966 and left in 1980 to join the U.S. Merchant Marine Academy

Some of the original cast members of *A Little Whale Told Me* ham it up for the camera in the fall of 1995. Left to right, front: Jeff Croucher, Lisa Miller, and Sky Craig; rear, Allison Cripe, Rob Carr, and Jon Balmous. Written by English teacher Vic Penuel, the play was a fund-raiser for the Texas Marine Mammal Stranding Network. Source: *Voyager,* 1994–95.

at Kings Point, where he served as associate academic dean. Generations of cadets handed down stories of standing watch on the ship and having to deal with McMullen's infamously difficult-to-answer "twenty questions" about maritime regulations, equipment, and practices.

In October the TAMUG Drama Club created a new way to educate children about the environment. Club members took the one-act play *A Little Whale Told Me* to the Houston Zoo and area elementary and middle schools; they also staged it at the local senior citizens' center. The play, written by TAMUG English teacher Vic Penuel, dramatized the communications between whales, dolphins, and people. It told audiences about the dangers of pollution and about what they could do to protect the environment. TAMUG students divided themselves into separate "white" and "maroon" casts so that they could present the play simultaneously in two different locations. Penuel originally wrote the play as a fund-raiser for the Texas Marine Mammal Stranding Network. It was based on the true story of a pygmy sperm whale calf stranded on Galveston Island with his mother in 1984.

An auto-pedestrian accident on campus that semester showed how supportive this university community was. Two freshmen women, walking from B-dorm to the classroom laboratory building, were crossing the road when a car plowed into them. The driver, also a freshman, said he could not see them because the sun was in his eyes. The two women were taken by ambulance to UTMB. Fortunately their injuries were relatively minor. Mostly they were banged up with bruises and scrapes, but one had a fractured tailbone. When they returned to campus, they could not believe their eyes. Balloons, flowers, and coloring books filled their dorm room. The top bunk had been moved down to the floor so that the injured woman would not have to climb. All of this was done by fellow students. Administrators got in on the act, too: the campus dean had flowers delivered to the dorm room. Shelly Henry, one of the injured women, later worked as student development specialist for TAMUG. She recalled that dorm life was always friendly: "When I moved into the first floor of B-Dorm, we had a blast. The entire floor of women were best friends. We'd go to cafeteria in a group of 30! Doors were always open along the hallway to encourage visiting. Sometimes we'd set up those hollow plastic bowling pins and do a little hallway bowling. One night the group went rollerblading at the human maze just off the Galveston seawall." After the accident, speed bumps were installed on campus. For a while they were nicknamed "Shelly bumps."

The education of cadets went high tech with the addition of a $1.2 million navigation and ship-handling simulator. Without leaving campus, students could now get the hands-on experience of navigating a 50,000-ton ship through the Panama Canal. The simulated ship's bridge included a radar scope, computerized visuals of seas and harbors throughout the world, radios, and standard ship controls. Students said, "It's like being in a normal ship." An instructor marveled at how technology had changed the way mariners learned: "It took me years at sea to get the kind of experience these students will get in a few months."

In November, students enrolled in introduction to biology got a chance to watch their instructor Tom Iliffe on the PBS television documentary "The New Explorers." Iliffe had been filmed exploring underwater caves on the Yucatan Peninsula.

The semester ended on a Tuesday that was treated as if it were Thursday. And the Monday before that was treated as if it were a Friday. No, it was not an Aggie joke. It was all done in the name of logic to fix the fall semester, which had always been short one Thursday and one Friday class because of the Thanksgiving holiday. The solution, said the faculty senate up at College Station, was to gerrymander the calendar so that from now on each semester would have an equal number of Mondays, Tuesdays, Wednesdays, Thursdays, and Fridays. No class would meet for fewer hours than any other. The awkward result was that in fall semesters the last two class days were redefined: you attended your Friday classes on Monday, your Thursday classes on Tuesday. A similar redefinition of the last Tuesday (now an Aggie Friday) occurred in the spring semester to replace the missing Good Friday holiday. Faculty and students found it easier to follow than to explain. And some didn't find it very easy to follow.

This year's Big Event, a one-day volunteer cleanup program in the community, concentrated on the Big Reef Nature Park. The park, along the North Jetty of Galveston Island, had suffered not only from use by tourists but also from a recent accident. A barge owned by Buffalo Marine Services had buckled and spilled more than 176,000 gallons of heavy fuel oil near the landing of the Bolivar Ferry. Students helped with shoreline cleanup.

In March TAMUG engineering undergraduates loaded the two-man human-powered submersible *Tiger Shark* onto a cattle trailer and drove for twenty-six hours to Escondido, California. They were to compete against thirty-two other North American teams, including from the University of Quebec, the U.S. Naval Academy, University of California–San Diego, and private industry groups like Batelle. Tom Powell, a member of the TAMUG Board of Visitors and the owner of Powell Industries, helped the students design, test, and paint the sub—it emerged complete with stripes, gills, and eyes. The team finished a respectable twelfth with a top speed of 3.25 knots. Students said they learned not only engineering but also "organizing, planning, time management, and team building."

Popular English teacher Sara Gragg passed away in April of 1996. She had taught writing and literature for eight years at TAMUG and had developed remedial reading and writing programs for at-risk stu-

1996

In 1996, TAMUG student engineers designed and raced a human-powered submarine. The entrance to the campus was landscaped. The maritime academy traded out ships. TAMUG appointed its first woman chief executive. The main campus donated the centerpole for the TAMUG bonfire.

dents. She also sponsored the publication of *Seaspray,* the campus literary magazine.

Also in April, a research building next to TAMUG's Fort Crockett building was temporarily closed after a rat was discovered carrying the potentially deadly hantavirus antibodies. The incident made front pages in newspapers around the region. The rat had been caught by a graduate student as part of a study on the mammal population of Galveston; but thirteen other rats also caught around the same time showed no such contamination. After a while, newspapers and the public lost interest in the incident, and the research project quietly continued. No repeat contamination was found.

The Pelican Island campus was freshened up dramatically that semester. Dilapidated tennis courts got a much needed facelift. The swimming pool, which had turned a deep shade of algae green, was refurbished and equipped with a wooden deck shaded by a horizontal fabric-screen suspended between two giant metal ATMs—supports in the form of the Texas A&M logo. Barbecue pits and picnic tables were installed near the dorms for students and their guests, and a major landscaping initiative lined the campus entry with shrubbery and trees. Even occasional visitors benefited from the changes: a permanent sign directed them to offices and points of interest on campus.

The 1996 *Voyager,* the campus annual, presented the year's events in a clever parody in an issue entitled "Changes . . . From Pelitraz to Fantasy Island." Students had first used the nicknames "Pelicatraz" or "Pelitraz" in the 1970s to describe Spartan conditions on Pelican Island, a sandy, dusty campus without a dormitory building, without a student center, without a library building, without a gym, without trees, without bushes, without even grass. Well, said the editors, things had now changed for the better.

In May about three thousand volunteers painted a 2.4-mile section of the seawall facing the beach with sea animals, birds, and people. Supervising artists, including former TAMUG student Jane Young, had spent seven weeks outlining the images and indicating what color they were to be painted by volunteers. It was billed as the largest paint-by-numbers project in the world. The Seaborne Conservation Corps and the Krewe of Thalasar (founded by TAMUG former students), always willing to lend a hand in the interests of community service, also participated. During the day volunteers filled in the background with blue primer; at night artists drew the outlines of the sea creatures by using overhead projectors powered by portable generators.

Texas Clipper II finally arrived at the campus in May. *Texas Clipper I* was towed out into the channel while her replacement took her old berth, and then the two ships remained tied up alongside each other for a few days. Texas maritime cadets and crew put in twelve- to fourteen-hour days getting used to the new ship before she departed on June 6 on her TAMUG maiden voyage. It was a short-distance cruise, designed to test

In May of 1996, *Texas Clipper II* (left) replaces *Texas Clipper I* (right) at the Pelican Island dock. The successor ship is the former *USNS Chauvenet*, a hydrographic survey ship, launched in 1968. At 393 feet long and 54 feet wide at her widest point, *Clipper II* is about 80 feet shorter and 12 feet narrower than *Clipper I*.

her out. Hurricane Bertha, packing winds of up to 115 miles per hour, caused *Clipper II* to wait in waters far south of Miami as a safety precaution to see what the storm would do before the ship sailed to her farthest port, Savannah, Georgia. Meanwhile *Texas Clipper I* was removed to Beaumont, where she was left to rust in the Ready Reserve Fleet moorings, a huge graveyard for ships that outlive their usefulness. Fittingly, Jack Lane, a former TAMUG faculty member who had captained her in 1975, was her last pilot in 1996; he took her as far as the Galveston sea buoy at twilight, transferred to the pilot boat, then saluted her as she was towed away.

In June David Schmidly resigned as campus dean and chief executive officer, a job he had held since 1992, to become graduate dean at Texas Tech University, his alma mater. A group of well-wishers bade him farewell in August at a reception at the Hotel Galvez. Schmidly was saluted for his dedication to students and his commitment to community service.

In August actress Bridget Fonda hosted the TBS television special "Dolphins in Danger," which featured Graham Worthy, a TAMUG professor and director of the Texas Marine Mammal Stranding Network. Many TAMUG students volunteered to help the two marine mammals rescued: Cole and Nemo, both bottlenose dolphins. Fonda helped release

David Schmidly, First and Last Campus Dean

David Schmidly, born in Levelland, Texas, earned bachelor's and master's degrees from Texas Tech University. He earned his Ph.D. in zoology from University of Illinois–Champaign/Urbana. His widely respected research focused on the conservation and natural history of mammals in Mexico and Texas, especially along the Gulf of Mexico. He was fondly known by the nickname "Batman" because of his popular books on bats, including *The Bats of Texas,* published by Texas A&M University Press. His latest book is *Texas Natural History: A Century of Change.*

Before coming to Galveston Schmidly was a faculty member at College Station for twenty years, spending the last six as head of the Department of Wildlife and Fisheries Sciences. His department administered the graduate program taught by TAMUG's Department of Marine Biology. In 1992 he became the first person named as campus dean (the previous campus leader having had the title of president) of TAMUG, now part of the newly merged College of Geosciences and Maritime Studies. He also co-chaired the Institute of Marine Life Sciences, which coordinated all the marine sciences in the Texas A&M University System. In 1993 he was elevated to the rank of chief executive officer and campus dean of TAMUG. After he stepped down, the title of campus dean was retired.

Schmidly left TAMUG in 1996 to become the graduate dean at Texas Tech University, where he was named president four years later. In January of 2003 he would become president of Oklahoma State University and CEO of the OSU System. He said that nothing prepared him better to rise in the ranks of academic administration than his five years at the helm of TAMUG.

Actress Bridget Fonda embraces Cole, a stranded dolphin. The two co-starred in the August, 1996, TBS documentary "Dolphins in Danger." For more than seven months, TAMUG volunteers in the Texas Marine Mammal Stranding Network helped nurse Cole back to health. Source: *Voyager,* 1996.

Nemo about ten miles offshore, but he washed back ashore nineteen days later, dead of apparent heart failure due to old age. After 227 days of tender loving care from TMMSN volunteers, the juvenile dolphin Cole recovered fully and was transported to Gulf World, Panama City, Florida. Because he had spent his early formative life in captivity, he had not learned to survive in the wild.

On August 16, Viola E. Florez became the first woman CEO of TAMUG. The former executive assistant to the president of Texas A&M and interim dean of the College of Education at College Station, she was named interim vice president and chief executive officer of TAMUG. Her one-year appointment was designed to allow TAMUG enough time to find a permanent CEO. The meager title of campus dean, held by her predecessor, was finally and officially recognized as inadequate for a person expected to have authority over all academic functions, buildings, and programs of an operation with three separate campuses in Galveston. Florez had told TAMU President Ray Bowen, "If this campus is as important as you say it is, you need to give us the title we deserve." He agreed. Bowen said the title change reflected the growing significance of the campus. What it meant in practical terms was that Galveston now had a seat at the president's conference table every Monday morning, would be able to voice concerns directly to the president, and would hear firsthand of any high-level discussion affecting its future. Such a seat had been denied for the past five years to anyone with the title campus dean, but a vice president had the ear—and the support—of College Station.

Florez held a master's degree from the University of Colorado at Boulder and a doctorate from Texas A&M University–Kingsville. She proved a popular leader during a difficult time when the campus was facing budget shortfalls. Much of the problem was due to old loans from main campus and some difficulties with accounts used to pay for research projects. She opened up the entire financial process to public scrutiny: the campus agreed to live within the means of a new need-based budget. The combination of belt tightening, writing off loans, fund-raising, and reconciling of accounts did the trick; TAMUG got out of the red. Meanwhile a national search for a permanent CEO continued.

In the fall of 1996, TAMUG was recognized as number one academically. For the first time, *US News & World Report* ranked TAMUG in its top spot in a category that included 423 schools (small liberal colleges in the West). The previous year, TAMUG had been number two. Students knew their school was good, but it was so small that they wondered how the magazine had discovered them; they also continued to wonder why it was placed in such a strange category.

Out on Bolivar Beach, students burned the fourth annual Sea Aggie bonfire to demonstrate their "burning desire to beat the hell out of t.u." (the Aggie nickname for the University of Texas). Students at College Station had donated the centerpole for the stack, estimated to stand thirty-five feet high. It was a nice payback for the forty-foot log that Galveston had contributed to the College Station stack twenty-eight years earlier.

In November, volunteers for the Texas Marine Mammal Stranding Network—most of them TAMUG students—worked around the clock to nurse a three-year-old female false killer whale that had washed up on Matagorda beach. They optimistically named the 450-pound, nine-foot whale Miracle. But the name was not enough to ensure survival: two hundred pounds underweight, the whale died.

The Houston Rockets were back at TAMUG to see if they could manage a third championship season, but it was not to be. However, they did provide an interesting diversion on campus with three future NBA hall-of-famers: Hakeem Olajuwon, Clyde Drexler, and the new addition Charles Barkley. The team raised money for scholarships in an intersquad game at the campus gymnasium. During halftime, the mayor of Galveston presented furniture-store huckster and Rockets booster "Mattress Mac" Jim Macinvale with a key to the city.

Harvey Roberts "Bum" Bright, chairman of the Texas A&M System Board of Regents and former owner of the Dallas Cowboys, spoke at the December commencement. "Progress never ceases," said Bright. "What you've learned is how to learn, how to change and how to adapt."

TAMUG took up the torch for the 1997 Mardi Gras five-kilometer run and kids' one-kilometer fun run after St. Mary's hospital, which had spon-

1997

In 1997, TAMUG appointed its eighth chief executive. Texas A&M mascot Reveille visited the Mitchell campus. The maritime studies degree was added.

sored the run for twelve years, closed its doors in 1996. About twenty-five hundred runners and walkers participated. The proceeds from the run went to scholarships for disadvantaged youth.

In March, Galveston College announced that it had sold its Fort Crockett building to TAMUG, but the announcement proved premature. The deal would eventually fall through. Instead, TAMUG began renting space in that seventy-seven-thousand-square-foot building, which stood just to the west of the TAMUG Fort Crockett building. While on-again off-again negotiations were under way to purchase the building, the first year's rental was just one dollar. In five years TAMUG would vacate the Galveston College Fort Crockett building and shift operations to Pelican Island in the Edison Chouest Offshore building adjacent to the Mitchell campus.

The Houston Rockets held their last practice on the TAMUG campus that April, ending a three-year run. They now had a newer facility. The team moved into a $3 million state-of-the-art practice center in Houston. A prescient sports writer for the *Houston Chronicle* argued that it might be unlucky for the Rockets to change their practice locale. After all, they had had great starts after their three TAMUG camps: 10–3 in 1994, 11–4 in 1995, and 15–1 in 1996. "If it ain't broke, don't fix it," he wrote. Sadly enough, the Rockets had a mediocre start in 1997, did not return to TAMUG, and did not win another NBA title. In 2003, seeking to revitalize the team into playoff contenders, the Rockets would once again hold their preseason practice at TAMUG. They made the playoffs with their star center, seven-foot, five-inch Yao Ming, but faltered in the first round.

The summer cruise had originally been scheduled to carry 106 cadets and 60 prep cadets to European ports. But a faulty pump delayed departure and forced the ship to shorten its cruise. Instead the ship went only as far as Montreal, Canada. Meanwhile back on campus, plans were under way to hold a fund-raising gala at the Texas Seaport Museum for the Seaborne Conservation Corps. Federal funding shortfalls had put the continued existence of SCC in jeopardy. About 450 partygoers raised more than $453,000 to show their appreciation for the SCC program and its exceptionally active commitment to community service.

After her one-year interim appointment was up, Vi Florez, who had been born and raised in New Mexico, accepted the post of dean of the College of Education at the University of New Mexico.

On July 25, W. Mike Kemp became CEO of TAMUG. Kemp had started teaching in the biology department at Texas A&M University–College Station in 1975; the next year, he became the head of the department. He was promoted to professor in 1982. From 1994 to 1996 he was the executive director for research at TAMU. He was president of the Federation of Societies for Parasitology and the American Society of Parasitologists. He would leave TAMUG in 2004 to assume the leadership for the Texas A&M branch campus in the State of Qatar.

In a 1997 interview with the *Nautilus,* Kemp said: "I grew up in a small west Texas town where there were no doctors or lawyers, and the

From 1996 to 1997 the top administrative position on campus was held by a woman for the first time. Viola Florez was interim vice president and chief executive officer of TAMUG. Here Houston Rockets head coach Rudy Tomjonavich (center) presents the proceeds from his golf tournament to Florez (left) and Galveston College President Bix Rathburn. The money funded student scholarships. Source: *Galveston Daily News,* December 29, 1996.

most educated people were the school teachers. So I grew up wanting to teach high school biology." He was attracted to the Galveston program for a number of reasons. On the personal horizon, it gave him the opportunity to spend more time with his wife Barbara, who was a research scientist at UTMB; professionally, he liked the TAMUG focus on the sea.

Like Florez before him, Kemp benefited from the continuing support of President Bowen and the College Station administration. But he also inherited an unhealthy enrollment problem: the numbers of undergraduates at TAMUG had been falling since 1994. The trend continued until the fall, when only 1,111 students showed up, a drop of almost 17 percent over the previous four years. At his first major address to students, faculty, and staff, Kemp announced that growing the student body would be his first priority.

Out at Moody Gardens, ground was broken for the blue aquarium pyramid and its two-million-gallon exhibit. It would be the third pyra-

Campus Goes to the Dogs

On August 11, 1997, the Pelican Island campus got a visit from a VID (very important dog). Reveille VI, official mascot of Texas A&M University, sat in on a physics class and fell asleep. Students joked that some students do exactly the same thing during class. Students had been hoping that Reveille would bark—which by Aggie tradition put an automatic end to any class. Luckily "Miss Reveille Ma'am" didn't have to pass an exam in the subject.

The dog is the highest ranking member of the Aggie corps of cadets, even higher than the student corps commander. Students lined up in the gym to have their photograph taken with Reveille; one enterprising group of students persuaded the handler to take the dog for a walk and had their photograph taken in the center of campus in front of the anchor of *Texas Clipper I*.

Then in the fall another dog won the hearts of students. No dogs are allowed in the dormitories, but the campus made a happy exception with a pilot program for Texas Hearing and Service dogs. Marine biology student Lisa Miller used a hand-clicker to train Abby, an eighteen-month-old golden retriever, for a College Station man paralyzed from the neck down. The dog learned to open and close doors and to function in a busy environment full of distractions.

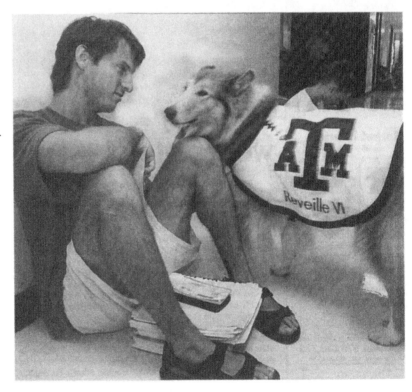

Student David Evans pets Reveille VI in the first floor hallway of the classroom laboratory building on the Mitchell campus. This was Reveille's first visit to TAMUG. The reigning collie is the mascot of Texas A&M and the highest ranking member of the corps of cadets. Source: *Galveston Daily News,* August 12, 1997.

mid built, joining the original clear glass greenhouse of the rainforest pyramid and the red discovery pyramid focused on space exploration, which had opened in June.

William E. Evans, the dean of the Texas Maritime College and super-intendent of the Texas State Maritime Program, spoke at summer commencement. The ceremony was held in the Hotel Galvez in the music room, formerly known as the Grecian room, the site where in 1958 the idea of a Texas Maritime Academy had been born.

Toward the end of September, a nearby shooting caused quite a stir on campus. Around noon some TAMUG students watched from their dorm balconies as two pickup trucks were speeding along Seawolf Parkway toward the Pelican Island bridge. The white truck pulled up even with the red truck. Gunshots popped, and one of the vehicles swerved off the road, hit a sign, and stopped in the marshy reeds; students ran to aid the driver. Campus police officers arrested the suspected gunman, who turned out to be a parole violator; he was charged with attempted murder. The shooting victim, a local wrecker service owner, was admitted to UTMB hospital in guarded condition with a gunshot wound to the neck; he was later released. The entire incident, Galveston police determined, seemed to have grown out of a domestic disturbance.

A year-long experiment with a student government association (composed of executive, legislative, and judicial branches) came to an end in September when the Student Senate voted to withdraw their support and to declare the SGA constitution null and void. Interest and participation in the SGA had fallen off drastically. Because the Student Senate was the only governing entity elected by the student body, it resumed its functioning as the student government of TAMUG. It would take another five years before a student government association was reborn on campus.

The *Nautilus* ran this spectacular front-page headline in October of 1997: "TAMUG's Link to Outside World May Be Cut Off." Overdramatic, perhaps. What had happened was much more mundane. The bearings that allowed the Pelican Island bridge open and close properly had been stripped by years of use, and the bridge was temporarily closed to marine traffic. Because the lifting arm had not quite meshed with the roadway, vehicular traffic had to slow down to go over a bump on the bridge until the bearings were fixed.

On October 16, the Texas Higher Education Coordinating Board approved the addition of the maritime studies (MAST) degree, the only bachelor of arts program on campus. It was the first new curriculum in fifteen years, since marine fisheries had been authorized. The program looked at the sea from a broad perspective of various disciplines, including anthropology, archaeology, ethics, history, and literature. It was expected that graduates with a MAST degree would find jobs in coastal planning, sea-related recreation and tourism, and economic and environmental development.

The Sea Aggie bonfire moved from Bolivar Peninsula to a closer location on Galveston's East Beach that November. Several hundred Aggie supporters gathered around the blazing fire.

In December George Mitchell donated another thirty-seven acres of land, worth more than half a million dollars, to the Pelican Island campus. Mitchell continued to be the major real estate benefactor for TAMUG. The newest addition, across the road on the north side of Seawolf Parkway, increased the campus by about one-third and significantly increased its access to the shore. When interviewed for this history, Mitchell said: "There is much work to be done in the Gulf. I believe that TAMUG can one day be the third leg of a group that includes Scripps Institution of Oceanography and Woods Hole Oceanographic Institution." TAMUG CEO Mike Kemp said Mitchell's generosity had given TAMUG a future: "If Texas A&M on Pelican Island doesn't grow, it won't be because it's physically constrained." At about the same time the Mitchell campus got a new neighbor: Newpark Marine Fabricators took over the site that had been occupied for about half a century by Todd Shipyards but had now been vacant for several years.

George F. Bass, president and founder of the Institute of Nautical Archaeology at Texas A&M University, spoke at the December graduation. Bass, arguably the most influential nautical archaeologist in the world, spoke to the graduates about the need for imagination in solving tomorrow's problems.

1998

In the spring, dropping enrollment forced campus layoffs. TAMUG faculty and students began helping with archaeological work on a sunken Civil War blockade runner. In the fall, undergraduate enrollment began a resurgence. A tropical storm with extremely high tides damaged the small boat basin on the Mitchell campus.

Colonel Bob Hickerson, founding executive director of the Seaborne Conservation Corps, resigned to accept a state job as the executive director of the Texas Commission on Volunteerism and Community Service for Governor George Bush. Hickerson had been with the TAMUG-sponsored Seaborne program since 1994. Al DeMadeiros replaced Hickerson. The TAMUG program was so well respected that secretary of the Navy John Dalton and national AmeriCorps director Debbie Joston visited Galveston and volunteered alongside the Seaborne Conservation Corps in picking up litter on the beach. Afterward, they all attended a Martin Luther King Day celebration.

TAMUG sponsored the Mardi Gras run for the second year in a row. This time it included the USA Track and Field twelve-kilometer women's national championship. More than a dozen of the nation's best middle-distance women runners competed in the event. Susannah Beck of Eugene, Oregon, won the title by four seconds over Shelly Steely of Albuquerque, New Mexico. It was a great finish for that particular race, but sadly it was also the last big Mardi Gras run held in Galveston. For economic reasons, Seaborne Conservation Corps decided it was no longer feasible to host the race.

The Center for Marine Training and Safety, at the TAMUG Offatts Bayou campus on Teichman Road, set up a state-of-the-art marine crisis management simulator. Trainees could use the simulator to learn how to

handle a variety of marine spills in just about any region of the world. After a trainee decided what to do in the imagined crisis, the computer would review all the decisions to evaluate their effectiveness. The simulator was run jointly by TAMUG and the Texas Engineering Extension Service.

During the spring semester, the Galveston campus of Texas A&M laid off staff members for the first time in its history. A projected budget shortfall of $1.3 million—due to a combination of cost increases and revenue loss from the enrollment decline—forced the university to eliminate nineteen positions. Campus CEO Mike Kemp said that during the past few years, when employees had retired or changed positions, TAMUG had not replaced them; that took care of eleven of the positions to be eliminated. Now "no alternatives" were left but layoffs. The campus worked hard to help those laid off obtain new jobs. About half of them found employment on the College Station campus. Still, the layoffs had a profoundly depressing effect on campus morale.

The only way to avoid future shortfalls, said Kemp, was to increase revenue by attracting more undergraduates. To accomplish that goal he increased funding and staffing for the recruiting office. Since the previous fall an intense campaign, overseen by Executive Associate Vice President Bill Hearn and led by Assistant Vice President of Academic Services Donna Lang, had been under way to recruit new students. The campus collectively held its breath as the fall application and acceptance numbers were tabulated. Things looked promising, but only the show-up numbers would tell whether the effort had been successful.

The Learning Resources Laboratory in the Williams library was upgraded with more computers, each with expanded memory, and more printers. Students were able to use the laboratory by telephone lines from anywhere off campus.

Mapping work began on *Denbigh,* a side-wheeler Civil War blockade runner that in 1865 had run aground near what is now the Bolivar ferry landing. The long-term project would eventually involve the work of several faculty members and a number of undergraduates from TAMUG. Artifacts recovered from the ship were stored in the archaeological laboratory of the maritime studies program. After the items were cleaned and treated, some were placed on display in the foyer of the library.

In May State Representative Craig Eiland addressed 139 graduating students, the largest number ever in a single commencement ceremony. The ceremony was held in the Grand 1894 Opera House, which holds one thousand audience members. But because the graduating class was so large, students were moved to the stage to make room for the audience. For the first time tickets had to be issued; each graduate was limited to eight guest tickets (supplemented by an active black market). The *Galveston Daily News* congratulated TAMUG for the record-breaking class and said the school was evidently "doing a good job of getting the word out to prospective students."

The summer was full of good news. College Station faculty taught education courses in Galveston to help certify TAMUG science majors to teach in middle and secondary schools. The courses were offered at Galveston's Ball High School. Also that summer a two-year renovation of dormitories began with the installation of a new door lock system. The next phase of renovations included refurbishing bathrooms, recarpeting rooms, and repaving driveways. In 1998 about half of the student population lived on campus; the dormitories could hold 655 students. Marine biologist Sammy Ray was honored by the chancellor of the Texas A&M University System that summer as one of eighteen people exemplifying service to the community. On its annual summer training cruise, *Texas Clipper II* carried not only prep cadets and its own Texas Maritime Academy cadets but also cadets from Massachusetts and Maine state academies and from the national academy in Kings Point. The maritime administrator of the U.S. Department of Transportation designated Texas Maritime Academy as a regional academy. The designation—approved by the governors of Alabama, Arkansas, Florida, Oklahoma, and Texas —doubled the amount of federal administrative support annually to two hundred thousand dollars.

The carefully orchestrated undergraduate recruiting push worked. Fall enrollment increased by about 5 percent and would continue its up-

Tropical Storm Frances Causes Campus Erosion

A poorly organized tropical storm named Frances did a great deal of damage in 1998 because of unusually high tides. On September 8, before the rain had begun, the tides were already high enough to back up storm sewers—curbside puddles were salty from water pushed up by the Gulf. By Thursday, September 10, tides had risen six feet above mean sea level. TAMUG closed at 2:00 P.M. and bussed students to College Station. Students were happily excited about the entire process—it was something new and interesting. Some enjoyed attending their first "hurricane party" (a tradition along the Gulf Coast) and then swimming in the streets when the wind had died down.

However, the aftermath of the storm was grim. On the West End of Galveston, about thirty feet of beach had disappeared, leaving some homes on the publicly owned side of the new vegetation line and thus marked for demolition according to the "Open Beaches" statute. The small boat basin on campus suffered severe erosion due to the winds, high tides, and rough waves that pounded the shoreline for about a week. Damage was so extensive that TAMUG had to get funding from state and federal agencies, like FEMA, to help rebuild.

First, workers cleaned out concrete, rocks, and metal that had been dumped there over the years. Then they encased the tip of the boat entryway in concrete and redid the brick matting system all along the basin. It took about eighteen months to get everything back into working order; the result was a better small boat facility than had existed before the storm. The intimate knowledge of the suffering caused by this tropical storm—not even strong enough to be labeled a hurricane—probably spurred the TAMUG community in its generous effort to contribute food, clothing, and money to Honduras two months later in the aftermath of the monster Hurricane Mitch.

ward trend, resulting in the third big growth spurt for the school. A larger student population meant more revenue to fund campus projects.

During the fall semester, TAMUG students worked to rehabilitate a six-foot dolphin. They called him Stormy, after Tropical Storm Frances, which was believed to have separated him from his mother and led to his stranding. He was found at Port Aransas and transported by the Texas Marine Mammal Stranding Network to a holding facility.

Later that semester, on October 10, students reveled in the first "maroon-out" football game at College Station: the idea was that all Aggie supporters were to wear maroon that day. The demand created a well-publicized nationwide shortage of maroon-colored clothing. At Kyle Field alone, fans bought more than thirty-one thousand maroon T-shirts. The sea of maroon electrified the crowd and may have helped A&M win 28–21 against Nebraska, a team ranked in the top ten. TAMUG students were there in force: "It seemed as if everybody from TAMUG went to the football games. We formed carpools from Galveston to College Station.

TAMUG first-year students pack up their belongings and head for buses to take them on to Sea Aggies Learning Traditions camp, August 28, 1998. During the weekend before classes start, upper class students impart to SALT camp participants what it means to be an Aggie. The camp began in 1994. Source: *Galveston Daily News,* August 31, 1998.

Once there, we had TAMUG radar—there may have been thousands of people in the crowds, but we always ran into Galveston folks. We all felt that the words of our alma mater song rang absolutely true: 'The Aggies Are We.' Texas A&M is *our* team."

The *Houston Chronicle* Sunday magazine *Texas* ran a cover story about TAMUG marine biologist Tom Iliffe. The seven-page feature, illustrated with breathtaking full-page color photographs, described his SCUBA-diving search for life forms in underwater caves. As a graduate student at the University of South Florida said, Iliffe "pretty much invented the field. If you don't think so, just try and find a significant academic paper on cave diving that isn't either by Iliffe or cites him." At TAMUG, Iliffe taught introductory biology, cave biology, and cave diving.

Seaborne Conservation Corps cadets still attended classes, trained, and ate in the cafeteria on the TAMUG Mitchell campus. Created by TAMUG and now run by the National Guard of Texas, the corps' continued existence had been in doubt most of the year. At the last minute, Republicans and Democrats who had been fighting over money and politics finally agreed to provide matching funds for the job-training program.

The parking lot next to C-dorm was expanded and paved. Previously the lot had been two separate, smaller areas divided by a ditch. The ditch was bridged and students responded enthusiastically: "It's great," said one, "there's no speed bump, there's more parking spaces. I give it a thumbs up."

Members of the TAMUG rowing team, without enough money even to buy their own oars, let alone their own racing sculls, won gold, silver, and bronze medals at the Pumpkin Head Regatta held in Austin on Halloween. The revamped rowing program, only in its first year, had a perfect record: team members won medals in each of the three events they entered. The team had been practicing three times a week using borrowed equipment at the Bay Area Rowing Club on Clear Lake. Not only did the team stun opposing teams from Rice, Tulane, Florida State, and Texas—they also shocked themselves. The gold medal went to coed crew Kenneth Hunt, Samantha Silkwood, Allison Buchtein, Aron Edwards, and coxswain Sarah Marsh. They made such a splash with their debut that they received donations from Newpark Shipbuilding and from the Austin Rowing Club—now they bought their own used shell. Rice University loaned them two oars. The next April the women's team won a gold and the men's team a silver medal at the Heart of Texas Regatta in Austin.

In November TAMUG marine biologist Bernd Würsig received a prestigious national award from the National Geographic Society, the Committee for Research and Exploration Chairman's Award. The society gave Würsig fifteen thousand dollars in recognition of the work he had done studying whales and dolphins, their behavior and habitat. "I've been interested in dolphins and whales ever since I was a kid," he said, "mainly because of the writing of Cousteau and John Lily about the intelligence of marine mammals."

The first "Mr. TAMUG Pageant" was held in the auditorium. Spoofing conventional beauty pageants, men competed in four categories: the walk or introduction; the swimsuit; talent; and evening gown. The crowd got to laugh at outrageous costumes, including a whipped cream bikini, as they watched men try to maintain their balance in spike heels. Some say the highlight was the interview, when contestants had to answer this question on stage: "If you were trapped on a deserted island what one type of ice cream would you bring and how does that flavor relate to being an Aggie?" Most contestants had thought the pageant a big joke, but one freshman took it seriously—he stole the show with his talented violin playing, and won. The next year, competition was even more spirited.

In February a group of volunteers worked with old-fashioned stencils, paint buckets, and paint brushes to let the public know that most of Galveston's storm drains empty into Galveston Bay. According to surveys, many residents believed erroneously that sewers sluiced paint, motor oil, antifreeze, and the like directly to some kind of waste-processing

1999

In 1999, TAMUG appeared in *Time* magazine's top five hundred list. Undergraduate enrollment continued to grow and, for the first time, achieved a near balance of men and women. The Aggie Bonfire collapse on main campus killed twelve people.

TAMUG students alert the public about nonpoint-source pollution, stenciling warning signs near storm sewers on the Strand in downtown Galveston: "Dump no waste. Drains to bay." Left to right: Jessica Gribbon, Alicia Foyt, and Eileen Johnson. Source: *Galveston Daily News,* February 22, 1999.

facility. TAMUG students, working with the Galveston County Health District, stenciled the phrases "drains to bay" and "dump no waste" on curbs and gutters throughout the city. The *Galveston Daily News* ran an editorial praising the volunteer program.

The Seaborne Conservation Corps changed its name to Seaborne ChalleNGe Corps, in recognition of its being part of the National Guard (NG) Youth ChalleNGe Program for the State of Texas. Seaborne moved many of its operations out of the houseboat barge tied alongside the Mitchell campus dock, though the barge would continue to be used for administrative functions; operations took up temporary residence at the former family care clinic of UTMB. When renovations were completed, Seaborne moved into its permanent home in the former Marine Corps Annex, part of the U.S. Army Corps of Engineers facility at Fort Point in Galveston. Seaborne would continue to use the Mitchell campus for training but the cadets would sleep and eat some meals at the annex.

In May *Time* magazine published its first *Princeton Review,* identifying the best five hundred universities in the United States. Only four public institutions in Texas made the top five hundred: Texas A&M University, the University of Texas, the University of Texas at Dallas, and Texas A&M University at Galveston. The rankings were based on selectivity of admissions. At TAMUG, in the previous year, 21 percent of the entering freshmen were in the top 10 percent of their schools, and SAT scores averaged more than 1,100. The recognition came a decade after TAMUG had first appeared in the *US News & World Report* rankings.

Award-Winning Proposal: Sea Aggies in Love

The summer of 1999 was a summer of love for TAMUG. Two former students made national news for winning the Beringer White Zinfandel's 1999 Irresistible Proposals contest. As a story in the *Houston Chronicle* reported, they had met and fallen in love as marine biology undergraduates at TAMUG in 1990; eight years later Chris Lowe (class of 1994) was working in the oil-spill recovery industry off the Louisiana coast and Andé Smith (class of 1993) was teaching at La Marque Middle School. In January, 1998, Lowe wrote an illustrated poetic proposal of marriage to Smith, put it in a bottle, and dropped it into the Gulf. The bottle, sealed with a wax-covered cork, also contained mailing instructions. Two months later he had switched his career to teaching science at Seabrook Intermediate School. They continued to date. The floating proposal was always in the back of his mind, but he said nothing.

Then one evening, as they were getting ready to leave for a dinner date in Galveston, he noticed that his girlfriend had received an envelope with a mysterious return address. "I think I know what this is," he said. "Can I read it to you?" Sure enough, it *was* the retrieved proposal. He read it; she accepted: "I was touched, surprised. It was perfect." The engaged couple sent out wedding invitations in—you guessed it—bottles. They were married onboard Galveston's tall ship *Elissa* by a judge dressed as a nineteenth-century ship's captain. In awarding the top prize (a week in California's Napa Valley), the Beringer wine company said what made their story stand out from other entries was their willingness to let fate take a hand. "Everyone else had a time frame, an offer and a response. This one had no time frame."

In the summer, Karl and Marilyn Haupt became the second married couple officially sanctioned to sail on a training cruise for the Texas Maritime Academy (Jack and Judy Held had sailed together in the late 1980s). Marilyn was the nurse on *Texas Clipper II*; Karl was the captain as well as a former TAMUG student. Duties kept them both busy, but they admitted it was nice to be together. After the cruise they adopted a family of three children; the new responsibility kept Marilyn from going on future cruises with her husband.

That fall semester, the campus reached a balance between the sexes: men barely outnumbered women on campus 656 to 632, or 51 percent to 49 percent. The freshman class, numbering 518, was the largest in the school's history. From concern just two years before about falling enrollment, TAMUG had now to deal with exactly the opposite problem. Since the fall of 1997 the student population had risen almost 16 percent, to 1,268. The campus housing shortage was so acute that sixty students were placed in the Howard Johnson motel near the entrance to Moody Gardens.

In October Captain Richard W. Lukens was named new superintendent of the Texas State Maritime Program at TAMUG. Lukens had been

Helping man the capstan aboard the 1877 tall ship *Elissa,* docked at Galveston's Pier 21, are TAMUG volunteers. Students have long played an active part in sail training and maintenance on the historic barque. Some have also worked internships at the Texas Seaport Museum, home of *Elissa.*

a department head and a teacher at the school for the past ten years. Informally, the Texas State Maritime Program still went by its original name, Texas Maritime Academy.

TAMUG student Brad Dawe was in the news that fall for a heroic wedding gift to the husband of a best friend. He donated one of his kidneys. The bride and groom to be—both graduate students at TAMUG—were overwhelmed by his generosity. They postponed their honeymoon so that the operation could be scheduled as soon as possible. "I figure I can make a difference," said Dawe. "This one [health problem] we can beat."

Unexpected tragedy struck that semester. On Thursday, November 18, at 2:42 A.M., the Aggie bonfire at College Station collapsed, killing twelve people and injuring twenty-seven others. The Galveston campus was stunned. Students were weeping openly. Friday classes were either canceled or held under solemn circumstances; many teachers gave students the opportunity during class time to talk about their feelings. In sympathy, the traditional bonfire in Galveston was dismantled. It was the first year since the 1963 assassination of President John Kennedy that there was no Aggie bonfire.

The Drama Club's November production of "A Gown for His Mistress" was the last show ever staged at the Upper Deck Theater, on the third floor of the Galveston College Fort Crockett building. Ticket prices were modest: one dollar for students; five dollars for others. Also in November the Academic Enhancement Office, which offered free tutoring for all students, had its official grand opening on November 23 in its new C-dorm suite of offices.

Toward the end of the semester the Galveston campus held its annual version of the traditional Aggie elephant walk. At 1:40 P.M. on November 30, graduating seniors (the so-called elephants) assembled in the student center to remember what had gone before and wonder about what would come next. Then they meandered around campus, arms linked, past buildings and places that were part of their undergraduate experience. One Galveston twist to this tradition was a procession underneath the peak made by the chain and anchor taken off the original *Texas Clipper.* Walking underneath this structure had by now evolved into a "senior privilege" (underclassmen caught underneath the anchor had to drop down and do pushups.) The seniors stopped for photos, a yell practice, and one final on-campus "Whoop!"

The decade of the nineties saw TAMUG tentatively assume its adulthood. The school proved itself mature enough to handle whatever resulted from accident or planning. It began the decade with surprisingly strong enrollment gains, bucking the national trend. Then, when nearsighted decisions to neglect recruiting caused enrollment to slide, the school took stock of what needed to be done and got back on the growth track. Most of the nineties were mired in the administrative morass of a clumsy merger between TAMUG in Galveston and the College of Geosciences in College Station. It was as if an upstart had married a princess who continued to live with her parents in the royal palace 150 miles away. The separation made it difficult for the upstart to know where he stood. Still TAMUG managed to forge on, building a physical education facility, replacing its first training ship, adding degree programs and campus acreage, dealing with the ravages of Tropical Storm Frances, climbing in the *US News & World Report* rankings, and being named one of the top five hundred U.S. colleges in the *Time/Princeton Review.*

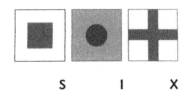

S   I   X

A New Century, 2000–2002
University for the Future

THE world marked the start of the twenty-first century: the mathematically correct start-year of 2001 was less celebrated than the year of 2000. International terrorism soon became the hallmark of the new century. The bottom seemed to fall out of the stock market as technology stocks, led by bankrupt dotcoms, lost their value. DVDs replaced videocassettes as the way to watch movies in your home. Scientific breakthroughs ushered in a whole new era of biotechnology.

Millions were glued to their television sets watching the reality show *Survivor*. The comic strip *Peanuts* ended original production, and then, when its creator died, went into reruns. Students used websites like Napster to copy recorded music onto their personal computers. International terrorists hijacked commercial passenger planes to attack the World Trade Center in New York and the Pentagon in Washington, D.C. In response, the United States launched a military invasion of Afghanistan. *Harry Potter and the Sorcerer's Stone* and *Shrek* were movie box-office hits. College Station scientists cloned the domestic cat, naming the clone CC. North Korea announced it had nuclear weapons, and the United States doubted Iraq's claim that it had no weapons of mass destruction. By 2002, it looked as if an invasion of Iraq was imminent.

TAMUG added new programs and continued to grow.

SeaWorld of San Antonio became a classroom for thirty-four TAMUG students during winter break. They earned college credit studying animal behavior, husbandry, veterinary measures, and biological research. Meanwhile they helped feed, weigh, and monitor livestock at the world's largest marine-life park. The hands-on program proved so worthwhile that a second was planned for the summer.

In January Bill Evans was named professor emeritus at TAMUG. Evans had retired as the U.S. undersecretary of commerce for oceans and atmosphere before joining TAMUG in 1989. On the Galveston campus

2000

Rankings in 2000 showed that facilities at TAMUG received heavier use than those of any other Texas public college. Ending a thirty-five-year tradition, *Texas Clipper* no longer carried prep cadets. Enrollment continued to grow. Women outnumbered men at TAMUG for the first time. A $2 million debt was wiped off the records.

198

he held several administrative positions, including department head of maritime administration, dean (superintendent) of the Texas Maritime College, and president of the Texas Institute of Oceanography. Evans has published internationally about the population of whales and other large marine vertebrates and about underwater bioacoustics. He retired from full-time teaching in 1999 but continued teaching part-time and advising graduate students. The rarely bestowed title *emeritus* (meaning "by meritorious service") recognizes those who have made extraordinary contributions to the university.

In February three maritime studies undergraduates—Heather Kelly, Laura Masters, and Eric Van Velzen—presented papers at the spring meeting of the East Texas Historical Association. Most campuses would find it extraordinary to have undergraduates deliver speeches at professional societies, but at TAMUG such an occurrence was not all that unusual. The papers concerned findings related to excavations at the *Denbigh*, a Civil War blockade runner submerged off Bolivar Peninsula. The students had conducted historical research and helped out in repeated dives on the site.

A TAMUG-sponsored public lecture series that spring proved highly popular. Three eminent figures talked about "Texans on the Potomac." The first two speakers, Lady Bird Johnson's press secretary Liz Carpenter and former speaker of the U.S. House of Representatives Jim Wright, drew overflow crowds at Ashton Villa. The last talk, by newspaper editorialist and humorist Molly Ivins, was moved to Levin Hall at UTMB to accommodate expected large crowds. Ivins attracted the largest audience ever for a TAMUG-sponsored lecture—more than seven hundred people. Faculty members Donald Willett and I put the series together.

In March, the TAMUG Student Senate held a "pimp-a-pal" extravaganza to raise money. Senators were auctioned off for seven to forty-four dollars each, and each high bidder got a dinner for two as well as a dinner companion.

Three years of having to borrow boats and equipment and of driving up to Clear Lake to train came to a happy end for the TAMUG Rowing Club in April. The club now owned two hand-me-down racing shells and one state-of-the-art shell. Restaurateurs Marion and Diane Duzich built the club a storage area and boat hangar underneath their Waterman's Restaurant at Galveston's West End and donated a floating dock so that the crew could row in adjacent Pirates' Cove. Club members still had to practice in the early morning hours because of their class schedules, but the nearer rowing site meant that they could remain in bed until 5:00 A.M. One of the rowers said, "Now we can stay out on the water longer instead of getting off early so we can get back to our classes on time."

In May, the *Houston Chronicle* ran a story under the headline "Texas A&M at Galveston Rated One of America's Best." In rankings published by the Texas Higher Education Coordinating Board, which oversaw all

Members of the TAMUG Rowing Club practice in front of The Waterman's Restaurant at Pirates' Cove on Galveston's West End. Left to right: Jessica Sharkey, Katie Woolven, Ryan Turner, Luke Morris, and Ashley Sutton. The club moved its home base from far away Clear Lake to this much more convenient location. Source: *Galveston Daily News,* April 7, 2000.

thirty-five Texas public colleges, TAMUG was named the most efficient in using its classrooms and laboratories. Its classrooms were occupied an average 46.6 hours every week, far exceeding the state standard of 38 hours. Its laboratories were occupied 30.2 hours, far exceeding the state standard of 25 hours. By comparison, main campus used its classrooms 38.5 hours and its laboratories 23 hours each week. TAMUG head Mike Kemp noted that the figures demonstrated not only "an exceptionally high level of efficiency" but also a critical need for additional classroom and laboratory space.

The summer marked the end of the prep program, a tradition since *Texas Clipper I* sailed on her 1965 maiden voyage. Newly graduated high school students, "preparatory" to their first fall semester in college, had enrolled in two college-credit courses on board the ship. The program had been an effective tool for recruiting new undergraduates. After learning about what upperclass maritime cadets did on training cruises, many preps decided to switch their college major to TAMUG degrees leading to a mariner's license.

But a new interpretation of U.S. Coast Guard regulations said that preps could not board the ship until after they had undergone lengthy training in safety procedures and seamanship. This requirement rendered the prep program impractical. Most prep cadets graduated from high school just the weekend before the cruise was scheduled to depart

—there was simply no time for them to spend weeks of training required by the new standards. So the program was discontinued. In some ways, however, the cancelation may have made a tough decision easier for the school. Recent growth in the Texas Maritime Academy left little room aboard *Texas Clipper II* for prep cadets. The prep program left behind a visible legacy: painted wooden plaques commemorating the ports and adventures of each summer cruise, often in humorous ways. Many of the collected plaques remain on permanent display on the ship.

That fall semester enrollment continued to increase, up almost 6 percent over the previous fall semester. It marked the first time that women outnumbered men on campus: 695 (51 percent) to 668 (49 percent). Back in 1973, the year that women were finally admitted as students, men had made up a whopping 94 percent of the total enrollment. Nationwide, women outnumbered men at many colleges. At TAMUG, the ratio had reached a comfortable equilibrium.

On November 15, an Army National Guard UH-60 Blackhawk helicopter landed in the field between Kirkham Hall and *Texas Clipper II*. It carried the adjutant general for the State of Texas, several members of the Texas National Guard, and a legislative assistant who had come to visit the Seaborne ChalleNGe Corps.

The TAMUG bonfire was canceled, as was the one in College Station, in remembrance of the deadly stack collapse of 1999. Many TAMUG students journeyed to College Station to attend the memorial service. Understandable issues of safety and legal liability threatened to put a perma-

Toward the end of each training cruise, prep (or fourth-class) cadets would design and construct a permanent display depicting events that had made their cruise memorable. As the prep program ended, so did their thirty-five-year tradition of colorful and imaginative cruise plaques.

nent end to the Aggie bonfire tradition. Reaction on the Mitchell campus was divided. Most students, angry about the cancelation, believed those who had lost their lives would have wanted the tradition to continue. Many others believed that no tradition was worth risking lives.

In December the Texas A&M Board of Regents forgave TAMUG a $2 million loan that had been used in 1992 to purchase the Offatts Bayou campus. That campus, south of Teichman Road, housed the Center for Marine Training and Safety and was used as the home of the undergraduate sailing club. Mike Kemp expressed understandable relief over the action: "What we were facing was beginning to pay that thing off at $100,000 a year for the next 20 years." Wiping out the debt was "like a $2 million gift" allowing TAMUG to "redirect these funds to develop educational and outreach programs."

2001

In 2001, the TAMUG-Geosciences merger ended. Pelican Island opened its only privately run dormitory. The school held its largest reunion of former students. An old-fashioned gazebo graced the campus. A one-act play by a former campus administrator took some of its inspiration from TAMUG.

In the spring of 2001 the last vestige of TAMUG's temporary merger with the College of Geosciences disappeared. The Department of Marine Sciences in Galveston officially separated from the Department of Oceanography in College Station. The nine-year experiment in hybrid administration came to a quiet and happy end. Now TAMUG resumed full control of its own destiny.

Dormitories took a new turn—privatization. Miguel Prida, TAMUG class of 1996, had noted the need for additional dorms when he was an undergraduate majoring in marine transportation. Now a developer, he built them. The two detached buildings were laid out parallel to each other, just across Texas Clipper Road (originally Bradner Street) from C-dorm and the tennis courts. Following the TAMUG alphabetical naming tradition, they were dubbed D-dorm and E-dorm. Architecturally, their relatively small windows were overwhelmed by the industrial-looking brick exterior. Some students said that from the outside the new dorms looked like jail cellblocks. But they were pleasant on the inside: single and double rooms with a laundry facility, study rooms, and kitchen facilities, including a microwave and refrigerator. "Gone are the days of cooking in the bathroom," said a student writer for the *Nautilus*. Outside was space to park 250 cars.

A single unit rented at $350 a month, a double at $470, all utilities paid. Residents also had satellite television and Internet access. However, the new era in housing was not as revolutionary as it sounded. Even though they were beyond the campus boundaries and privately run, the new dorms enforced all the rules that applied to on-campus housing. Whether your dorm was private or public, if you lived on Pelican Island you had to follow university rules. Still, rumor had it that D- and E-dorms were convenient sites for weekend partying.

The Office of Academic Enhancement inaugurated a program to recognize honor students. In February, they were presented an Aggie Scholar pin. The pin, in the shape of Texas, was first given out in a brief ceremony in the lobby of the Northen Student Center. A faculty and staff committee came up with the idea when someone pointed out that TAMUG had many programs for students in academic difficulty but almost nothing for students who excelled. Recipients of the pin had to maintain a grade point average of 3.5 or better for the academic year. In keeping with the spirit of Mardi Gras season, the honor students also received green, gold, and purple beads.

On the fourth weekend of April, the school held its largest student reunion ever. A committee of former students had planned activities and sent out invitations. Lots of familiar faces from the 1960s, '70s, '80s, and '90s showed up. The opening Friday night event packed at Connolly's Bar (formerly Foam Depot) on 22nd Street, where live entertainment was provided by Relix, a band led by former student John Machol (class of 1976). Saturday morning and afternoon activities were for families. Barbecue was served under a tent pitched in the quadrangle. All around were carnival-type games and a popular inflated "moonwalk" structure for young children. There were tours, visits to the ship's simulators, presentations by faculty members—the weekend had something for everyone. On Saturday night about 250 people enjoyed a dinner and dance on board Galveston's tall ship *Elissa*. The organizing committee got rave reviews for the weekend. One committee member said, "Casual and easy —that's what our former students like and come back for. We are a blue-

D-dorm and E-dorm, the first private dormitory buildings, were constructed in 2001 for TAMUG students. The two buildings lie outside campus boundaries, across the road from C-dorm and the tennis courts. Each dorm has laundry and kitchen facilities. Source: TAMUG files.

jeans-and-happy-hour bunch, not a formal-dress-and-cocktails crowd."

■ The next reunion was tentatively scheduled for spring, 2005.

Chapter 6   In June Tropical Storm Allison stalled over Houston and Galveston for five days, dumping as much as 35.7 inches of rain in Greens Bayou in Harris County. Flooding in Houston was catastrophic and deadly: underground parking garages in downtown Houston were filled with water to street level; houses in subdivisions along the southern loop of the Sam Houston Tollway (Beltway 8) were submerged up to their eaves. Pelican Island and Galveston were not as hard hit—as the old-timers say, you can't stack water on an island. But during the storm many members of the TAMUG community found themselves stranded, unable to drive to or from school; some suffered water damage to their cars, their homes, or both. The nation's death toll was at least forty-three from this storm, which took twelve days to complete its path of destruction from Texas to New England.

That same month TAMUG announced that it would create the nation's only seagrass nursery, a project coordinated by faculty member James Webb as part of a Wetlands Study Center. When completed in 2004, the center would include a self-guided nature trail around the campus, exhibits, and a pavilion.

In spring, 2001, students begin enjoying the brand new gazebo built in the shadow of eucalyptus trees between C-dorm and the swimming pool. Picnic tables and barbecue grills make the gazebo an inviting gathering spot.

The profit from the soft-drink machine contract on campus went into building a wooden gazebo between the swimming pool and C-dorm. The project was the idea of students who the previous year had voted a gazebo as number one on their wish list. Dorm residents could hear the hammering of the TAMUG maintenance workers every morning, starting at 7:00 A.M.—it was more effective and annoying, they said, than an alarm clock. But the finished gazebo was charming, designed in the Victorian style. Wooden railings, arcaded posts, and architectural gingerbread ornamented its open structure; a shingled roof peaked at the center of the octagon. Some students said it reminded them of the housing for old-fashioned carousels.

Nearby tables and barbecue grills made the gazebo a popular spot for hanging out after hours. Dormitory residents could be seen picnicking or just taking in the weather; one English instructor used it for outdoor student poetry readings. Nestled amid so many functional-looking buildings, the gazebo added a touch of whimsy to an otherwise practical campus. Not everyone, however, found it an improvement. Before it was built, rain had often turned the spot into a playing field for mud football—a spectacular sport for dorm residents. Now that the gazebo was smack in the middle of that temporary field, football mudders had to play where they were not so easily seen from dorm balconies.

All of us remember where we were and what we were doing on that pretty September 11 Tuesday morning when the world was changed by passenger planes forced by hijackers to fly into the World Trade Center in New York City and the Pentagon in Washington, D.C. Members of the TAMUG campus, like all Americans, were sick at heart. Those awful images of the collisions and then later the collapsing towers were repeatedly broadcast on TV. You could hear the collective "Oh my God" groan from those crowding around the TV in the lobby of the classroom laboratory building. Some classes were canceled; many were shortened—it was a difficult day to teach and a difficult day to learn ordinary academic things. Like most other people throughout the nation, the TAMUG community wept and prayed. American flags and red-white-and-blue bunting could be seen all over campus. We were part of a country united in pain and in resolve.

On October 4, Texas A&M celebrated its 125th anniversary. College Station had the day off. The day had originally been designated on the published academic calendar as a holiday for TAMUG students as well. But after the semester had started, teachers unhappy with losing a class day politicked successfully to reinstate classes, and it turned out to be a class day after all. Needless to say, most students and many faculty members were miffed. "If we really are Aggies," the sentiment ran, "then we need to be treated like Aggies." Students had also complained twenty-five years earlier when the Galveston campus, unlike main campus, held classes on the 100th anniversary of Texas A&M. Regardless of the official edict, sympathetic teachers canceled many classes on the 125th anniversary.

Two days later the Texas Navy, an honorary historical organization devoted to the memory of the Galveston-based navy during the Texas Revolution, held its annual barbecue on *Texas Clipper II*. Members of the organization are appointed by the Texas governor, and every one of them is called an admiral. The admirals had to seek shelter in the ship's enclosed hangar when cold October winds forced the event off the flight deck (the aviation terms are a throwback from her days as *Chauvenet*, when she used to carry helicopters). Over the years the Texas Navy has supported the campus and has nominated some of its former students and faculty to its honorary rank of admiral.

Later that month the one-act comedy *The Boating Party* was produced as a fund-raiser for Galveston's Strand Theatre. William "Bill" Merrell, former president of TAMUG, was the amateur playwright. Although he denied that the fictional Gulf Coast campus was based on TAMUG, he admitted that he had drawn inspiration from his experiences as a faculty member and administrator at A&M campuses at both College Station and Galveston. Along with serious treatment of themes like love, racism, and ecology, the play poked fun at college politics. The opening night performance was sold out. Reviews were mixed but it was all in fun.

Two years after the bonfire tragedy on main campus, the TAMUG Student Senate passed a strongly worded resolution supporting the College Station decision to suspend bonfire for at least another year. The resolu-

Graduating seniors link hands for the traditional elephant walk, held just before the last regularly scheduled Aggie football game. Their usefulness to the student body over, they wander around the campus like dying elephants, remembering good times and bad as they revisit landmarks—the dorms, quad, gym, swimming pool, tugboat propeller, library, wooden triptych, dock, and *Texas Clipper I* anchor.

tion specifically addressed widely discussed rumors that it might be okay to circumvent the suspension by building privately organized bonfires. While recognizing that bonfire would "remain a symbol of Aggie Unity and Aggie Spirit," the senate discouraged "construction of or participation in any outside activities that could endanger the lives of present or future Aggies or in any way damage Aggie Unity." TAMUG Bonfire crew members remained active by putting their energy into other causes, cleaning up the Offatts Bayou campus at Teichman Road and helping the Krewe of Thalasar stage their Mardi Gras ball and parade.

In December, the Houston Endowment awarded a $250,000 grant to help TAMUG pay for upgrading its ship simulator, used in training cadets. The simulator's computerized images and motions duplicate the control room on a ship when entering or leaving port. The 180-degree view of the old simulator was broadened to 210 degrees, and some elements could be expanded to a full 360 degrees. It was so realistic in creating the effects of weather and sea conditions during a demonstration that some onlookers reported feeling seasick, even though the simulator never moved from its fixed location inside a building. "The simulator is state of the art now," said academy superintendent Lukens, "and we intend to keep it that way."

That same month, the ship *Caribbean Mercy* arrived at Pier 21 in Galveston. The vessel is one of a three-ship fleet of mercy ships providing free medical care worldwide to those who need it most. Captaining it was Jonathan Fadely, master of the ship since 1994, a former student of TAMUG and married to a former prep cadet.

In January marine biologist Sammy Ray was inducted into the Texas Science Hall of Fame along with ten others, including three Nobel laureates. Ray, now a professor emeritus, was still working as the associate director of continuing education at TAMUG. One month away from his eighty-third birthday, Ray said his greatest passion in life had been his work. The award acknowledged his internationally renowned work in oyster research.

In February, the Association of Former MASE students was born. It had grown out of discussions the previous year about the benefits of interaction between current students and former students. Maritime systems engineering students and faculty are a tight-knit group; they had kept in touch informally. Now they adopted a constitution to formalize the arrangement. The following spring the association would present its first scholarship to a current MASE student, Kerri Ludwig.

Increased numbers of TAMUG students participated in that year's Big Event, showcasing Aggie volunteerism. They filled trash bags with litter strewn along Seawolf Parkway, painted a building at Galveston's Scholes air field, spruced up the city recycling center, landscaped City Hall, washed trucks for the fire department, cleaned pet cages at the animal shelter, and cleaned up Seawolf Park.

2002

The TAMUG Sail Club made national headlines with a heroic rescue. Enrollment broke the fifteen hundred mark for the first time. TAMUG added two new degrees: the undergraduate program in ocean and coastal resources and its first independent graduate degree—marine resources management. The school marked forty years of existence.

On February 23, 2002, a TAMUG practice regatta turned into a dramatic rescue of all five passengers in a submerged minivan. The Aggie rescuers were (front) Robin Reger; (middle row) Brence Bedwell, Danna Svejkosky, Julie Svaton, Joseph Richardson, and Jake Scott; (back row) Jenipher Cate, John Gross, Jeffrey Daigle, Chris Noll, and faculty coach Gerard Coleman. Scott and Gross were students at College Station; the rest were at Galveston. Rescuers not pictured were TAMUG students Kevin Gunn, James Loynes, and Bill Self; former TAMUG students Luckey Reed (class of 2001), Shannon Galway (2000), and Laura Stover (2000); University of Texas at Austin student Spencer Ogden; and Scott Marsden of Houston. Source: *Galveston Daily News,* March 22, 2002.

For evening entertainment, twenty-first-century Sea Aggies would go on Thursday nights to Diggy's bar or Market Street Tavern; the long-standing popular hangout at Vibes had finally shut down. The I-Hop restaurant on the seawall was hands-down the most popular off-campus destination to cram for exams. "It's where everyone goes to pull all-nighters," said a student. "It's open 24 hours, and you can get a bottom-less cup of coffee for $2.95."

A routine simulated regatta turned into a brave rescue by members of the Sail Club. On Saturday, February 23, faculty sponsor Gerard Coleman had arranged a noncollegiate sailing regatta at Offatts Bayou to give team members practice. The six-person teams included students from TAMUG, TAMU, and the University of Texas and some former students. Just as they were ready to start, a minivan came from nowhere, sped up, left the road, catapulted eighteen feet out, and sank in about twelve feet of muddy bay water. Their regatta forgotten, the sailors quickly made their way to the crash site. Only one man surfaced from the vehicle. When questioned in Spanish, he said he was the driver and that five other people—women and children—were still underwater. The sailors went into action. One marked the site by standing in chest-deep water on the roof of the van. The sixty-degree water was murky; it was impossible to see anything clearly. The sailors dragged rocks from the shoreline to smash the van's windows (many of the rescuers suffered cuts) and began pulling out unconscious passengers one by one. Those on the shore administered CPR to the victims until an emergency medical team arrived. The last passenger was a seven-month-old girl, still stuck underwater in her baby seat. Luckey Reed, a former TAMUG student, spent

one and a half minutes under the surface until he finally freed her. The
baby, blue and without a pulse, was hooked up to a life-support system and driven to the hospital, where she was thought dead on arrival.
Miraculously, after one of the paramedics kissed her, the baby began
breathing. The driver was arrested and taken in for psychiatric evalua-
tion. Every one of the van's occupants, even the baby, was later released
from the hospital.

According to TAMUG sailing team captain and Coast Guard reservist
Jeff Daigle, members of the three rival schools forgot their differences
as they worked together for a higher cause. "Everyone just pitched in.
We all found something to do and did it. No one sat down and said, 'Ok,
you do this and you do that,' everyone just jumped in and the teamwork
of everyone involved amazes me," said Daigle. Fire Department Safety
Officer Captain Jeff Smith summed it up, "These people are alive because
of the reaction of these students. We've been involved in several rescues
and in a rescue such as this, it is not uncommon to lose one of our rescue workers due to the water temperature, depth, and the murky condition of the water. It's very easy to get disoriented down there. I feel that
if it had been any other group of college students, these people would not
be alive today. These are sailors and mariners and they spend their lives
in and around the water. The Aggie leadership I've heard talked about
was very true today."

On March 21, the Texas A&M University System Board of Regents
presented the rescuers with a proclamation recognizing their efforts.
"Sometimes remarkable events occur in our midst," said Erle Nye, chairman of the Board of Regents. "Today, we're honoring these students for
their heroic actions during trying circumstances. We are amazed at the
courage they showed without regard to their own welfare." The incident
received regional and national television coverage and was the subject of
a seven-page story on everyday heroes in the September, 2002, issue
of *Reader's Digest*. The back cover of the magazine featured a full-page
photo of three of the TAMUG rescuers: student Joseph Richardson, faculty coach Gerard Coleman, and former student Luckey Reed.

TAMUG received approval that month to build a $14.8 million engi-
neering building. At more than thirty-five thousand square feet, it would
dwarf every other structure on the Mitchell campus. Under the headline "TAMUG Celebrates 40 with New Building," the *Galveston Daily
News* described how necessary the new construction was. "For the past
10 years, TAMUG has held the dubious distinction of having the highest
classroom usage in the state," said CEO Mike Kemp. "We have not added
more classrooms since the '70s, when enrollment was under 500. A high
percentage of our classrooms are typically in continuous use from 8 A.M.
until midnight." The three-story building was designed to wrap around
two sides of the existing engineering laboratory building. Groundbreaking took place in 2003, and the building was scheduled for completion
in the spring of 2005.

In April the TAMUG sailing team got back to the more mundane business of competing in regattas. They hosted their district competition and took first place among the coastal states from western Florida to Texas and adjacent interior states north to Nebraska. TAMUG won out over teams from College Station, Tulane University, UT-Austin, the University of Southern Alabama, Baylor, and the Universities of North Texas, New Orleans, and West Florida. Their victory qualified them to travel to Hawaii in June for the Intercollegiate North American Championship.

Back on campus the staff basketball team in red shirts outscored the faculty team dressed in blue. The game, which looked like the beginning of a traditional annual matchup, featured play-by-play and color announcers, cheerleaders, inexperienced and experienced players—altogether, it was a great deal of fun.

The university saw a fine example that spring of how one person can make a difference by speaking up for what is right. Because of her commitment to the environment, a TAMUG student got to write the text for a newspaper advertisement for the local restaurant Brothers Petronella. Sarah Hayes, a junior in the ocean and coastal resources program, told her boss that he should not be serving Chilean sea bass because this fish, in danger of becoming commercially extinct, was mostly being caught illegally. Frankie Petronella, her boss, agreed. He paid for the ad. "We can all make a difference, as Frankie has become aware," wrote Hayes in the ad, which appeared in the *Galveston Daily News*.

Two new structures were added to TAMUG that spring. Bennison Place, a hipped-roof beach cottage on stilts, was built on the Offatts Bayou campus. The cottage became a convenient staging facility for the sailing club, marine science students, and faculty. Its construction was made possible in part by an extraordinarily generous donation from an

A member of the TAMUG Sail Club leaves the dock next to Bennison Place on the Offatts Bayou campus. The cottage, financed through a twenty-five-thousand-dollar student donation, is a homey and comfortable place to meet, eat, and set up sailing regattas. Source: *Voyager*, 2001–2002.

undergraduate student, Jane Sherrod (Bennison is her maiden name and her daughter's first name). The Student Senate authorized the first twenty thousand dollars—revenue from soft drink vending machines on campus—for the building; Sherrod put up the remaining twenty-five thousand. "Sailing is for all kinds of people and they need a place to be able to meet and have support, as does the crew team," said Sherrod. The cottage satisfied one other important need—"it has bathrooms."

The other structure was a three-story clock tower, donated by Elizabeth and Searcy Bracewell, back on Mitchell campus. Searcy Bracewell, A&M class of 1938, was a longtime member of the Board of Visitors. The clock tower, completed just before the end of the spring semester, could be programmed to chime or play songs on the hour and half hour. Not surprisingly its first two musical selections were "We Are the Aggies" and the Aggie War Hymn. A campuswide poll taken the previous year had shown that more than 80 percent of students surveyed were in favor of putting the clock tower in the middle of the quad and moving the *Texas Clipper I* anchor to a new spot next to the library entrance. The move was made.

The tower quickly became a meeting place for students. Before construction was completed, its doorframe remained open; romantically inclined students could go inside. Afterward, doors were bolted on and locked. Students joked that the clock kept Aggie time because none of its four sides agreed with any other. The anchor, which had occupied that spot since 1995, retained its evolving traditional significance in its new location: any student could rub the anchor for good luck, but only seniors were allowed to walk underneath the inverted V made by the anchor and its welded chain.

Two new degree programs made headlines that year. In May the first

The memorial anchor from *Texas Clipper I* formerly occupied the central spot in the quad, where the Bracewell clock tower stands. Now the anchor graces the exterior of the Williams library, to the left of its entrance. TAMUG tradition permits only seniors to walk underneath the passageway made by the chain and anchor. But anyone may touch or rub the anchor for good luck, especially in an upcoming exam. TAMUG files.

six students to receive a bachelor of science degree in ocean and coastal resources (OCRE) walked across the stage of the 1894 Grand Opera House: Christina Alegria, Brian Bader, Jana Hartline, Alicia Rea, Samantha Tompkins, and Nancy Voss. Jerry Gaston, deputy chancellor of the Texas A&M University System, gave the commencement address. One of the poignant moments in the ceremony occurred as the Arthur B. Hansen Rescue Medal was awarded to the Sail Club.

In August, Stephanie Marsh became the first graduate student ever to receive a master's degree from TAMUG. She walked across the stage in the Pelican Island campus auditorium to receive her master's cowl and degree in the new program of marine resources management (MARM). "Our faculty have been working with graduate students for over 30 years, but this is the first time a TAMUG graduate program is based solely in Galveston," said TAMUG Vice President and CEO Michael Kemp. He was referring to the long-standing M.S. degree in wildlife and fisheries sciences, which could be earned by study in Galveston but which was granted by College Station; the newer graduate degree was a 100 percent Galveston product. "This is another signal regarding the continued academic maturation of TAMUG and is a tribute to the faculty and staff whose efforts have made the degree possible," he said. The Department of Marine Sciences created MARM as a nonthesis master's degree for graduate students with strong science backgrounds who want to learn about managing coastal and ocean resources.

The upcoming fortieth anniversary of TAMUG helped raise awareness of the school's educational impact. According to the registrar's office at College Station, TAMUG (under various names) had awarded 3,682 undergraduate degrees from September, 1962, to August, 2002. Current students were paying about $4,400 a semester ($7,700 for out-of-state students) for tuition, fees, and room and board. This meant that a student could expect to pay from $35,200 to $61,600 for all four years. Training cruises cost cadets about $3,200 each summer. Considering the going rate, it was a pretty good deal, even for out-of-state students. Back when the Texas Maritime Academy had opened in 1962, the bill for all four years plus three training cruises had come to $6,720 (adjusted for inflation, that would be about $40,000 in 2002 dollars).

During the summer training cruise, the quarterdeck of *Texas Clipper II* began to be outfitted as a nautical museum with its first artifacts: the wooden binnacle and large wooden steering wheel from *Texas Clipper I*. A photographic exhibit of the history of that first training ship was also mounted. Cadets stripped paint from the grand piano, a relic from the nuclear merchant vessel *Savannah*. The piano graced the forward promenade lounge of *Texas Clipper I* from the 1960s until May of 2002, when it was transferred to her successor *Texas Clipper II*. James Michener had sung songs from *South Pacific*, the musical based on his book of the same name, with an impromptu group gathered around that piano during the 1984 cruise.

The maneuver of moving the piano was a tricky one. Crew members boarded the older ship, unbolted the piano from the deck, then removed the legs and turned the instrument on its side. Since they had no dollies they had to improvise by rolling the piano over wooden rods made from numerous pieces of broom handles. A supply boat crane removed it from the ship and ferried it to a waiting trailer onshore. The crew members drove the piano to Mitchell campus, where a ship's crane hoisted it onboard.

That summer the *Clipper* detoured north on its way to Norway so that cadets could be initiated as bluenoses. She passed between the Shetland and Orkney islands on her way to cross the Arctic Circle at Greenwich. To get them into the right frame of mind, cadets were served blue eggs for breakfast, and then they shivered their way through an icy ceremony. Afterward they painted the bow of the ship blue to celebrate their new identity as bluenoses.

The weekend before classes started, the Sea Aggies Learning Traditions camp was larger than ever. Back in 1994, its first year, SALT camp had been small enough for all participants to fit comfortably into a single bus. Now they were jammed into five buses. The camp continued to be run entirely by upperclassmen, who paid to be part of this continuing event to ensure that Galveston students would remain a cultural part of Aggieland. Does it work? The answer may lie in a survey of how many students attend Aggie football games at main campus. About 33 percent of all TAMUG students buy season tickets and make the two-and-a-half-hour drive to College Station for home games. Just 18 percent of College Station students buy season tickets—and they have only to travel across town.

Fall semester opened up with a record enrollment of 1,556 and a new building that expanded the campus to the east, past the small boat basin. The student body continued to be almost evenly split between men and women: for the past two years women had held a slim majority of 51 percent; now men were back in the lead with 52 percent of total enrollment.

TAMUG had executed a lease-purchase agreement to acquire the building and property owned by Edison Chouest Offshore (formerly owned by Western Geophysical). The building was renamed Sea Aggie Center. The bookstore, faculty offices, research management, educational outreach, and some classrooms moved there. Money needed to refurbish its interior completely was unavailable. One way to cut costs was to avoid installing individual ductwork for cooling and heating each room. Instead walls were left open at the top and there were no drop-down ceilings. That way the air could circulate freely throughout the building.

But so could noise. Students and faculty members found the building's acoustics troublesome. It was difficult to distinguish what a teacher said from what was in progress on the other side of those interior walls, especially when a loud air-conditioning unit cycled on. It was a lot like

In the fall of 2002, the campus expanded its acreage and classroom space significantly with the addition of the Sea Aggie Center.

an open-concept arena with large office cubicles. TAMUG maintenance workers adjusted the cooling units so that they did not engage during class hours. Still the background sounds of an opening truck bay door, a neighboring lecturer, or even a telephone conversation from a nearby office disrupted quiet classrooms. About the best that could be said was that "it's not as bad as it was at the start of the semester." There were plans to fix the noise problem when more money became available. By the fall of 2003, classroom walls would finally be extended all the way to the ceiling.

After thirteen years of representation by a student senate, led by a president, TAMUG undergraduates reorganized under a student government association (SGA). It was the third kind of body in this sphere. The Student Advisory Committee (SAC), led by a chairman, had represented undergraduates from 1973 to 1989. The Student Senate, led by a president, took over from 1989 to 2002. In 1996–97 TAMUG had briefly tried the student government association model, as noted, but after a promising beginning the model had been abandoned because of confusion over purpose and concern over inadequate student participation. However, in 2002 the SGA model was firmly established. SGA, like the federal government, is divided into executive, legislative, and judicial branches. For the first time, TAMUG now formally established the office of student body president; previous student leaders had used that title unofficially. Shepherd "Sales" Shelton was the first student elected to that office.

Tropical Storm Fay blew into town on Friday, September 6, bringing with it above-average high tides and plenty of rain. Although the Galveston Independent School District had canceled classes that Friday, TAMUG did not close or order evacuation. However, as street flooding worsened, making it difficult to get to or from the Mitchell campus, the school canceled afternoon classes. As Tropical Storm Frances had done in 1998, this storm carried away beach sand, especially from the West End of Galveston. Fortunately the small boat basin on campus had been

On September 11, 2002, at a memorial ceremony beside the Bracewell clock tower, the Mitchell campus pays tribute to the victims of 9/11. Most of those in attendance wore red, white, and blue. Following the remarks about the significance of the day a lone bugler played taps, and the crowd remained at attention for a moment of silence.

so well reconstructed after Frances that it stood up well to pounding from Fay.

To mark the anniversary of the terrorist plane bombings of 9/11, TAMUG held a memorial ceremony by the clock tower. A crowd began to gather just before 9:00 A.M., the time when the first commercial jet was forced into the World Trade Center. TAMUG Vice President and CEO Mike Kemp spoke to those assembled about the significance of the day: "For you students who are here, I would like to remind you that each generation seems to have a single defining moment that marks its lifetime. For your grandparents, it was probably Pearl Harbor. For your fathers and mothers, perhaps the death of President John Kennedy. For you, most assuredly, it will be 9/11." Kemp concluded: "We can best honor the memory of that tragedy, and its victims, by resolving to keep our nation and its freedoms strong against any adversary. In that way, no force, regardless of how evil or treacherous, will ever win against us."

That commemoration, coming less than a week before the fortieth anniversary of the school, rightly got most of the attention. A quiet ceremony, sponsored by the residence advisors association in the lobby of the Northen Student Center, recognized the passage of four decades of Galveston's A&M undergraduate program. On September 17, 1962, the first twenty-three cadets of the Texas Maritime Academy had begun attending classes. The celebration included brief remarks on the history of the institution, followed by the cutting of a sheet cake on which was written in icing: "Happy 40th Anniversary!"

Hurricane Lilli, a deadly category 4 storm with sustained winds of 145 miles per hour, scared residents along the Texas-Louisiana coast at the start of October. This time the Galveston Independent School District held classes as scheduled, but Texas A&M University at Galveston canceled classes from Wednesday, October 2, through Monday morning and ordered an evacuation of the campus. A campus van driven by a resident advisor took fifteen dorm residents to the College Station campus, where arrangements had been made for them to stay. Some had already planned the trip anyway to see the Aggies play Texas Tech; to help make their evacuation sweeter, the TAMUG administration made sure every one of those fifteen had football tickets.

Happily, by the time the storm came ashore at midmorning of Thursday, October 3, near New Iberia, Louisiana, it had weakened to a category 2 hurricane with winds of 100 miles per hour. The Galveston area was hot and sunny, a bit breezier than normal; only someone who was paying close attention to weather news would have known that there was a storm to the east of Texas. Students were allowed to return to their dorms on Friday afternoon. However, many preferred to stay on the main campus to take part in festivities surrounding Saturday's classic football game dominated by offense: the Aggies were outscored 48–47.

On October 10, a record-breaking seventy-four fish (freshmen) cadets were sworn into the maritime corps of cadets. Standing at attention in company formation on the dock next to *Texas Clipper II,* they recited in unison the words of the cadet oath. Then their names were called alphabetically: Fish Adams, Fish Benson, Fish Carlson, and so on. One by one they marched up to man the rails, joining upperclassmen already there. When the ceremony concluded, every space along the upperdeck rails on the ship's starboard side, facing the campus, was filled. They had taken their place symbolically in the corps. The sheer size of this freshman class was impressive. It had taken the Texas Maritime Academy all of its first four years, from 1962 to 1965, to reach a total four-class enrollment larger than the single freshman class of 2005.

TAMUG Student Services now began employing the medium of email to describe some old Aggie traditions. The first in the series of electronic communications to all students and faculty members described the origins and practices of "Midnight Yell." At Galveston on the Thursday night before home football games at Kyle Field in College Station, students followed Galveston Yell Leaders into the gymnasium to chant the old army yells, sing the Aggie War Hymn, and listen to "fables" of how A&M was going to "beat the hell" out of its opponent. When lights were turned off, those present kissed their dates or "flicked their Bics" (lit their cigarette lighters)—whichever was appropriate. Then the fish ran after Yell Leaders, caught them, and threw them into the swimming pool. Afterward Yell Leaders led the crowd in more yells. Interestingly for Galveston, the modern version of Midnight Yell at main campus began in 1931 on the steps of the YMCA building, where in 1962 the superintendent would open up the first administrative office of the new Texas Maritime Academy.

On November 1, at 4:30 P.M., the campus formally dedicated the Elizabeth and Searcy Bracewell clock tower. Searcy Bracewell, A&M class of 1938, had served as a Texas state senator and state representative. The ceremony had been postponed repeatedly due to inclement weather (it was not the only event to be affected by weather—Galveston was more than twenty inches ahead of its annual average rainfall for the year). At the ceremony and at the reception following, the TAMUG community got the chance to thank the Bracewells for their gift. So great was Searcy Bracewell's love for the school that one of his last public appearances, a week before he died, would be to participate in the TAMUG commencement in May, 2003.

Also in November the TAMUG community was recognized for giving a gift of its own. UTMB gave TAMUG an award for the highest percentage participation of local area colleges and universities in the November blood drive.

The year ended with a special commencement in the 1894 Grand Opera House. In recognition of the fortieth anniversary, TAMUG for the first time invited one of its former students as the main speaker. Rear Admiral William Pickavance, class of 1968, had retired after thirty-two years with the U.S. Navy, including as director of operations for the Pacific

Command. He had gone on to manage the Florida operations of the U.S. Space Alliance at the Kennedy Space Center. Pickavance, a member of the TAMUG Board of Visitors and recently inducted into "Legends of Aggieland," told students they would find, as he had, that their undergraduate institution had given them the tools they needed to succeed. The Reverend Lawrence Carter gave the invocation and benediction. Carter had been a cook during the first cruise of *Texas Clipper I* in 1965 and had retired after more than thirty years with the food services department of TAMUG. In his poignant benediction, he urged graduates to remember gratefully all those—including faculty and staff—who had made their education possible.

The class of 2002 took its place alongside all others in the history of TAMUG. The school for which the impetus in 1958 had been little more than a promising reply to a casual question, the school that in 1962 opened the doors of its College Station YMCA office to twenty-three students, that expanded in 1973 to include marine sciences, was almost shut down in 1986, and then in the 1990s gained national academic prominence—well, what a remarkable, unexpected, and wild ride its first forty years had been. Who could have predicted it? And who in 2002 could imagine where the next forty years would take the school?

Ground was broken for the new two-story engineering building on October 17, 2003. The L-shaped building wraps around the north and west sides of the old engineering lab building (barely visible jutting out to the left). At fifty-eight thousand square feet, including the renovated interior of the older building, the new one will be by far the largest structure on campus. Its signature design element is a fifty-foot-tall tower, housing a crane. The $15 million building was expected to be ready for use in the spring of 2005. TAMUG files.

The start of the twenty-first century saw TAMUG self-assured, academically respected, and growing. Construction on campus gave evidence of this firm foundation. A student-designed outdoor adjunct to the cafeteria was finished in spring, 2004. The outdoor wetlands center opened in 2004. The mammoth engineering building was to be completed in 2005. A new science building was in the planning. Faculty members had established TAMUG as a center for groundbreaking research. Undergraduate enrollment, at a record high of more than sixteen hundred, continued its upward trend. Students boast that there is no grade inflation on their campus. If it is true that the worth of a degree is backed by the current reputation of the educational institution, then the students have cast their lot wisely with TAMUG.

TAMUG is of, for, and by the sea. It educates men and women about the science, engineering, business, and humanities involving the ocean. It measures time by the names of tropical storms and hurricanes. A thin bascule bridge links its campuses on two fragile barrier islands. It is connected to the larger world by a small fleet of sea-going vessels that train merchant mariners, collect marine specimens, and extend its reputation globally. Like an ocean wave, it has had its share of falls and rises. Its energy has swelled into amazingly beautiful and complex forms. The wind of history playing on its surface has filled the air with a fine spray—the tang of salt, the spume of water, and the savor of life.

Appendix

Institutional Name Changes
1962	Texas Maritime Academy
1971	College of Marine Sciences and Maritime Resources
1972	Moody College of Marine Sciences and Maritime Resources
1977	Moody College
1979	Texas A&M University at Galveston

Chief Executive Officers of the Galveston Campus of Texas A&M
1962–67	Bennett Dodson, Superintendent
1967–71	J. D. Craik, Superintendent
1971–86	William H. Clayton, Dean, 1971–74; Provost, 1974–79; President, 1979–86
1987	Sammy Ray, Interim President
1987–92	William Merrell, President
1992–96	David Schmidly, Campus Dean, 1992–93; Chief Executive Officer and Campus Dean, 1993–96
1996–97	Viola Florez, Interim Vice President
1997–2004	W. Michael Kemp, Vice President and Chief Executive Officer
2004–2005	William Hearn, Interim Vice President and Chief Executive Officer

Chair, Board of Visitors
1962–67	Sherman B. Wetmore
1968–70	Charles H. Glenwright
1970–77	Emmett O. Kirkham
1977–78	Melvin Maltz
1979–81	Joe H. Moore
1981–83	Marilyn Schwartz
1983–89	John W. Caple
1989–91	Searcy Bracewell
1991–93	John P. Baxter
1993–97	Bernard A. Milstein
1997–99	Thomas W. Powell
1999–2002	Jerry E. Finger
2002–pres.	Michael E. Cokinos

Student Body Leaders
Student Advisory Committee Chair
1974–75	James Dodson
1975–76	Bert Scott
1976–77	Bradley L. Jetton
1977–78	Allen Zschiesche
1978–79	Allen Zschiesche
1979–80	Mark Sanders
1980–81	Karl Haupt
1981–82	Laurie Guthrie
1982–83	Peter Ravella
1983–84	Skeeter J. Braun
1984–85	Vel Lena Steed
1985–86	Ed O'Donnell
1986–87	David Dale
1987–88	Patrick Fallon
1988–89	Walter Littlejohn III

Student Senate President
1989–90	Walter Littlejohn III
1990–91	Chris Perrocco
1991–92	Ashanti Suné Johnson
1992–93	Ashanti Suné Johnson
1993–94	Paul Hille
1994–95	David Houston Jr.
1995–96	Steve Wilson
1996–87	John Michael
1997–98	John Michael
1998–99	Alex Strogen
1999–2000	Alicia Foyt
2000–01	Chris Little
2001–02	Eric Van Velzen

Student Government Association President
2002–03	Shepherd "Sales" Shelton
2003–04	Matthew Johnson
2004–05	Catherine Gorga

Commander, Maritime Corps of Cadets
1963–64	Jack H. Smith
1964–65	Danny Miller
1965–66	William Radican
1966–67	Jim Marcontell/William Pickavance
1967–68	William Pickavance
1968–69	Kenny McWilliams
1969–70	Michael Clyde Bandy
1970–71	Charles Russell
1971–72	James F. Moore
1972–73	C. E. Larsen

1973–74	William Paul Ricker
1974–75	Scott Wesley Craig
1975–76	James Ellis Heap
1976–77	Mark Pittman
1977–78	Joe McCormack
1978–79	Joseph G. Stephens
1979–80	Mark Grinstead
1980–81	Mike Godinich/Jim Brown
1981–82	Frank Lee
1982–83	Will Heidel
1983–84	Jane Bedessem/Hugh Flinn
1984–85	Frank K. Kemery
1985–86	Joseph S. Snook/Trent Thornton
1986–87	William R. Walwork/Bruce Pflieger
1987–88	Richard R. Ritter
1988–89	Matthew W. Hahne
1989–90	Amy K. LaCost
1990–91	Steven Moneymaker
1991–92	Kristine M. Groth
1992–93	Todd A. Bridgeman
1993–94	Christos Sotirelis
1994–95	M. Scott Platz
1995–96	Daniel K. Polk
1996–97	Brent J. Allison
1997–98	John Davis/Amy Wagner
1998–99	Abel L. Strickland
1999–2000	Aaron Leatherwood
2000–01	Marie Hancock/Bianca K. Cowan
2001–02	Andria E. Steger
2002–03	Matthew H. Glass
2003–04	Jonathan P. Willett
2004–05	Jack Curtis

Most Effective Teacher Award (by student vote)

1974	Francis Tormollan
1975	Carol Congleton
1976	Robert Mearn
1977	Robert Graves
1978	Charles Mickey
1979	William McMullen
1980	Joseph Dawson
1981	Ralph Davis
1982	Robert Freehill
1983	William Ruefle
1984	Peter Vanderwerf
1985	Michael McConachie
1986	Donald Willett
1987	Ching-Yun Suen
1988	Stephen Curley
1989	Arthur Blackwelder
1990	Andre Landry
1991	James Kanz
1992	Tom Illiffe
1993	Robert Cooper

1994	Graham Worthy
1995	Bernd Würsig
1996	Jaime Bourgeois and Sara Gragg
1997	Deborah Maceo
1998	James Perrigo
1999	Susan Knock
2000	Jon Stern
2001	Ching-Yun Suen
2002	Donald Willett

William Paul Ricker Distinguished Faculty/Staff Award

1986	William Hearn
1987	Stephen Curley and William Seitz
1988	Ernest Estes
1989	Sammy Ray
1990	Su-Zan Harper
1991	Donald Harper
1992	Andre Landry
1993	Willie Crayton

Divided into separate awards for faculty and staff

1994	Melanie Cravey and Rita Talley
1995	Donald Willett and Elizabeth Ward
1996	Ching-Yun Suen and Josephine Mejia
1997	Richard Lukens and Pat Erwin
1998	Gary Gill and William Gomez
1999	Fred Schlemmer and Donna Lang
2000	Wyndylyn vonZharen and Cathy Palmer
2001	James McCloy and Terry Lovell
2002	William Wardle and Jose Portillo
2003	Thomas Schmalz and Grant Shallenberger
2004	Victoria Jones and Lupe Aaron

Edwin Eikel Outstanding Student Award

1978	Wayne R. Stolz
1979	Charmaine Walter
1980	Robert Hayes
1981	Michael Godinich
1982	Frank Lee
1983	Jonathan Fadley
1984	Deborah Robinson
1985	Frank Kemery
1986	Keith Palmer
1987	Weston Griffiths
1988	Andrew Grose
1989	Matthew Hahne
1990	John E. Cook
1991	Amy Baylor
1992	George Englemann-Rogers
1993	Ashanti Suné Johnson
1994	Heather Madsen
1995	Buck Defee
1996	David Houston

1997	Todd Wolf
1998	John Michael
1999	Alex Strogen
2000	Robert Paterno
2001	Nicole Cass
2002	Kristin Hiltunin
2003	Angela Lefler
2004	Emily Douce

Training Cruises of Texas Maritime Cadets

1963. *Empire State IV* at Fort Schulyer, New York, to Dublin, Ireland; Bremen, Germany; Antwerp, Belgium; Naples, Italy; Palma, Majorca (1st training cruise for Texas Maritime cadets; 1st voyage with New York Maritime; see 1995)

1964. *State of Maine,* Castine, Maine, to Cartagena, Colombia; Curaçao; San Juan, Puerto Rico; St. Thomas, U.S. Virgin Islands; Bridgetown, Barbados (only voyage with Maine Maritime; only spring cruise, February through April)

1965. *Texas Clipper* to Halifax, Nova Scotia; Southampton, England; Copenhagen, Denmark; Edinburgh, Scotland; Hamilton, Bermuda (maiden voyage of *Texas Clipper,* used for all cruises 1965– 94; start of prep program)

1966. Dublin, Ireland; Bordeaux, France; Malaga, Spain; Las Palmas, Canary Islands; Nassau, Bahamas

1967. Port of Spain, Trinidad; Rio de Janeiro and Recife, Brazil; Willemstad, Curaçao (shellback cruise, crossing the equator)

1968. New York, New York; Oslo, Norway; Amsterdam, Netherlands; Lisbon, Portugal; Gibraltar; Canary Islands, San Juan, Puerto Rico; Corpus Christi, Texas

1969. Las Palmas, Canary Islands; Barcelona, Spain; Piraeus, Greece; Naples, Italy; Funchal, Madeira Islands; New Orleans, Louisiana; Port Arthur, Texas

1970. Cobh, Ireland; Le Havre, France; Hamburg, Germany; Aalborg, Denmark; Plymouth, England; Ponce, Puerto Rico; Brownsville and Port Lavaca, Texas

1971. Cadiz, Spain; Copenhagen, Denmark; Rotterdam, Netherlands; Las Palmas, Canary Islands; Cork, Ireland; St. Thomas, U.S. Virgin Islands; Mayport, Florida

1972. Valencia, Spain; Split, Yugoslavia; Palma, Majorca; Las Palmas, Canary Islands; New Orleans, Louisiana; Freeport, Texas

1973. Tenerife, Canary Islands; Barcelona, Spain; Naples, Italy; Funchal, Madeira Islands; St. Thomas, U.S. Virgin Islands

1974. San Juan, Puerto Rico; Sint Maarten, Netherlands Antilles; Willemstad, Curaçao; Cartagena, Colombia; Guantanamo Bay, Cuba; Vera Cruz, Mexico

1975. Mayport, Florida; Santo Domingo, Dominican Republic; Caracas, Venezuela; Saint Nicolaas, Aruba; Ponce, Puerto Rico; Miami, Florida

1976. Boston, Massachusetts; Halifax, Nova Scotia; Alexandria, Virginia; New York, New York; Charleston, South Carolina; New Orleans, Louisiana (Bicentennial cruise)

1977. Ponta Delgada, Azores; Amsterdam, Netherlands; Cork, Ireland; St. Thomas, U.S. Virgin Islands; New Orleans, Louisiana

1978. Dry Tortugas; Norfolk, Virginia; Fort-de-France, Martinique; Balboa and Cristobal, Panama Canal Zone; Callao, Peru; Vera Cruz, Mexico (shellback cruise)

1979. Dry Tortugas; St. Georges, Bermuda; Bridgetown, Barbados; Oranjestad, Aruba; Vera Cruz, Mexico; New Orleans, Louisiana

1980. Jacksonville, Florida; Halifax, Nova Scotia; Puerta Plata, Dominican Republic; Cozumel, Mexico; New Orleans, Louisiana; Freeport, Texas

1981. New Orleans, Louisiana; Mayport, Florida; Amsterdam, Netherlands; Southampton, England; Nassau, Bahamas; Lake Charles, Louisiana

1982. New Orleans, Louisiana; Mayport, Florida; Roosevelt Roads, Puerto Rico; Oranjestad, Aruba; Kingston, Jamaica; Vera Cruz, Mexico; Port Arthur, Texas

1983. New Orleans, Louisiana; Norfolk, Virginia; Boston, Massachusetts; Sint Maarten, Netherlands Antilles; La Guaira, Venezuela; Vera Cruz, Mexico; Houston, Texas

1984. New Orleans, Louisiana; Cork, Ireland; Edinburgh, Scotland; Lisbon, Portugal; Funchal,

Madeira Islands; Vera Cruz, Mexico; Beaumont, Texas

1985. St. Georges, Bermuda; Las Palmas, Canary Islands; Naples, Italy; Cadiz, Spain; Ponta Delgada, Azores; Freeport, Texas

1986. Puerto Plata, Dominican Republic; Aalborg and Copenhagen, Denmark; Helsinki, Finland; St. Petersburg, Russia; Ponta Delgada, Azores

1987. Freeport, Texas; Grand Bahamas; St. George's, Grenada; Rio de Janeiro, Brazil; Port of Spain, Trinidad; St. Thomas, U.S. Virgin Islands (with 83 cadets from Massachusetts Maritime)

1988. Baltimore, Maryland; Montreal, Canada; Reykjavik, Iceland; St. Georges, Bermuda; Dry Tortugas (blue nose cruise, crossing the Arctic Circle)

1989. Port Arthur, Texas; Port Canaveral, Florida; Lisbon, Portugal; Palma, Mallorca; Tenerife, Canary Islands

1990. Corpus Christi, Texas; Funchal, Madeira Islands; Stavanger, Norway; Rotterdam, Netherlands; Tampa, Florida

1991. Puerto Plata, Dominican Republic; San Juan, Puerto Rico; Willemstad, Curaçao; Fort-de-France, Martinique; Cristobal, Panama; Belize City, Belize; Vera Cruz, Mexico

1992. Barcelona, Spain; Genoa, Italy; Piraeus, Greece; Ponta Delgada, Azores; Miami, Florida

1993. Las Palmas, Canary Islands; Cork, Ireland; Gdynia, Poland; St John's, Newfoundland; Baltimore, Maryland

1994. Montevideo, Uruguay; Pointe-à-Pitre, Guadeloupe; San Juan, Puerto Rico; Vera Cruz, Mexico (shellback cruise; last voyage of *Texas Clipper I*)

1995. *Empire State VI* at Fort Schulyer, New York, to Albany, New York; Norfolk, Virginia; Toulon, France; Naples, Italy; Vera Cruz, Mexico (2nd voyage with New York Maritime: see 1963)

1996. Maiden voyage of *Texas Clipper II* to Vera Cruz, Mexico; Ponce and San Juan, Puerto Rico; St. Georges, Bermuda; Savannah, Georgia; Port Canaveral, Florida; Dry Tortugas; New Orleans, Louisiana

1997. Sydney, Canada; Montreal, Canada; Charleston, South Carolina; Port Everglades, Florida; Ponce, Puerto Rico; Willemstad, Curaçao; Vera Cruz, Mexico; New Orleans, Louisiana

1998. Balboa, Panama; Valparaiso, Chile; Galapagos Islands; Punta Arenas, Costa Rica; Colon, Panama; Key West, Florida; Port Arthur, Texas

1999. Las Palmas, Canary Islands; Lisbon, Portugal; Cork, Ireland; Le Havre, France; Port Arthur, Texas

2000. Alexandria, Virginia; St. John's, Newfoundland; St. Georges, Bermuda; Ponce, Puerto Rico; Cozumel and Vera Cruz, Mexico; New Orleans, Louisiana; Port Arthur, Texas (discontinuation of the prep program)

2001. Bridgetown, Barbados; St. Johns, Antigua; Miami and Key West, Florida; Port Arthur, Texas

2002. Philadelphia, Pennsylvania; Stavanger, Norway; Aalborg, Denmark; Port Everglades, Florida; Port Arthur, Texas (blue nose cruise)

2003. Boston, Massachusetts; Portland, Maine; Charleston, South Carolina; New York, New York; Key West, Florida; Houston, Texas

2004. Port Everglades, Florida; Cork, Ireland; Falmouth, England; San Juan, Puerto Rico; Corpus Christi, Texas; Freeport, Texas

Sources

The archives of the Jack K. Williams Library—by far the most important source for any history of Texas A&M at Galveston—contain pamphlets and brochures, official memoranda and letters, transcribed interviews, photographs, news releases, and newspaper and magazine clippings. The archives have the only complete run of the yearbook *Voyager* 1968–2001, and the most complete collection of the newsletter/newspaper *Channel Chatter/Nautilus,* irregularly appearing student publications. They also contain the private papers—including letters and memoranda about the Texas Maritime Academy from 1960 to 1966—of Peter J. La-Valle, Texas state representative and later Galveston County judge. I filled in archival gaps with visits to files kept in a number of departments and units on the TAMUG campus.

"The Establishment of the Texas Maritime Academy, 1958–1962" (1969) by Sherman B. Wetmore, with the collaboration of John A. Parker and Peter J. LaValle, is a fifty-five-page typed manuscript giving the definitive account of the founding of the school. Wetmore's private papers are available in the archives of Rosenberg Library, Galveston's public library. Henry C. Dethloff, in *A Centennial History of Texas A&M University, 1876–1976* (College Station: Texas A&M University Press, 1975), recounts that early history, relying almost entirely on Wetmore's manuscript. I used Dethloff for background information about what was going on at the main campus during the period. Donna

Lang's unpublished thirty-five-page essay "A Brief History" extends Wetmore's account to the 1970s. Mary Gardner's sixteen-page booklet "The Twenty-Fifth Voyage of the *Texas Clipper*" (Galveston: TAMUG, 1989) contains first-person memories of faculty and former students. Gene Gurney and Brian Sheehan, in *Education Guide to U.S. Service & Maritime Academies* (New York: Van Nostrand, 1978) summarize the histories of the national and state maritime academies. Stan Blazyk's *A Century of Galveston Weather (1900–1999): People and the Elements on a Barrier Island* (Austin: Eakin Press, 2000) contains details about storms that disrupted routine for students, faculty, and staff in Galveston.

The appendix represents my best attempt to fashion authoritative and comprehensive lists about the history of the school. Since there were no complete lists of student body leaders and corps commanders, I had to cobble them together from a combination of sources: award plaques, student government archives, newspaper articles, and interviews with former students. The list of cruise ports is based upon an online list compiled by the office of the maritime corps of cadets, extended and corrected with reference to archival material, interviews, and cruise plaques. Trying to reconstruct historical lists from spotty sources demands patience, problem solving, and—of necessity—some educated guesswork. I invite comments and corrections.

Index

Photos are indicated with *italic type*.
Page numbers with "c" indicate information in the caption only.

CPSIA information can be obtained at www.ICGtesting.com
Printed in the USA
LVOW03s0049250914

405774LV00001B/1/P